**Oxford Resources
for Cambridge**

Pix

Cambridge IGCSE® & O Level

Complete

Global Perspectives

Third Edition

Dean Roberts

Annette Borchert   **Rashima Varma**

Karem Roitman   **Elena Morgan**

Stuart Wire   **Geetika Pawar**

OXFORD
UNIVERSITY PRESS

OXFORD
UNIVERSITY PRESS

Great Clarendon Street, Oxford, OX2 6DP, United Kingdom

Oxford University Press is a department of the University of Oxford.
It furthers the University's objective of excellence in research, scholarship,
and education by publishing worldwide. Oxford is a registered trade mark
of Oxford University Press in the UK and in
certain other countries.

© Oxford University Press 2023

The moral rights of the authors have been asserted.

This edition published in 2023

British Library Cataloguing in Publication Data

Data available

9781382042598

10 9 8 7 6 5 4 3 2 1

MIX
Paper | Supporting
responsible forestry
FSC® C007785

The manufacturing process conforms to the environmental regulations of
the country of origin.

Printed in the UK by Bell & Bain

Acknowledgements

This Student Book refers to the Cambridge IGCSE® Global Perspectives
syllabus published by Cambridge Assessment International Education.

This work has been developed independently from and is not endorsed
by or otherwise connected with Cambridge Assessment International
Education. IGCSE® is the registered trademark of Cambridge Assessment
International Education.

We would like to extend our gratitude to Elena Morgan, Rashima Varma and
Geetika Pawar for their subject knowledge, insight, and engagement with
the project.

We would like to thank Sawangwong Roberts for her continued support
for the series editor when the project kept him pinned to his office chair.
Julie Wire for her insight, input, and expertise. Isaac and Simon for inspiring
approaches to teaching and to Huckle for his editorial eye.

The publisher would like to thank the following for permissions to use
copyright material: Extract from 'Subcultures in Tokyo' written by Time Out
Tokyo Editors Wednesday 26 September 2018. ©Time Out England Limited and
affiliated companies owned by Time Out Group Plc. Reprinted by permission of
Time Out England Limited. Extract from 'The carbon-free energy of the future:
this fusion breakthrough changes everything' written by Arthur Turrell;
13 December 2022, © Guardian News and Media Ltd, reprinted by permission
of Guardian News and Media Ltd. Extract from the article 'Is Climate Change
Causing More Wars?' by Vishva Bhatt, 1 February 2022, The Years Project
Blog. Reproduced with permission of The Years Project Blog. Extract from 'A
New Era of Conflict and Violence'; published by United Nations. Reproduced
with the permission of the United Nations. Extract from 'Managing a world of
free trade and deep interdependence', Renato Ruggiero, published by, World
Trade Organization, 1996. Reprinted with the permission of World Trade
Organization. Extract from 'Fast Fashion and Its Environmental Impact', written
by Rashmila Maiti; 1 December 2022; published by Earth.Org. Reprinted by
permission of the publisher. Extract from 'Cryptocurrency in Vietnam - statistics
& facts' written by Minh-Ngoc Nguyen, 17 November 2022, reprinted by
permission of Statista. Extract from 'From Maldives, with hope: Climate change
has brought a sea of uncertainties for children and families in Maldives',
written by Stuti Sharma. Reprinted by permission of Unicef.org. Extract from
'Christopher Hitchens obituary' written by Peter Wilby; 16 December 2011, ©
Guardian News and Media Ltd, reprinted by permission of Guardian News
and Media Ltd. Extract from 'The greatest banned songs of all time – ranked!'
written by Laura Snapes; 14 February 2019, © Guardian News and Media
Ltd, reprinted by permission of Guardian News and Media Ltd. Extract from
'What sport means to me', written by Adam Paton, published by The Glasgow
Guardian, 12 October 2020, © Glasgow Guardian. Reprinted by permission
of the publisher. Extract from 'Could 2022 be sportswashing's biggest year?'
written by Karim Zidan; 5 Jan 2022, © Guardian News and Media Ltd, reprinted
by permission of Guardian News and Media Ltd. Extract from 'What Is Big Tech
and Why Is the Government Trying to Break It Up?', written by Shannon Flynn,
published in makeuseof.com. Reprinted by permission of the publisher.

The publisher and authors would like to thank the following for permission to
use photographs and other copyright material:
Cover: Andriy Onufriyenko/Moment/Getty Images;

Photos: p4: Rawpixel.com / Shutterstock; **p10(t):** d3verro /
Shutterstock; **p10(b):** Sono Ringo / Shutterstock; **p13:** Denis Gorelkin
/ Shutterstock; **p14:** Photo Kozyr / Shutterstock; **p18(t):** Igor Zoiko /
Shutterstock; **p18(b):** SFIO CRACHO / Shutterstock; **p24(l):** Jorge Royan /
Alamy Stock Photo; **p24(r):** Mark Gstohl; **p25(l):** imageBROKER / Alamy Stock
Photo; **p25(r):** Keith J Finks / Shutterstock; **p26:** PA Images / Alamy Stock
Photo; **p28:** LHBLLC / Shutterstock; **p29(t):** rasid aslim / Shutterstock; **p29(b):** tichr
/ Shutterstock; **p36(tl):** zummolo / Shutterstock; **p36(tr):** topten22photo/
Shutterstock; **p36(bl):** Kobby Dagan / Shutterstock; **p36(br):** Plamen
Galabov/Shutterstock; **p38:** Rena Schild / Shutterstock; **p40(l):** Isacco /
Shutterstock; **p40(r):** icosha / Shutterstock; **p44:** Kingcraft/Shutterstock; **p48:** Dean
Roberts; **p52(l):** Images & Stories / Alamy Stock Photo; **p52(m):** asharkyu/
Shutterstock; **p52(r):** Mike Flippo/Shutterstock; **p62:** Skorzewiak / Alamy Stock
Photo; **p72:** Fran / Cartoonstock; **p75:** Ralph Hagen / Cartoonstock; **p78:** Julie
Pop/Shutterstock; **p84(t):** Faizan qadeeri / Shutterstock; **p84(b):** Sergiy
Kuzmin / Shutterstock; **p86:** evan_huang / Shutterstock; **p92(l):** pixinoo
/ Shutterstock; **p92(r):** Kathrine Andi / Shutterstock; **p96:** Kjpargeter /
Shutterstock; **p99:** Michelle D. Milliman / Shutterstock; **p100:** Monkey
Business Images / Shutterstock; **p101:** fizkes/Shutterstock; **p104(l):** Nacho
Calonge / Alamy Stock Photo; **p104(r):** SeventyFour / Shutterstock; **p113:** Ron
Coleman / Cartoonstock; **p120:** BJ FlavioMassari / Alamy Stock
Photo; **p122(l):** Steve Photography / Shutterstock; **p122(m):** Jorgen Udvang /
Alamy Stock Photo; **p122(r):** Yavuz Sariyildiz / Shutterstock; **p124(t):** Hagen /
Cartoonstock; **p124(b):** Volodymyr Burdiak / Shutterstock; **p128:** Rich Carey /
Shutterstock; **p132:** Bradford Veley / Cartoonstock; **p134(tl):** Ground Picture
/ Shutterstock; **p134(tr):** Ground Picture / Shutterstock; **p134(bl):** Natasha
Breen / Shutterstock; **p134(br):** Rawpixel.com / Shutterstock; **p137:** AlexLMX
/ Shutterstock; **p146:** Hugh Mitton / Alamy Stock Photo; **p148:** Yandry_kw
/ Shutterstock; **p149(l):** Hemis / Alamy Stock Photo; **p149(r):** Birgit Reitz-
Hofmann/Shutterstock; **p156:** Sander van der Werf / Shutterstock; **p164(l):** Cluff
/ Cartoonstock; **p164(r):** Edgar Argo / Cartoonstock; **p168(l):** arogant
/ Shutterstock; **p168(r):** qvist / Shutterstock; **p172(tl):** Branko Devic /
Shutterstock; **p172(tr):** Mikhail Leonov / Shutterstock; **p172(b):** Tim Cordell /
Cartoonstock; **p180:** Radiokafka / Shutterstock; **p182(a):** Monkey Business Images
/ Shutterstock; **p182(b):** Wuttisit Somtui / Shutterstock; **p182(c):** Fishman64
/ Shutterstock; **p182(d):** fizkes / Shutterstock; **p182(e):** Followtheflow /
Shutterstock; **p183:** Everett Collection Inc / Alamy Stock Photo; **p193:** William
Potter / Shutterstock; **p197(t):** Alex Mateo / Alamy Stock Photo; **p197(b):** Rose
Makin / Shutterstock; **p204:** michelmond / Shutterstock; **p205:** Just Jus /
Shutterstock; **p218(l):** dreamerroom / Shutterstock; **p218(m):** BearFotos /
Shutterstock; **p218(r):** 1000 Words / Shutterstock; **p221(tl):** Alexander Tolstykh /
Alamy Stock Photo; **p221(tr):** PictureLux / The Hollywood Archive / Alamy Stock
Photo; **p221(bl):** Collection Christophel / Alamy Stock Photo; **p221(br):** Pictorial
Press Ltd / Alamy Stock Photo; **p229:** James Boardman / Alamy Stock
Photo; **p230:** Hugh Brown / Cartoonstock; **p232:** Vectorium/Shutterstock; Hugh
Brown / Cartoonstock; **p233(bkg):** Raevsky Lab/Shutterstock; **p233(bl):** Shaun
Botterill/Getty Images; **p233(br):** Jonathan Larsen/Diadem Images /
Alamy Stock Photo; **p236(l):** frantic00 / Shutterstock; **p236(r):** DisobeyArt /
Shutterstock; **p240(l):** JPL-Caltech; **p240(r):** JPL/Colleen Sharkey; **p241(l):** NASA/
JPL-Caltech; **p241(r):** JPL-Caltech; **p243:** kentoh / Shutterstock; **p252:** Ammit
Jack / Shutterstock; **p254:** red mango / Shutterstock; **p256:** Grigory Kubatyan
/ Shutterstock; **p260(l):** reisegraf.ch/Shutterstock; **p260(r):** saiko3p /
Shutterstock; **p264:** Anton Watman/Shutterstock; **p267(tl):** Longfin Media
/ Shutterstock; **p267(tm):** dramaj/Shutterstock; **p267(tr):** Drazen Zigic /
Shutterstock; **p267(bl):** Sk Hasan Ali/Shutterstock; **p267(br):** tolga ildun /
Shutterstock; **p268:** Colored Lights / Shutterstock; **p269:** John Robertson /
Alamy Stock Photo; **p272:** Cezary Wojtkowski / Shutterstock; **p276:** Piyaset/
Shutterstock; **p277:** Christian Mark Inga Osorio / Getty Images; **p280:** V_ace/
Shutterstock; **p281:** Suwin/Shutterstock; **p284:** dkroy / Shutterstock.

Artwork by Aptara.

Every effort has been made to contact copyright holders of material reproduced in
this book. Any omissions will be rectified in subsequent printings if notice is given to
the publisher.

Links to third party websites are provided by Oxford in good faith and for
information only. Oxford disclaims any responsibility for the materials contained
in any third party website referenced in this work.

Contents

Answers to the tasks and questions in the Teaching and Learning sections of each unit can be found on your free support website. Answers to the Moving towards assessment sections are given in the Teacher Handbook. Access the support website here.

Introduction

Studying Global Perspectives

Congratulations on choosing to study Global Perspectives. This gives you an exciting opportunity to consider significant global issues and to develop an approach to studying them using a range of different, and sometimes alternative, perspectives.

Global issues – such as poverty or climate change, access to clean water or human rights – and people's perspectives on them are extremely important in our modern world. It is interesting to see what the United Nations (UN) has to say about global issues.

▲ Fig. 1

The United Nations' statement on global issues

As the world's only truly universal global organization, the UN has become the foremost forum to address issues that transcend national boundaries and cannot be resolved by any one country acting alone.

To its initial goals of safeguarding peace, protecting human rights, establishing the framework for international justice, and promoting economic and social progress, in the seven decades since its creation the UN has added on new challenges, such as AIDS, big data, and climate change.

While conflict resolution and peacekeeping continue to be among its most visible efforts, the UN, along with its specialized agencies, is also engaged in a wide array of activities to improve people's lives around the world – from disaster relief, through education and advancement of women, to peaceful uses of atomic energy.

The UN suggests that the following topics are important global issues at the present time:

- Africa
- ageing
- AIDS
- atomic energy
- big data
- children
- climate change
- decolonization
- democracy
- disarmament
- ending poverty
- food
- gender equality
- health
- human rights
- international law and justice
- migration
- oceans and the law of the sea
- peace and security
- population
- refugees
- water
- youth.

This student book will support your study of IGCSE® and O Level Global Perspectives, and help you to embrace the following challenges:

- take your place in a changing, information-rich, and connected world
- analyse and evaluate global issues and their causes and consequences
- suggest actions that use evidence to respond to and sometimes address these global issues
- approach global issues from the objective of sustainability
- consult and research a wide range of sources and information in a critical manner, reaching judgements based on clear lines of reasoning
- engage with different perspectives and viewpoints, questioning them to understand the links between them
- develop and modify your own perspectives and viewpoints on a wide range of issues.

In doing so, you will become familiar with using the following study skills:

- working collaboratively, in pairs and in groups, and work independently to take responsibility for your own learning
- developing your communication skills in writing, speaking, and responding appropriately to others
- reflecting on your learning in a structured manner on a frequent basis.

1. What do you think about the UN's statement that a global issue cannot be solved by any one country alone?
2. What do you think about the argument that the past is of little use in solving current global issues?
3. Do you agree with the UN's list of contemporary global issues? What issues would you add to the list?
4. How ready do you think you are to take on the challenges?
5. What might you need to change about your existing study skills to study this Global Perspectives course?

The last six pages of each unit will help you move towards assessment. There are two pages for each of the following:

- Individual Report (Component 2)
- Team Project (Component 3)
- Written Exam (Component 1).

Every Moving towards assessment – Written Exam section has up to four sample sources available via the QR code printed on the relevant page in this book and at www.oxfordsecondary.com/IGCSECompleteGP You should use these sources alongside the tasks included for examination practice.

How the student book has been designed

This student book has 22 units, to match the topics list in the Cambridge International syllabus. Each unit has 12 pages, split into six double-page sections. Each section has been designed to give you the opportunity to gain further knowledge about the relevant topic and to practise important skills that will help you do well on the Global Perspectives course.

It is very likely that you will not study all 22 topics. Some topics will not suit your circumstances or context, and that is fine. The student book has been designed so you can focus on just those topics you have decided to study, probably in agreement with your teacher. You can choose from a wide range of topics and each unit in the student book offers you a stand-alone programme of study.

This student book offers you the opportunity to choose a pathway through the Global Perspectives course. You may decide to study several topics that are inter-connected, and this makes very good sense. However, you might like to study topics that are very different from each other. Whichever pathway you choose, you will find new knowledge and key skills in each unit, with a balance across the whole book. Of course, the more units you can study, the more knowledge you gain and the more advanced your skills become!

Kerboodle online resources: Additional support can be found on Kerboodle. There are resources for every topic, including assessments, skills interactives, and reports. You can also access the digital book.

Teaching and learning sections

The first six pages of each unit focus on teaching and learning. These sections provide springboards from which you can explore specific topics. They do not try to cover all aspects of a topic but, instead, spotlight some interesting ways to look at it.

You can start by exploring what you already know about a topic by spending 10–15 minutes discussing the points raised in A line of enquiry. You can give examples from your own experience and start to look at the topic from different viewpoints and perspectives. You can also start to think about big questions that you can investigate as you progress through the unit.

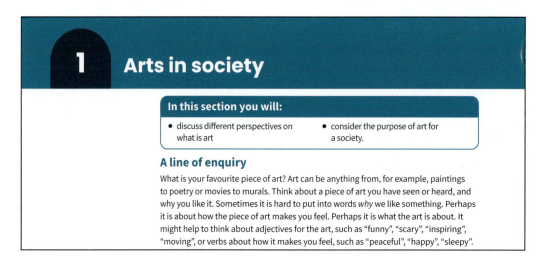

1 Arts in society

In this section you will:

- discuss different perspectives on what is art
- consider the purpose of art for a society.

A line of enquiry

What is your favourite piece of art? Art can be anything from, for example, paintings to poetry or movies to murals. Think about a piece of art you have seen or heard, and why you like it. Sometimes it is hard to put into words *why* we like something. Perhaps it is about how the piece of art makes you feel. Perhaps it is what the art is about. It might help to think about adjectives for the art, such as "funny", "scary", "inspiring", "moving", or verbs about how it makes you feel, such as "peaceful", "happy", "sleepy".

Each double page in the teaching and learning section also has expected outcomes to enable you to look back after six pages and see how much you have learned and progressed.

The teaching and learning sections offer a range of sources for you to engage with: primary and secondary sources, articles, visual sources, talks and dialogues, graphs, cartoons, etc. Each source is then followed by a task. You will have plenty of opportunity to work collaboratively as you explore the sources and work together to analyse, evaluate, and respond to them.

The tasks have been designed to help you practise the following useful skills:

Useful skills

Remember – Can important information be identified and described?

Understand – Can important ideas and concepts be explained?

Analyse – Can the parts be distinguished, and can connections be seen?

Apply – Can knowledge and understanding be used in a different context?

Evaluate – Can a stand, decision, or judgement be justified or opposed?

Create – Can a new idea or a new dimension be suggested?

1. Have you decided yet which topics you are going to study? What factors are involved in making your choice for a pathway?
2. How would you describe your current knowledge of the topics you are likely to study? Which areas in these topics do you want to spotlight to know more about?
3. Do you already engage with primary and secondary sources that you think will be useful on this course? How much and how often?
4. Look at the list of useful skills. In which other subjects that you study are these skills developed? How strong do you feel you are in these skills?

Other features in the student book

In the teaching and learning sections, there are various types of feature box (as shown on page 8). Each feature has been designed to achieve one of these three outcomes:

- to provide **information** to extend the teaching and learning of the topic and the spotlighted theme
- to give **examples** that further explain and illustrate a point, a skill, an appropriate piece of knowledge, etc.
- to prompt further **thought** and **enquiry**, often using rhetorical questions.

Here are the aims of the 12 different types of feature box:

Sustainability

You will soon realize that studying Global Perspectives involves analysing issues and evaluating what changes need to be made to ensure a better world and a better future for us all. Change should be sustainable, and this feature challenges you to think about how your ideas can made sustainable.

Evidence

Evidence is information that you use to make a judgment about whether something can be proved to be true. The evidence you use therefore underpins your argument or viewpoint about an issue. These feature boxes ask you to consider evidence in this way and to think carefully about how you intend to present it in your work.

Viewpoints

These feature boxes offer ways of looking at perspectives. For example, you might be asked to look at topics from the following viewpoints (as if looking through a lens): economic, political, scientific, psychological, ethical, environmental, technological, etc.

Ever-changing world

The relationship between global issues in the past with those in the present, and issues that can be predicted in the future, are explored in these feature boxes.

Research

Research is organized and methodical study to establish facts, find evidence, and develop new understanding. These feature boxes provide specific ideas to help you dig out appropriate research and deepen your knowledge and understanding of global, national, and local issues.

Mindfulness

To be mindful is to focus your awareness on the moment, to concentrate on what is happening or to gain inner calm. You can also think of it as taking "time out" to reset your feelings about something. You are faced with some big, impactful issues in this course and these feature boxes prompt you to think about them in a mindful way.

Reflect

These feature boxes prompt you to reflect. They aim to focus your reflections to give them structure, usually by asking you to think about important issues of global concern and how they affect you personally.

Quote

Quotations often stimulate thought and reactions, and these boxes include quotations from historic and contemporary thinkers to add value to the issues and topics you are studying. Sometimes you will have to interpret the quotations and work out what they mean.

Empathy

We empathize by putting ourselves in other people's positions to try to understand how they feel. These feature boxes ask you to think of others, by presenting situations that relate to the relevant topic. It is often difficult to imagine how another person might feel, especially when the situation and conditions they are experiencing are unpleasant and challenging.

Argument

An argument contains reasoning and evidence to support a claim. These feature boxes give examples of arguments that extend the points made in the unit you are studying.

Causes and consequences

Sometimes these feature boxes focus just on causes. Others explore consequences. Where appropriate, causes and their specific consequences are included.

Perspectives

The student book covers a wide range of perspectives held by different individuals and groups of people across varying social, cultural, and geographical contexts. The perspectives could be: personal, local, regional, national, international, or global.

Looking back at the three intended outcomes at the bottom of page 7, copy and extend the table to include all 12 types of special feature. Give examples which you think meet the aims of each special feature. You can use topics from the UN list on page 5 or any of your own ideas.

Special features	Reason for using it	Example
Sustainability	Thought and enquiry	I wonder why so many people are against nuclear energy?
Viewpoints	Examples	1. A government minister for economics wants controlled migration to boost her country's labour force. 2. A migrant escaping a civil war is not looking for a job.
Causes and consequences	Information	Sometimes a cause has an indirect consequence that could not be predicted. Don't always think of immediate and direct consequences – look for longer term impacts that are not easy to foresee.

Key skills for success

One aim of the course is to support you in developing interdisciplinary skills. These skills will also help you in other subject areas by, for example, being better prepared for gaining artistic, scientific, and academic knowledge.

The word cloud includes some of these skills.

▲ **Fig. 2** *Word cloud showing key skills*

Identifying global, national, and local issues

An issue is an important topic or a problem for debate and discussion.

A global issue is therefore one that has relevance and an impact across much or most of the world.

A national issue is prominent in a specific country. The same issue may be an issue in more than one country. An issue that is important in several countries in Latin America, for example, is a regional issue.

A local issue has relevance and impact in a smaller area such as a village. The issue may not have any relevance beyond that small area. The same local issue may be an issue in other areas in the same country or in other countries. However, it is still regarded as a local issue unless it spreads to a wider area.

▲ **Fig. 3** *Example of a national issue*

▲ **Fig. 4** *Example of a local issue*

Examples of issues that you might meet in the course

a. Future wars with people fighting over water supply

b. Using the science of nuclear weapons to develop nuclear energy

c. Colonizing Mars

d. The state of fish farming in the Andaman Sea

e. Transport costs for people aged 70 and over in a township in South Africa

f. Modern youth is spending half their waking time using digital tools

g. Flooding in some parts of the world and droughts in others

h. Secondary education in Finland is a model of education for others to follow

i. Development of sport for women across the European Union

j. Coral degradation on the Florida coastline

k. Increasing reliance on artificial intelligence in daily life

l. Increase of knife crime in south-east London in the last decade.

Identifying global, national, local, and personal perspectives

An issue is often a matter of opinion. For example, the idea that the human race should explore alternative locations in space to further its existence is a view held by some people but not all. A value judgement is often involved. Those who feel we do need to expand the space exploration programme value its aim of building colonies on the Moon and planets other than Earth. They might suggest that the new colonies will offer equality and be cross-cultural, with no poverty or conflicts.

All issues can be looked at from more than one, if not a range of different viewpoints or perspectives. For example, a person, group of people, formal organization, government, or an international organization could all hold different viewpoints about investing money and time in a space programme. These perspectives will have personal, local, national, and global elements, and use opinions, arguments, assumptions, and evidence to make their point. For example, NASA's perspective will argue that space exploration is vital, because space exploration is why the organization exists. On the other hand, you will be able to find many people who hold a counter-perspective and do not agree with space exploration at all.

Perspectives can change over time. A well-known astronaut who went on several missions into space has changed his viewpoint significantly. In his older years, he changed his mind and argued against further space travel – his personal perspective has done a complete about-turn.

One of the aims of the Global Perspectives course is to encourage you to be open-minded to different viewpoints and to appreciate different perspectives. Be open-minded and be prepared to be flexible. You might modify your viewpoint, or you might not, but do consider a wide range of other perspectives before you defend your own.

1. Which types of content would you regard as primary and / or secondary sources on the internet and social media? Think about blogs, tweets, chats, etc.

2. Did you realize that such a wide range of sources are available to you? Are you happy that research is not all about reading long articles and extracts from books? Which alternative sources would you like to research?

3. Now you know that the provenance of some sources is not reliable, what will you be careful about when looking for sources?

4. You should analyse a source's content before evaluating it. What is the difference between analysing and evaluating?

5. Using the elements at the bottom of page 14, which ones are present in the list of statements on page 15?

6. You understand why you have to use citation and referencing systems for your extended research work on the course. Do you know which system you will use?

Using graphs as sources

During your Global Perspectives course you are likely to engage with statistical sources when you are doing research for your Individual Report; doing research while planning your Team Project; preparing for and taking your Written Exam; and undertaking general reading and skills work.

The range of statistical source material includes bar graphs, line graphs, infographics, and other data sets. The student book contains plenty of practice in obtaining information from data presented in these forms. You will engage with them for three main reasons:

- to locate specific and important information
- to identify trends and patterns
- to interpret information, trends, and patterns.

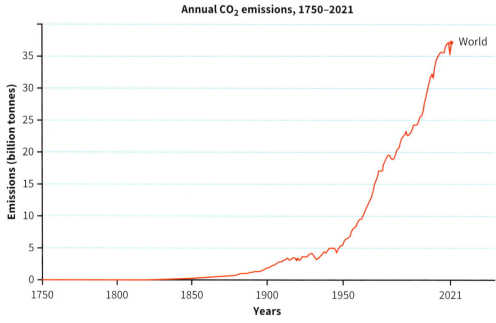

Annual CO_2 emissions, 1750–2021

▲ **Fig. 7** *Example of the type of graph you can analyse to identify a trend*

Example statements relating to causes and consequences

a. Climate change is a human-made problem.

b. There's no doubt in my mind that, if we had not developed the nuclear bomb in the 1940s, we would not have developed nuclear power.

c. Consequences are not always negative. Think about how much cleaner parts of our world are now that we know more about pollution.

d. More megacities, more migration, more social issues, more conflict.

e. It has all resulted in increased poverty, and the gap between poorer and wealthier people is greater than it has ever been in human history.

f. When the first humans saw the sun they believed it was the centre of the universe.

g. 35 years ago, 90 per cent of crops were grown outside. In 2022, 35 per cent of crops are grown inside.

h. The transport union has announced three further one-day strikes as their demand for a pay rise of 12 per cent has not been met by the employer.

i. Cultures always change. That's what culture means. For example, if you put some bacteria on a culture tray, it will usually grow, quickly or slowly.

j. It's not joy that these people see in purchasing art – it's money, it's investment.

k. The cause of all wars is that wars exist and have been fought before.

l. Gender equality in education has not happened by chance. It has been the constant pressure of action groups, politicians, and educators to seek change.

m. Since the new prime minister took office, human rights laws have benefited.

n. Electric vehicles are the future. They are clean and popular. However, they are expensive. The only way forward is to make them a lot cheaper. Governments can start by giving money to support new manufacturers in the industry.

o. The more people who play sport, the less taxpayers will need to pay for healthcare. But, then again, more people will end up getting injured.

p. Helping poorer countries by giving them financial aid creates more bad things than good things.

q. The graph clearly shows that 25 per cent of people are not receiving any state support and are still unemployed.

Proposing courses of action

After an issue has been identified, researched, described, explained, analysed, and evaluated, courses of action can be proposed.

In Global Perspectives, you are likely to be recommending global, national, regional, and local courses of action. You will come across courses of action that range from very reasonable, sensible, perhaps obvious, to others which seem exaggerated, unlikely to succeed for a variety of reasons, or perhaps only theoretical. What matters most is whether the proposed course of action was fully considered in the light of alternative courses of action that were available and viable.

An aim of your course of action is to raise awareness of an issue and / or suggest a solution to the problems an issue raises. In both cases, you should be seeking a positive outcome. You should show that you are able to consider a range of potential courses of action based on research. It could be your own research or the research of others, for example, when you collaborate with others on the Team Project.

Courses of action can be suggestions expressed in writing, for example in a report about an issue. Alternatively, they can be actions carried out in a more active way as in a presentation, a video, a display, or an interview.

Examples of courses of action

a. A government decides to create a new department called the Department of Social Inclusion. It will be staffed by five people who will have responsibility for more opportunities for women, more jobs for people with eye conditions which have resulted in partial sight, and loans of $20,000 for people who employ socially excluded staff.

b. A mobile network company has been researching the accessibility of smartphones for teenagers aged 11–17 in Japan. Their research showed that 72 per cent of teenagers in that age range in Tokyo had their own phone. To address the shortfall, they have decided to donate phones to 28 per cent of the teenage population aged 11–17 in Japan.

c. In her report on innovation, a professor found that the main barriers to innovation in the energy industry were a) lack of specialist knowledge, b) lack of time for research and development of new concepts, and c) a lack of money to fund new research. Her task was to suggest just one suitable course of action. She opted to prioritize the lack of specialist knowledge, recommending that universities offer places for students to study innovative technology with all costs paid.

d. My research was to study crimes globally, highlighting one country where crime is way above average. The evidence I found was that globally crimes are decreasing, but that crime in the highlighted country had increased by 30 per cent in two years. As a solution, I recommend that the national police from the problem country visit the national police department of a country which has average crime levels.

e. Global Happy Days is a group of like-minded people spread around the world with member organizations in almost every country. Our research shows that in some countries people respond to our surveys with amazing results showing high levels of happiness. Unfortunately, in some other countries, people appear to be much too sad. What we propose is a global Funny Day. Our social media and website will be open to all to post a joke, a funny story – whatever you want to make us all laugh.

f. Our team focused on the local issue of how arts and music in our town have been declining over the past few years. We assigned each other roles to research several different perspectives on this, and our research produced a list of factors explaining the decline. We felt we could solve all of these, so we set about finding solutions to each one. As a consequence of our action, we were faced with 22 factors and 22 possible solutions.

1. What do you think the phrase "I can't follow your line of reasoning" means? Where, other than on a Global Perspectives course, might you hear people say this?

2. Think of the common phrase, "Have you considered the consequences of your actions?" When is this used and what is the usual tone of the question? What about the consequences of non-human actions, such as an asteroid hitting the Moon. Does that change how you think about consequences?

3. Look at the example statements about causes and consequences on page 19. Using the checklist below, identify, analyse, and evaluate each statement.

   Checklist

   ✓ Is there a clear cause?

   ✓ Is there a clear consequence?

   ✓ Are there any statements where the causes were not entirely responsible for the consequence?

   ✓ Is there more than one cause and / or more than one consequence?

   ✓ Are there any implied causes and / or implied consequences?

   ✓ Are there any consequences that are not given in the statement but you think are likely to happen in the future?

4. Look at the examples of courses of action on page 20. Using a table like this, evaluate each one.

Global, national, regional, local, or individual?	Were alternative courses considered?	Is the chosen course of action reasonable?	Was the research solid and secure?

5. Think about any consequences of the actions proposed in Question 4. Do all the courses of action generate positive outcomes? Would you modify any of the courses of action to improve them? How?

Reflecting and concluding

The noun "reflection" has several meanings:

- the image of something in a mirror or on any reflective surface
- in physics, the return of light, heat, sound, or energy from a surface
- something that shows, expresses, or is a sign of something
- serious or careful thought.

In the Global Perspectives course, reflection is a good thing, and you should reflect as much as possible on the new learning you are experiencing. You might also like to think about how you are learning, your learning style, and how you might improve this.

Reflection is a valuable process when it is well targeted. For example, reflecting on issues and perspectives will help you to take other people's ideas seriously and be open to new ideas and new ways of looking at something. It might even change some of your previously strongly held views. Reflecting can also help develop your mindfulness.

You will be asked to show evidence of reflection in the work you submit to be assessed.

Concluding is a skill that is equally important on your course. In this context, if reflection is the cause, conclusion is the consequence. For example, if a student writes the following, it shows that they have reflected and come to a conclusion.

"Finding out that the death sentence still applies in certain countries made me reflect on my own position on this. I changed my mind, concluding that such severe punishment for crimes should never happen."

Another person might disagree with this statement and, after reflection, might argue for the death penalty to remain and perhaps be used in more places.

It is important to show that you have gone through a process of reflection and used this to make balanced judgements with conclusions. If you have, other people reading your work or listening to you speak will consider your judgements and conclusions much more objectively and seriously.

How you will study your course

During your Global Perspectives course, you will work with your classmates on a regular basis, probably more than for any other school subject. Much of the work in the teaching and learning sections of each unit will be done in pairs and groups. This will help you to develop the skill of collaboration – a key skill that you are assessed on by your teacher and the external assessors.

You will have to work with a small group of two to five people to produce a Team Project, and your collaborative skills will be very valuable. The process of looking at issues and perspectives at the global national, regional, and local levels should not be done working entirely alone. Therefore, many tasks in the student book have been designed to involve sharing ideas, views, judgements, and reflections.

There are, of course, times when it is appropriate to work individually, for example, in writing your 2,000-word Individual Report. Even so, research and planning for the report should involve engaging with others – it is not intended as completely isolated study.

Some students like to keep a learning journal to record their ongoing thoughts, ideas, and reflections as they work through their course. However, it's a personal thing – you can choose whether keeping such a journal will be helpful to you or not.

How you take notes is also a personal choice. The content – the topics, themes, and spotlighted areas – is not assessed directly so you do not *need* to make any 'content-based notes'. However, feel free to do just that if you want to develop a collection of Global Perspective appropriate content. Knowledge of your chosen topics – the specific areas that you have decided to investigate in depth – is, of course, important.

What is most important is that your learning journey can be seen by others looking at your work and listening to your spoken output. Ideally, this will be a reflective learning journey.

Communication and language

Communication is important for your Global Perspectives course and you will need your English language skills to communicate well. Communication involves:

- making sure your output has a clear purpose
- targeting the specific audiences who will read, hear, and watch your work
- sequencing your research, evidence, responses to enquiry, and reasoning in a logical, coherent manner
- structuring the range of perspectives you have engaged with and communicating your own viewpoints and perspectives with clarity
- providing clear answers to questions you have raised about issues you have chosen to investigate
- using consistent and clear citation and referencing systems
- listening and responding constructively in class discussions and debates
- performing well and positively in project-based teamwork.

It is important to be as accurate as you can be with your English language. However, as long as you have clarity and you can meet the above standards, your work can be assessed for its skill and knowledge of Global Perspectives. Don't over-stretch yourself, therefore. Use a language level that works best for you, that you feel comfortable with, and that means you will only be making minor language mistakes.

---

1. Why do you think you should reflect as much as possible during your Global Perspectives course? Is reflection always a good thing? Can you think of occasions where over-reflection has consequences?

2. Under which conditions on your course do you think it would be acceptable to reach exactly the same conclusion you held about an issue before you started your research?

3. How do you think teaching and learning on this course will be different from other subjects? Where is it likely to be similar?

4. How do you think you will organize your own learning? How will you approach note-taking? Will you keep a learning journal?

5. From the list of ways to ensure good communication:

   a. pick out ten words that you think are vital. What do they have in common?

   b. Sort the skills into receptive (listening, reading) and productive (writing, speaking) skills. What do you notice?

A line of enquiry

What is your favourite piece of art? Art can be anything from, for example, paintings to poetry or movies to murals. Think about a piece of art you have seen or heard, and why you like it. Sometimes it is hard to put into words *why* we like something. Perhaps it is about how the piece of art makes you feel. Perhaps it is what the art is about. It might help to think about adjectives for the art, such as "funny", "scary", "inspiring", "moving", or verbs about how it makes you feel, such as "peaceful", "happy", "sleepy".

Art is not an easy thing to define. People disagree on what is art. Have you ever shared a piece of art with a friend and been surprised at how differently they feel about it from you? You might think of a piece of music as energizing art, while they find it annoying noise!

Perspectives on art

One of the reasons defining art can be challenging is that art reflects local cultures. Your country's art is likely to show local landscapes, local patterns, and local ideas of what is beautiful. Some of what you have grown up with and are used to, however, might appear strange and perhaps unpleasant to someone from another culture.

Art is global. International artists such as Banksy influence art that is being produced around the world.

Task 1

In small groups, discuss the following questions.

1. How would you define graffiti?
2. Is graffiti art? Should graffiti be allowed and if so, where?
3. What is the purpose of visual art? Think about this from a range of perspectives, such as creating art, showing art, selling art, and studying art. Add more perspectives to discuss.

▲ **Fig. 1.1** *Grafitti in Italy*

▲ **Fig. 1.2** *Graffiti by Banksy on a 19th-century building in Treme, USA*

Art for the people

If we think about art from a national perspective, we can consider what role a government has in supporting art.

▲ **Fig. 1.3**

▲ **Fig. 1.4**

Task 2

In small groups, answer the following questions.

1. Look at the two examples of art above. Discuss how these make you feel.

2. Does your local town or city have any similar art? Would you like to have more of this kind of art? What would it be and where would you put it?

3. The Amherst Public Art Commission states:

   "Public art adds enormous value to the cultural, aesthetic and economic vitality of a community. It is now a well-accepted principle of urban design that public art contributes to a community's identity, fosters community pride and a sense of belonging, and enhances the quality of life for its residents and visitors. Towns gain real value through public art."

   What are some arguments for and *against* having public art?

4. Write a proposal for your government, asking for funding for public art. In your proposal, address these questions.
   - Economic: Who would decide which artist gets the money and how much?
   - Social: Should art reflect local cultural values?
   - Political: Should the government decide on what topics an artist covers?
   - Sustainability: Should the art be sustainable?

Empathy

Putting into words how something makes you feel can be a great exercise. It helps you learn about yourself and communicate your feelings. As you discuss how different pieces of art make you feel, try to use verbs to describe your feelings and adjectives to describe the art. Also take time to actively listen to how others feel about art. Try to understand their experiences, their reasoning, and their feelings.

Argument

"Subjective" means based on personal views or opinions. "Objective" refers to something based on facts, not affected by personal opinions. Many argue that art, like beauty, is subjective – art is a personal opinion not an objective fact. Those who think art is subjective might say that art is "in the eye of the beholder".

Art that reflects communities

In this section you will:

- discuss how your community is represented in art
- consider why some art is controversial and has been pulled down from public spaces.

A line of enquiry

Art can be a powerful tool to help you reflect on your own views and ideas. It can also help you to explore your community. What about art from your community or country? Consider what the art expresses. Look at its components. Is there anything that particularly shows how the art is relevant to you?

What are your country or your community's most beautiful aspects? Do you feel that local and national art represents this well? What about the challenges, and art that represents those?

Should some art be pulled down?

Because art shows what is important to us, what art is displayed, where it is displayed, and how it is displayed are points that are often debated.

There has been much debate about public statues that portray individuals who owned people as slaves or who benefited from the trade of humans as slaves. Community members have asked for these statues to be pulled down or at least relocated to museums. Indigenous peoples have made similar demands about statues that portray colonisers.

Quote

When the monument to the merchant and slave trader Edward Colston was torn down in Bristol in June 2020, the mayor of London, Sadiq Khan, stated, "Imagine what it's like as a Black person to walk past a statue of somebody who enslaved your ancestors. And we are *commemorating* them – *celebrating* them – as icons…".

▲ **Fig. 1.5** *Protesters in the UK pull down a statue of Edward Colston, who was a merchant involved in the slave trade in the 17th and 18th centuries*

In Mexico, the debate has centred on whether statues of Christopher Columbus should be pulled down. Read a summary of the debate below.

Should Columbus statues in Mexico stay or go?

In its most simplified version, the debate has two opposing fronts. The opposition party, *Partido Acción Nacional* (PAN), calls for the preservation of monuments as a vital representation of a country's history and an important connection to the past. Christopher Columbus statues represent an unavoidable and ineffaceable truth: the statue is part of the country's scenery and history, and as such it cannot and should not be negated. PAN accused President López Obrador of "manipulating history for political purposes". On the other hand, López Obrador and others who call for revisionism conceive statues as more than a representation of a static, collective past. Under this lens, monuments do not offer a neutral perspective: they can be divisive, they can misrepresent history, and to some, they can be hurtful reminders of a darker past.

From *Latin American Policy Review*

Task 3

In pairs, answer the following questions.

1. Who was Christopher Columbus?

2. In your own words, explain the arguments for and against pulling down Columbus's statue in Mexico.

3. Explain what the word monument means. How about the word monumental?

4. Imagine you work for United Nations Educational, Scientific and Cultural Organization (UNESCO), advising governments on culture and art. Discuss what you would do in each of the following scenarios. Provide an argument and explain your viewpoint in each case.

   a. A country is coming out of a civil war. Government leaders think all art that might remind people of the two sides that fought should be destroyed.

   b. An artist has created an expensive piece of art in the centre of a large city. Some of the city members find the art rude and feel it offends their religious beliefs. They want the art torn down.

   c. A group of students want university art that depicts individuals who held sexist or racist beliefs to be taken down from public display. They want the art moved to a museum where explanations can be given about who the individuals are and what they did.

Viewpoints

'Indigenous people' refers to the original inhabitants of an area. Sometimes the terms "First Peoples" or "Native Americans" are used, depending on the geographic context. Around the world, indigenous people are among the most impoverished and isolated populations. As indigenous peoples have gained political power, they are asking for public art that represents their values and acknowledges their history, struggles, and triumphs to be recognized.

Art all around us

In this section you will:

- consider the impact that art has on us
- think about how art can be used as a communication tool.

A line of enquiry

Humans like to be surrounded by beautiful and interesting things. This is why we decorate our houses in ways we find pleasing. We also design objects and spaces we use to make them attractive. In a way, we could say that art is all around us.

To create spaces and things that people like, designers need to understand people's tastes. They might choose to carry out primary research to learn more about what people do and don't like, and why. Primary research means gathering data that has not been collected before. Secondary research means using data that has already been gathered by other researchers.

Research

When writing research questions, avoid writing questions that might bias respondents to a particular answer. These are called leading questions and will produce biased data. For example, don't ask the question, "Smart people think this is a beautiful design for an airport. What do you think?" Instead, you could ask, "What do you think about the design of this airport?"

Task 4

Imagine your city's authorities have hired you to develop a new airport. They want the airport to be functional and beautiful. With a partner, design a research project to understand how stakeholders in your city view the airport's design.

1. Consider whose opinions you want to find out. Who is in your research population?

2. What perspectives might you consider?

3. Discuss how each of the research methods below

▲ **Fig. 1.6** *Phoenix Sky Harbor International Airport, USA*

might be particularly suitable, or unsuitable, for your research.

   a. Interviewing people to ask them for their views.

   b. Creating a survey.

   c. Appointing a focus group.

   d. Conducting observations.

   e. Reviewing existing documents.

4. What data and evidence are you looking for? How will you present the data?

5. Discuss how you would ensure that your research is ethical.

Communicating using art

Art is a powerful way to communicate ideas. Art can be used to remind people about the past or to warn them about the future. Through art, subtle ideas and feelings can be expressed, even when words are not allowed.

Task 5

1. In small groups, look at Figures 1.7 and 1.8 but don't read the text alongside. How does each image make you feel? What do you think each image is about?

2. Now read the texts. Discuss whether you think each image is effective at communicating its message.

3. Think of a piece of art that you feel expresses an important message. Explain the message to your group.

▲ Fig. 1.7

'Little Amal' is a giant puppet representing a ten-year-old Syrian refugee girl, created by Handspring Puppet Company. The puppet has travelled over 9000 km, across 13 countries, to help people to think about the experiences of children who are escaping from war, violence, and persecution. Little Amal hopes to attract attention wherever she goes, reminding people, "Don't forget about us".

▲ Fig. 1.8

Picasso painted *Guernica* in 1937, and it might be his most famous painting. The Basque town of Guernica in Spain was bombed by German Nazi forces on 26 April 1937. Picasso's painting depicts some of the horrors of war. Its deformed and broken shapes can feel nightmarish, taking us into the moments when bombs tore people's bodies and lives apart.

Quote

"There are some who argue that art reflects society, and others who think that society reflects art. Therefore, some worry that if violent art is made, a society will learn violence. Others respond that violent art is only produced because society is already violent." (Anon.) "Art is not a mirror held up to reality, but a hammer with which to shape it." (Berthold Brecht)

Sustainability

When considering what is beautiful, you could argue that sustainability should be considered. For example, an airport is beautiful if it does not create hazardous fumes or if it protects and preserves wildlife and insects; an airport that can help collect rainwater can be a beautiful building and a work of art. This is a refreshing way of thinking about what is beautiful and what is art, and which considers the impact of our creations.

Considering different perspectives

In your **Individual Report** of 1,500 to 2,000 words, you should aim to answer your own research question by reflecting on what you have learned through your research and by considering different perspectives. Your conclusion needs to show how the research you did helped shaped your answer to the question.

Skills focus – reflecting on your learning

Reflecting on how your perspective might have changed as you learn about other perspectives is an important skill. Consider the research question below and decide on your position on the issue.

"Should countries restrict art from other countries?"

1. What might each of the following people say in responding to the research question:
   - a local artist with a small following
   - a world-famous musician planning a world tour
   - a researcher (1) whose research shows that art exchanges can inspire new ideas
   - a researcher (2) who looks at how art by native cultures has been erased by Western art?

2. How does each viewpoint help develop your perspective?

Viewpoint to consider	New ideas it made me consider	Does this change my view a lot/some/not at all?
Artist		
Musician		
Researcher 1		
Researcher 2		

3. Now consider the question again, taking into account the new information you have gained. Has your perspective changed? Why or why not?

Proposed research questions

Look at the four research questions that have been suggested for Individual Reports on the topic of *Arts in Society*.

Evaluate each one. How suitable are they as research questions? How could they be modified to ensure that they meet the expectations of a full report?

1. Should a country return all art it has obtained from other countries, even if obtained them hundreds of years ago?
2. Should art be a mandatory part of school curriculums for students aged 16–18?
3. Can art result in war?
4. Is art good?

Sample student reflections

Three students examined the issue of whether art education should be an integral part of education globally. Read the three extracts from the students' conclusions, then answer the following questions.

1. To what extent does each of the students respond to the main issue?

2. How does Renata note that her point of view has changed as she learned from research?

3. Does Jeremy's approach make clear his personal perspective and how it has changed?

4. Which of the three students best discusses how their perspective has been impacted by learning about others' perspectives?

Renata

To answer whether art education should be an integral part of education around the world, I considered the views of Clain and Mark (2018), who argue that art education is a luxury that can be done away with in times of financial crisis. Their argument considered only how much education costs, not the effect it has on young people. I think governments should consider art education as a long-term investment, not just for economics but for the wellbeing of their population. Researchers highlight that art can help mental health (Argona 2010) and support people after conflicts. The stories of those impacted by art education, such as Luz and Veronica (2015), further convince me of the importance of art education.

Azul

I have had to do art classes every year in school. I was never interested in art and found this a waste of my time in school. Some researchers argue that art education has positive effects like helping people be more creative and resilient. But I never found this happened to me. On the other hand, there is the argument that art is a luxury that we cannot waste money on. I don't think art is a luxury.

Jeremy

When I started this project I thought art should not be a global priority. It seemed like something private – you like art or you don't. However, I learned about the impact of art in helping people affected by war and by disasters. I also learned about art projects that have been used to bring people of different religions together to resolve conflict. I learned about musicians from Israel and Palestine playing together and growing in friendship. I started to see art in a new light, as a tool for global peace. I think governments and international organizations like the United Nations should focus on supporting art, because it helps individuals and it helps the world become more peaceful.

Assessment tip

It is important to remember that you need to provide a clear answer to your research question. In this case, Azul fails to provide an answer. Your answer must be based on your reflections on other perspectives and evidence found through your research. Jeremy does well in clearly presenting an answer and explaining how his answer came from reflecting on his research and other perspectives.

Common misunderstanding

Your reflection does not need to show that you changed your point of view, but it does need to show how your point of view has developed – as Renata does. As you learn more about an issue, your views might not change, but they should evolve. Your understanding should also be greater and the reasons for your view better informed.

Supporting art in local communities

In many places funding for the arts is being cut. This does not affect everyone equally. If your family has art in their home and access to the internet, you can see and hear wonderful art. However, for some people these cuts might mean missing out on experiencing many cultural treasures. It might also affect how a society develops. Imagine if no one in your community knows how to make music or paint. What might your world be like for the next generation?

Skills focus – assessing a project's success

Use the crossword puzzle below to discover some ways to measure a project's success.

▲ Fig. 1.9

Across

2. Large paintings on walls that can tell stories or share information.

5. Art that can be hung on walls to teach, inspire, or motivate.

6. Counting the number of _____ to an event.

7. Measuring how much _____ you collect to help fund an art project.

Down

1. A way to measure how many times something online is watched.

3. Number of people who sign a _____ to ask a government or organization for change.

4. Used to collect responses to understand what people have learned.

Proposed projects

Look at the following four ideas that have been suggested for a Team Project on the topic of *Arts in Society*.

Evaluate each one. How suitable are they as projects? How could they be modified to become more appropriate and viable?

1. Organize a group of famous international artists to create a series of murals. Each mural will depict ways of helping the environment.

2. Record a music video to encourage communities around the world to be mindful of the beauty in their surroundings.

3. Work with a local primary school to organize an art fair where young students can learn about local artists.

4. Raise all of the funds to build a new theatre for your community.

Sample student reflections

Three students have reflected on how successful their projects were. Read their reflections and then answer the following questions.

1. Does each student explain clearly what the goal of their team project was? Can you summarize these goals in your own words?

2. What other information do you think Jen needs to supply in order to explain whether her team's project was successful?

3. Is Mirena's approach to this reflection successful?

4. Which of the three teams do you think was most successful in their project? Why?

Jen's team

I think our project was successful enough. We made posters that looked nice. Each poster had a picture of a different local artist's work. We made 40 posters and put them in shopping centres.

Mirena's team

Our project aimed to raise funds for local artists who struggle. Our goal was to raise enough funds for them to rent a community space and run an exhibition which would allow local community members to attend and the press to learn about the artists. We raised funds by selling T-shirts with the artists' work printed on them. We raised quite a bit but miscalculated how much the T-shirts would cost, so we did not get enough for the exhibition. But the artists were still happy. While the exhibition might be delayed, it will take place next year, allowing the artists to show their art to the community. I think, therefore, that our project was partly successful.

Zamir's team

The goal of our project was to help school children access art education. We worked with volunteers to run two art workshops open to children from our city. We had only 15 children at the first workshop but 50 at the second, as we realized that letting people know about the workshops was key to success. The children enjoyed and laughed in the workshops, and, when they left, 80 per cent said they were inspired to continue making art. Each child was given a small bag of paints to continue their artistic journey. We succeeded in exposing children to the wonders of art and providing them with resources to make more art.

Assessment tip

To be able to assess the success of your Team Project, you need to have a clear sense of what your goal was. If it was to raise awareness, you need to think about how to measure how much awareness was raised. If your goal was to fundraise, you need to think about how you kept track of the funds you were collecting. In Jen's case, we are uncertain what the goal of the project was and, therefore, how successful it was.

Common misunderstanding

You are not being assessed on how successful your project was but on how well you can evaluate whether and why the project was successful. You need to demonstrate that you understand what the project tried to do, what it did well or poorly, and what its impact was. If you created art posters, for example, you could consider the impact that the posters had in the local community. Did this meet your expectations?

Scan here to obtain the source material you need to carry out this examination practice work.

Question 3 in your **Written Exam** is a question based on a source that presents different arguments about the global issue. Candidates answer by writing an extended response. Candidates are required to analyse and evaluate the arguments, and make a reasoned judgement about the quality of the arguments.

Q3. Study Source 4.

Which argument do you find more convincing, Rosa's or Lin's?

Your answer should:

- consider both arguments
- evaluate their reasoning, evidence, and use of language
- support your judgement with their words and ideas.

Read the three sample student answers, then answer the questions that follow.

Aki's response

There is much debate about where art should be held. Should art be kept in museums, where it is safe, or in places where all people can access it? We also need to consider if art should be kept where it was originally made or where it has ended up now for some reason. I think art needs to be where it is safest, so that it can be enjoyed not just by us but by generations in the future. While both arguments presented in the source make valid points, Rosa about art belonging to its makers and Lin about art needing to be kept safe, in the end art should be where it is safer.

> Gives his views but this is not what the question calls for. Needs to focus on deciding which argument in the source is stronger and why.

> This is too vague. It makes no use of the source to explain what the points are.

Marisa's response

Art should be kept where its creators wish. If I was making a piece of art I would want to be able to choose where it goes. This is why I agree with Rosa's position. I think the artist should decide where art goes. As Rosa points out, art has been stolen in wars, and it is the correct thing to bring it back to its place of origin. The example of art stolen by the Nazis sheds a light on the injustice behind these actions. As Rosa notes, this is a matter of addressing an injustice, and it does not matter how long ago the injustice happened, it still needs to be addressed. Rosa's argument is logical. Lin's argument, on the other hand, might be biased because she is an art collector, and she might be more interested in possessing the art than in ensuring it is in the right place.

> Makes use of a clear example from one of the sources.

> Is there any evidence to prove bias? If yes, then show it.

> Does not engage equally with both arguments. The answer needs to be more balanced, considering strengths and weaknesses of both arguments.

Darva's response

To decide where art should be housed, one must consider several perspectives. Rosa, as an artist, presents the view that the location of art should be determined by its makers. She argues that art taken from a country is stolen, which she illustrates with how the Nazis stole art from Jewish victims. This argument, however, only holds for art that has been stolen. What about art that has been legally bought? Rosa further argues that art can bring tourism to a country. This is a good economic argument, but she provides little evidence that this might happen. There are only a few pieces of art famous enough to attract large crowds. Lin's argument comes from a different perspective, that of an art collector. Thus, Lin might not be as emotionally invested as Rosa. Lin's main argument is that art must be kept safe as it is a world treasure. This argument only holds if one agrees with the idea of 'global ownership'. If art belongs to a person or to a culture, then it is up to them to keep the art safe or not, and not for others to decide where to move it. On the other hand, as Lin notes, taking art back is not always safe. While art in a large museum is accessible to many, it is not accessible to all. After all, not everyone can go to museums in London or Paris. Thus, Lin's argument has some blind spots and is likely to be made by someone with a wealthy perspective. While both arguments have some merit, I think Lin's argument is stronger because it provides stronger examples and considers not just a personal perspective but also a global one.

> Evaluates the logic of Rosa's argument.

> Notes that an argument is logical, but also that it lacks evidence.

> Good consideration of possible vested interests.

> Good analysis of the argument's logic.

> Provides a clear answer to the question and arrives at this response by carefully considering both arguments.

> Analysis of the author's perspective. Good consideration of flaws in the argument.

Engaging with Question 3

1. Which student engaged most effectively with the source? Why do you think that?

2. How could Aki turn his questions into an evaluation of the sources?

3. Do you agree with Darva's final assessment of the sources? Explain your answer.

In this section you will:

- explore diverse examples of cultural heritage, including your own country's
- consider how the global community is changing
- investigate newly emerging online communities.

A line of enquiry

We are all familiar with communities. A group of people living in the same place, and sharing the same characteristics and interests, is a community. People within a community usually feel a "sense of community", wherever they are in the world. The term 'community' is also used in ecology to describe a group of interdependent plants or animals growing and living together in a specific habitat.

Can you think of some examples of human communities – groups of people that share the same attitudes, values, characteristics, and a sense of community? These could be local, national, and / or global. And what about non-human communities?

You may be less familiar with the idea of culture. What is culture? How would you define it and what examples could you give? Cultures have to grow and, of course, this means they change.

Cultural heritage

One way to look at how much, or how little, cultures around the world have grown and changed is to look at cultural heritage. We can think of heritage as historic buildings and cultural traditions that have been passed down from previous generations, or things of a special nature that are preserved by a nation. Look at the examples in the photographs.

▲ **Fig. 2.3** *Music is often an important part of a country's culture*

▲ **Fig. 2.4** *New buildings, like Dubai International Airport, are built all the time in United Arab Emirates*

▲ **Fig. 2.1** *Traditional Japanese tea ceremony*

▲ **Fig. 2.2** *Floating markets are a way of life in Thailand*

Task 1

In pairs, answer these questions.

1. What cultural heritage is being preserved in each photograph? As a group, what do they tell you about the nature of culture?

2. Do any of the photographs suggest change? Or that any change has taken place?

3. What role do you think religion plays in preserving cultures?

4. Do you think there may be elements of a country's past that it does not wish to show as its heritage? Explain, with examples.

5. Think about your own country and its cultural heritage. What comes to mind? Do you think of historic buildings or other things? What elements of your own culture are being preserved?

6. You have been invited by your country's tourism authority to design a brochure or poster for a new cultural heritage centre. What aspects of your culture would you include? What aspects of cultural heritage would visitors from a very different country be interested in?

New communities

Cultural heritage is mostly about preserving and showing a country's past. However, many communities are in the process of developing, perhaps making significant changes to how they lived in the past. There is also a growing number of new communities, including global ones, emerging in various parts of the world. For example, "New Age" communities are made up of people who share a particular philosophy of how to live together. "Utopian" societies are communities of people who seek to live a perfect, balanced life.

Perhaps the most significant modern development of culture and community is online. Think of how many times you have been on the internet and seen references to online communities.

Task 2

1. While you have been surfing the internet, how often have you been invited to "join our online community"? Think of support, discussion, and action communities. Give some examples.

2. Are online communities a good idea? Are they safe? What are some advantages and disadvantages of online communities?

3. If you were to develop your own online community, what would it be? What rules would you have for your members? Who might you not want in your community? Why not?

4. Imagine a new community that you would like to be part of that is not online. What would be the community's aim and mission? What would bring its members together? Would you like to start such a community? Where would it be based?

Argument

The book *Utopia* was written in 1516 by Thomas More. It explores the idea of an imaginary, perfect society which exists for the good of everyone in society. This idea was turned upside down in 1945 by George Orwell's book *1984*. In it, Orwell saw such a dream as impossible – an apparently perfect society becomes a dystopia (an undesirable or frightening community). A lively argument still remains about how to achieve a perfect, harmonious community.

Research

As people strive to protect their futures, for themselves and their families, many are looking to join "New Age" or "New Earth" communities. Many of these communities can be found online. You can join a "new music" community based in Sri Lanka or a "new consciousness" community based in Canada. Research new communities to get a sense of how they want to protect the future.

Popular culture

▲ **Fig. 2.5** *Toni Morrison was presented with a Presidential Medal of Freedom at the White House in the USA in 2012*

A line of enquiry

Popular culture is sometimes called contemporary culture. This tells us that culture is usually in the process of changing. Think about how popular culture was different when your parents were 25 years younger.

We are going to look back 50 years to the 1970s and get a sense of what was popular in culture in the USA at that time. That era in US history saw the Vietnam War come to an end and people were looking for peace. Environmentalism and feminism became much stronger movements, and the hippie culture of the 1960s was fading out. Read these extracts, which give one person's viewpoint.

The **cinema** became a force to be reckoned with.

- *The Godfather* ranks as one of the most highly rated movies of all time. The film was about the life of a mafia leader and was full of violence. Yet, it was the highest-grossing movie in US history, contradicting the activists' cries for peace and exposing the desire of a cultural transformation that the people looked forward to.
- *The French Connection* was another addition to the thriller category of anti-mafia movies that cinema was delving into.

The 1970s was an iconic era for the US **music industry**. Progressive rock dominated the industry and saw various bands and solo artists create havoc through this genre.

- The 70s saw the British band Led Zeppelin rise to the skies on their 'Stairway to Heaven' when the song became an emblem of rock and roll in US culture. The song features the most played guitar solo of all time.
- The Bee Gees came up with their super hit album *Spirits Having Flown*, which set them parallel to the Beatles and Elvis Presley when they had a run of six US chart-toppers in only a year. This album made disco the most popular genre of the 70s.

Termed the 'polyester decade' of **fashion**, the 1970s was a time of big transformation, going from hippie culture to modern culture. Men and women wore tight, fitted outfits with platform shoes and went around in bright colours.

- The decade saw a rise in the number of women working in corporate jobs, which increased the number of women wearing suits.
- Long, straight hair was the preferred choice and little to no jewellery.

New forms of **art** like photography, graffiti, feminist art, and environmental art were incorporated into the culture.

- With the development of the digital camera, Eric Fischl provided a new way to look at things, making photography a new form of art.
- Impressed by the hip-hop disco culture, Michael Craig Martin took graffiti to a whole new level.

Books were a prominent part of pop culture in the 1970s. Although television, music, and disco were the main focus of people, literature found its way through and never really died.

- Gabriel Garcia Marquez's *One Hundred Years of Solitude* was released in the USA and became a major hit. People related to magical realism instantly.
- *Bluest Eye* and *Song of Solomon* by Toni Morrison started the movement for African American people.

Task 3

In pairs, answer these questions.

1. Why is it a good idea to look at the USA when exploring popular culture? Where else would you look? Why?

2. Why do you think the cinema became 'a force to be reckoned with' in the 1970s?

3. What do you think of the new genre of mafia and anti-mafia movies that began in the 1970s? What does it tell you about US culture at the time?

4. Progressive rock, guitar solos, and disco are mentioned in the text. What does this tell you about music culture in the 1970s?

5. Bright colours, women wearing suits, long hair, no jewellery, platform shoes – what does this tell you about how US fashion culture was changing?

6. Did the USA really introduce new forms of art in the 1970s? Or did some of the forms of art mentioned exist long before the 1970s? What do you think might have been different about art in the 1970s?

7. Literature is centuries old. Why do you think this period attracted the attention of writers?

8. The article focuses on cinema, music, fashion, art, and literature.
   a. Does this match your views on what popular culture is? Explain your answer.
   b. Which aspects of popular culture do you think are missing from the article?

9. Analyse and evaluate this source. How much do you accept it as a reliable source exploring US popular culture in the 1970s? Find some 'facts' you would challenge as doubtful.

10. Focus on your country or region. Compare the current popular culture to the popular culture of 50 years ago. On a scale of 1–10, where 10 is "massive cultural change", where would you place your country?

11. With another pair, hold a panel discussion on: "Popular culture in the future, where we live and globally". Among other things, talk about:
    - how much popular culture has changed in your country
    - what has caused the changes and some consequences
    - whether popular culture is dominated now by globalization.

Sustainability

Forms of popular culture such as fashion, music, movies, comic books, hi-tech gadgets, gaming consoles, internet streaming services such as 24-hour news channels, social media, and similar forms could be argued to be non-sustainable. While popular culture brings people together to enjoy society and community, the way it goes about doing this could be a lot more sustainable.

Viewpoints

Not everyone enjoys popular culture. By its nature, it is contemporary and, as such, might not be welcomed by people who prefer traditional things or who choose to live in traditional societies. One viewpoint is that "popular" is a term to be wary of; it might have negative connotations for some people. For example, a political regime may not approve of popular culture because it changes the way society behaves.

Subcultures in Japan

In this section you will:

- explore examples of subcultures in Japanese society
- plan your own new subculture.

A line of enquiry

A subculture is a group that exists within a larger culture. Although it has some connections to the larger culture, a subculture has some beliefs, values, interests, norms, and / or cultural patterns that set it apart from the larger society it is part of. A group that does not have any connections to a larger culture is not a subculture.

Read about two examples of subcultures in Japanese society.

Kendama

Kendama, the traditional Japanese skill toy, has seen a boom in the last few years, presumably driven by social media. There are many videos and posts about the impressive tricks you can do with the toy, which has demonstrated that playing with a wooden ball on a string is a lot more exciting than it sounds. Organizations like the Tokyo Kendama Team (which hosts the Tokyo Kendama Grand Prix), high school and university clubs, as well as specialist shops and designated kendama hang-out spots, have all forged a larger community where players of all ages and levels can get together, share tips, and show off their skills.

▲ **Fig. 2.6** *Kendama toys*

Itasha

You've probably seen anime characters appearing on smartphones or as nail art. However, the ultimate declaration of love for your favourite fictional 2D muse is itasha. A portmanteau [a combination of words] combining itai (painful) and sha (vehicle), it sees owners decorate their cars with huge stickers and custom artwork featuring anime, manga, and video game characters. These big investments are an extreme form of fandom; a grand gesture to demonstrate one's devotion. The cars are proudly displayed at conventions and at weekend gatherings in the Akihabara UDX parking garage.

▲ **Fig. 2.7** *A decorated car, itasha style*

Task 4

In pairs, answer these questions.

1. What is it about kendama that suggests it is a subculture?

2. Why could it be argued that kendama is no longer a subculture?

3. In the description of itasha, other subcultures are mentioned. What are they?

4. Itasha is described as an extreme form of fandom. Can you think of any other examples of fandom?

5. What is it about these two subcultures that shows they are part of a larger culture?

6. Discuss these viewpoints. Can you think of any more viewpoints?
   - "Young people these days need their subcultures. It makes them feel part of a secret group that they think we know nothing about." (A parent)
   - "Life would be dull without our subcultures. I'd have to do traditional stuff all the time." (A teenager)
   - "There's money to be made in these subcultures. I invested in itasha and made a fortune." (A businesswoman)
   - "These subcultures are fine if they remain harmless. We keep an eye on them to ensure they remain morally and legally safe." (A politician)

7. Do you engage with any subcultures or with groups of like-minded people that you now see are subcultures? Share your experiences.

8. Plan your own subculture. Think about how and where you will introduce your subculture to others and how many members, or followers, you want. Here are some tips.
   - Be sure to have a specialist theme you want to share with a specific group of people.
   - There should be a feeling among members that they are an in-group and that outsiders don't really understand what they are doing or why they do it.
   - Your subculture must share some beliefs, values, etc. with the larger culture it exists within, but it should also have differences.

Argument

There is a counter-argument to the wonderful world of subcultures – that the people of planet Earth will not be able to move forward as one community while there are groups of people who either follow different pathways to others or are part of counter-cultures set against the dominant culture. Surely in order to achieve global peace, we need a one culture, one language, one race planet Earth?

Research

The world is full of wonderful and wide-ranging subcultures. Some examples are hipsters, hackers, new age, surf culture, cosplayers, skaters, goths, beatniks – it is a long list. In music, there are emos, hip-hop, grunge, K-pop, mods, punks, reggae. Sometimes, people are suspicious of such subcultures as they fear they are counter-culture and will change society radically. It is an interesting area to research.

Moving towards assessment – Individual Report

Developing global and national perspectives

In your **Individual Report** of 1,500 to 2,000 words, you should show understanding of different perspectives. You must include a global perspective and either a national or a local perspective. Engagement with the chosen perspectives needs to be sustained and detailed.

Skills focus – covering different perspectives

A core skill is being able to identify different perspectives.

Consider the research proposals below. Then answer the questions that follow.

Research proposals: general

- The effects of war on wheat supplies and how local conflicts have global impacts.
- Do invasive species have the right to remain where they are?
- Should child vaccination be compulsory in just urban areas of Canada?
- Should swimming be taught in all schools?

Research proposals: on the theme of cultures and communities

- Do indigenous peoples have a fair voice in national governments?
- Can music help solve cultural disharmony?
- Is football a global sport?

---

1. Look at each proposal from a global perspective. How global is each one?
2. Now look at each one from a local, regional, or national perspective. Do any proposals cover more than one geographical perspective?
3. What would you change to develop the way each proposal incorporates perspectives?

Proposed research questions

Look at the four research questions that have been suggested for Individual Reports on the topic of *Change in culture and communities*.

Evaluate each one. How suitable are they as research questions? How could they be modified to ensure that they meet the expectations of a full report?

1. Is getting a tattoo in a foreign language "cultural appropriation"?
2. Can food culture travel to different countries and still be considered authentic?
3. Describe how some cultures in the Pacific region have adapted to survive.
4. When is preserving cultural traditions a good idea?

Sample student extracts

Three students wrote reports exploring the impacts of the rise in popularity of foreign language films in mainstream cinema. Read through the report extracts, which explore some perspectives. Then answer the questions that follow.

Jelena

In 2021, one of the biggest-selling films worldwide was the story of a young woman's fight to preserve her Pacific island's traditional dance culture. It was a global hit despite being spoken entirely in Fijian. UNESCO (2022) said the film helped raise awareness globally of the fragility of the island way of life. The film was part of a growing trend in mainstream global cinema that uses the character's native language to enhance the authenticity of the story. While here in Fiji we benefited generally from the exposure in sharing our plight with the world, the nation also experienced a huge upsurge in interest in our dance traditions, which then spawned 'traditional' Fijian dance classes around the world. Unfortunately, these classes tended to teach their own interpretation of our culturally traditional dance, thereby having a negative impact on the very thing they set out to preserve.

Stuart

Attendance figures for cinema audiences in the USA for 2021 show a 7 per cent rise in the number of people watching main feature films that are not in English, compared with 2020 (Wicks, 2022). This rise demonstrates a renewed interest in world cinema among cinemagoers. The rise in demand is helping to fuel the cinema industry in less developed countries where there is a ready pool of talent waiting to be tapped into. The cinema of South East Asia is particularly popular, and local actors are able to become big stars as a consequence of this new global reach. In so doing, they are able to support their local communities.

Kelsy

The recent surge in interest in films not in English has had a diverse effect on the cinema industry. Cinema audiences are becoming more sophisticated than before and are willing to focus on a subtitled film in order to enjoy the full cultural experience of watching a story unfold in a different language. This can promote positive connections with new cultures. However, some local cinema industries, such as here in Hanoi, are beginning to tailor their output to cater for a more westernized audience and are watering down the very cultural experience that attracts filmgoers to their productions in the first place. If this process goes the full distance, we will simply end up with a Hollywood-style film in Vietnamese.

> **Assessment tip**
>
> Different perspectives do not necessarily have to be opposing. So, in this case, they might be seen as beneficial from a social, economic, or even environmental viewpoint. It may depend upon your choice of topic. For example, Stuart's extract highlights benefits from both cultural and economic perspectives.

> **Common misunderstanding**
>
> To gain credit for including a global perspective, students need to mention in their work a formal organization that is truly global such as UNESCO, the United Nations (UN), the World Health Organization (WHO), or a group of like-minded individuals with a common global identity such as vegans. Simply mentioning three or four countries or, as in Stuart's extract, a region, does not make a report global. They are simply various national examples.

1. Can you identify a supported global perspective in Jelena's extract?

2. Which types of perspectives are seen in Stuart's extract?

3. Does Kelsy's extract include a clear and supported national perspective?

4. Do any of the extracts offer more than one perspective? How are they identified?

Community growing spaces

Community gardens have many benefits for a local community. At the core of the concept is the desire to bring people together and build bonds around growing healthy and free produce. These gardens encourage community cohesion, teach new skills, support wildlife, and encourage local people to enjoy a fit and healthy lifestyle in a friendly and sustainable manner.

▲ Fig. 2.8

Do you think a community garden can be set up anywhere? What size might it need to be to function as a viable growing space? What different skills and benefits can members of a community bring to such a project? Does everyone benefit?

Skills focus – completing tasks and supporting others

A local council wants to improve sustainability and social cohesion in the area. Part of the plan is to encourage community group projects to convert patches of wasteland, road verges, and abandoned parkland into free-to-access community spaces for growing food. In addition, the groups involved will be encouraged to share their projects online with national and global audiences to show what can be achieved.

Imagine you want to organize and run one of these projects.

1. Decide where you would like to establish your garden, who it will serve, and how you will share your project progress on social media.

2. Think about the roles needed. Each person should contribute equally to the project. How will the roles differ from each other?

    Remember, you will need to demonstrate the strength of your performance in this process, so you need to consider:

    *   which tasks you can complete alone and when you will need to ask for help from others

    *   when you should make decisions about working alone or with help, and why

    *   at what point you should offer to support others in the team by sharing your own ideas and solutions

    *   how you should discuss and consider the ideas of others if they offer help and advice

    *   whether there should be a specific leadership role in the group.

3. What problems do you think you will encounter in this project? How do you think you might plan ahead to avoid or prepare for them?

Sample student reflections

A team of three students has completed an action. They have established a community garden and shared their progress online.

Read the notes each of them made in their journals at the end of the first growing season about their individual contributions to the whole project. Then answer these questions.

1. Who do you think was most engaged with the project? Explain why.
2. If you were Sanjay, what would you have done to change your situation?
3. How do you think Nina's role compared with Trish's role?
4. How well do you think Nina dealt with her issue with Sanjay and the blog?

Sanjay

My role was to coordinate the blog entries. I did this as best I could, but it was very time-consuming and I felt that I was constantly having to ask the other members of the group for their contributions. I should have been more outspoken about this, but I felt that it was easier for me to write my impressions of what was happening rather than struggle on. I allowed myself to become very detached from the project as I was writing about it but not actually getting involved. The others then began to suggest that I was not helping enough. I felt very left out.

Nina

The council had very clear guidelines as to how they wanted us to proceed, and it was a lot of work for me to ensure that everyone else stayed on task, but I think I managed to achieve this well. I was very efficient in this as I was always checking in on everyone in the group to make sure they didn't have any issues and, if they did, I was the one they came to for help. I did often have to ask Sanjay what was happening with the blog as he stopped talking to the group and the blog was an important element.

Trish

I am good with people so the task of organizing the work groups fell to me. I drew up work rotas and made sure everyone who volunteered had a task to do. I really enjoyed the process and the feel of everyone joining in and looking to me for leadership. The other group members did help out occasionally, but they seemed far more focused on their own elements of the project, which I guess is how it was supposed to work.

Assessment tip

You need to demonstrate that you were an asset to the team. This means that you did what was expected of you in your agreed role and that you were able to step in and help others when the need arose. For example, Sanjay appeared to be struggling with the blog. If you had been in the team, you might have described how to speed up team contributions to the blog to help Sanjay.

Common misunderstanding

Complaining about everyone else is not optimizing your own performance. Making excuses as to why another team member stopped you carrying out your role effectively is not useful. You need to focus on what you did that was positive even in the face of ineffective teammates. For example, Nina complained that Sanjay stopped talking to the group, so she needed to explain what she did to help Sanjay reconnect.

Moving towards assessment – Written Exam

Scan here to obtain the source material you need to carry out this examination practice work.

Question 2 in your **Written Exam** is a structured question based on a source that describes some research or evidence about the global issue. There will be two parts to the question. Candidates are required to evaluate the research or evidence, and suggest ways to research or test a claim related to the global issue.

Q2. Study Source 3.

a. "Supporting national cultural institutions is the responsible thing to do."

Explain the strengths and weaknesses of the research outlined in Source 3.

b. "Most people would be happy to pay for keeping their national heritage safe."

Explain how this claim could be tested. You should consider the research methods and evidence that could be used.

Read the two sample student answers, then answer the questions that follow.

Liam's response

a. The tone of this source comes across as very passionate. By using phrases such as "patriotic duty" and "preserving their own heritage", the researcher is attempting to raise support for their ideas by appealing to a reader's nationalistic pride. I think this makes the argument full of bias towards their personal opinion. Also, the researcher clearly states what ought to be done and how they think it would happen but really fails to justify these comments with detailed evidence. For example, they state, "One good solution" without actually clarifying who thinks it is good or who exactly it is good for. In addition, they say that people need to be pleased to help but without giving any counterview. With the exception of one reference to UNESCO, there is no link to any supporting evidence. This somewhat undermines the credibility of this source.

However, the researcher is not completely one-sided in their tone. They do suggest that "one might argue", suggesting that they are open to other views. Also, they do offer some justification as to why they take the position they do: "It is important to value our heritage". And then goes on to show where such efforts might lead, with the whole nation benefiting. On the whole, it appears to be a politically driven document and. because of that, this source is largely one-sided, however, it hints at alternative possibilities being available but not worth mentioning.

Annotations (left):
- Highlights the purpose of the research.
- Reinforces the evaluation.
- Uses source material to emphasize a point.
- Introduces the counter-perspective, the positives.
- Concluding summation of the evaluation.

Annotations (right):
- Signposts this as an issue but not as a possible weakness.
- Rather emotive. Stay neutral in tone to avoid suggestion of bias.
- Gives interim conclusion on the evaluation.
- Direct use of source material helps to highlight the researcher's personal perspective.

Starts by outlining the complexities to come.

Kamir's response

b. ==This is a difficult statement to== test. Measuring happiness is never straightforward as there are so many possible factors that can influence a person's state of mind and degree of happiness. However, if we are to test this claim, I would look to use a wide range of research methods to see it from several different perspectives. But, before we even get to that stage, the idea of "people" covers such a big group that ==I would consider it unwise to lump everyone together in the same category==. It might be more effective to narrow down the field of view to a single age group of men or women of specific socioeconomic qualities. If not, the research would be so varied as to prove almost meaningless.

People most clearly demonstrate their willingness to do something via ==their spending behaviour==. Their willingness to pay for something can be used as a measure of their acceptance or, in this case, "happiness" to do something. I would choose a group of wage earners, and therefore are most likely to have an element of disposable income. This group can be surveyed either by asking them directly for their views or indirectly by assessing their spending habits. The higher their spending, the more willing they would be to pay and so, by implication, be happier. This is a better method than simply asking them because people tend to distort their answers when asked about money.

Explains how the research needs to be defined.

Relates to the testing procedure.

Engaging with Question 2

Responses to Question **2a** should balance strengths and weakness of the research that underpins an argument.

1. Has Liam provided a balanced assessment of this research? Can you list the strengths and weakness he has detailed?

2. Liam considers the tone of this research passionate. How would you judge Liam's own tone?

Responses to Question **2b** should test the claim using relevant research methods to obtain useful evidence.

3. Do you think Kamir's approach is valid? Explain your reasons.

4. Can you think of additional research methods that would provide useful evidence that Kamir has not discussed?

3 Climate change, energy, and resources

In this section you will:

- understand the impact of climate change reform
- analyse the fairness of paying compensation to developing nations
- evaluate strategies for adaptation and survival.

Quote

"Our planet is still in the emergency room."

"Greenhouse gas emissions keep growing, global temperatures keep rising, and our planet is fast approaching tipping points that will make climate chaos irreversible."

"We are in the fight of our lives, and we are losing."

(Antonio Guterres)

A line of enquiry

The science is clear – climate change is happening. Global temperatures are rising with devastating effects on countries located mainly in the global south. International organizations such as the Intergovernmental Panel on Climate Change (IPCC) are warning that catastrophic impacts can only be avoided by drastic cuts in greenhouse gas emissions. However, some governments and people believe that the extent of the problem is exaggerated.

At the UN Climate Change Conference COP27 in November 2022, many countries agreed to wide-reaching reforms which will affect many areas of our lives. Pledges made by governments at summits do not always turn into reality. Questions such as where the finances to make these reforms should come from and what role technology should play in this need to be answered along the way.

Governments promise to create a better world

Begin by thinking about some proposed reforms. Study Figure 3.1.

Then read the actual pledges made at COP27 in 2022.

COP27 implementation plan

- Enhance a clean energy mix, including low-emission and renewable energy.
- Transform energy systems to accelerate transition to clean and renewable energy.
- Restore nature and ecosystems, including mangroves and forests, to achieve temperature goals.
- Reduce global warming to 1.5°C by cutting emissions.
- Establish a four-year programme on agriculture and food security.

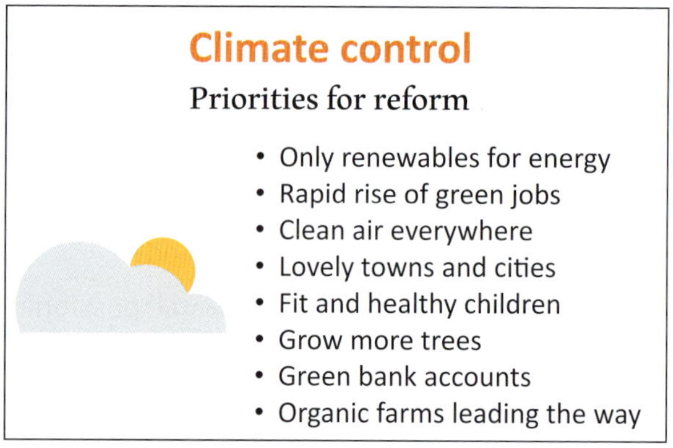

Climate control
Priorities for reform
• Only renewables for energy
• Rapid rise of green jobs
• Clean air everywhere
• Lovely towns and cities
• Fit and healthy children
• Grow more trees
• Green bank accounts
• Organic farms leading the way

▲ **Fig. 3.1** *Climate control presentation slide*

- Move to sustainable lifestyles and patterns of consumption.
- Transform financial systems, including banks, to establish a low-carbon global economy.

Task 1

In pairs, answer the following questions.

1. Discuss whether each reform on the presentation slide has been achieved, partly achieved, or not achieved.

2. Which reforms on the slide do you think are easiest or most difficult to implement?

3. Choose three of the pledges made at COP27. Explain what their impact could be for your country.

Empathy

Consider the exploitation of resources and cheap labour for profit in developing countries. If Western businesses use cheaper goods and labour in other countries to make more money, should they also be responsible for paying part of the loss and damages? And where does this leave us as consumers of these cheaper goods?

The loss and damage fund

At COP27, over 200 nations agreed that a fund should be set up to help pay for the damage that climate change is causing in developing countries. Here are some viewpoints and opinions that arose during the meeting.

Some estimate that damages will cost around $580 billion. Such a fund will bankrupt the USA and Europe.

Poorer countries have the same right to develop as developed countries, but they have a more difficult start because of climate change.

It's not the fault of developing countries that global temperatures are rising. Developed nations are responsible for this disaster.

Helping developing nations to be more resilient and build better infrastructure now can reduce the risk of climate migration.

Wealthy countries and individuals should be happy to donate their money for the good of all countries.

It's no longer clear who the rich countries are. Developed nations have a lot of debt and some emerging economies are big polluters. They should pay into the fund, not take out.

Task 2

1. In pairs, analyse and evaluate the viewpoints expressed above.

2. What are the strengths and weaknesses of a loss and damage fund? Suggest a strategy to decide how the fund could work.

- When should a country be paid from the fund? Give examples, such as the one in the table below.
- Who decides who will pay and who can receive money?
- How would you assess which countries are eligible for funding?

Pay in	Take out	Strengths	Weaknesses
EU countries, each according to GDP	Pakistan for flood damage	Helps Pakistan to rebuild infrastructure and repair damage caused by floods	Pakistan becomes dependent on the EU; some EU countries also have damages to pay for

The way net zero could become a reality

In this section you will:

- discuss how daily energy consumption can be reduced
- evaluate the impact of fusion energy.

A line of enquiry

Energy has become an expensive necessity. In many countries, it is used throughout the day from charging mobile phones, tablets, and laptops to cooking or washing clothes. Many people enjoy using new electronic gadgets, but saving money and reducing energy consumption are becoming increasingly important.

How could you help to reduce your family's energy bills?

Task 3

In pairs, answer the following questions.

1. Explain which of the actions in the table you and your family already do, which you want to do, or which you do not want to do. Explain your answers.

Unplug everything you are not using	Put your laptop to sleep when you are not using it	Turn your PC off if not using it in the next hour	Turn off lights when you leave a room
Change to LED light bulbs	Turn home thermostat down by 1–2 °C	Turn down the brightness on your screens and phone	Use natural light as much as possible
Make radiator reflectors to save heat	Use extra blankets and wear more clothes to keep warm	Warm up by being active, walking the dog, etc.	Try playing board games rather than computer games
Match the pan size to the hob ring or flame	Use the microwave more than the oven or hob	Use lids when cooking	Boil only the amount of water you need
Wash clothes at 30–40 °C	Defrost food overnight in the fridge	Switch to a green energy provider using renewable energy	Check energy ratings before buying new electronic devices
Track your carbon footprint	Challenge your friends to take action	Share your actions online	Recycle or donate old electrical items and cables

2. "Modern appliances and electronic gadgets have made our lives less environmentally friendly and more expensive. It would be best to ditch them." Discuss this statement from several different perspectives.

Sustainability

Solar energy is sustainable because it is natural, renewable, widely available, and has a low environmental impact. But what about the toxic waste created when solar panels reach the end of their lives? The International Renewable Energy Agency estimated there was about 250,000 tonnes of solar panel waste in the world in 2016, which could reach 78 million tonnes by 2050. Recycling solar panels is time-consuming and expensive, so most end up in landfill.

Carbon-free clean energy that powers stars

Read the following extract and answer the questions that follow.

This is a moment that scientists have dreamed of for well over half a century. The US's National Ignition Facility (NIF) has smashed the longest-standing goal in the quest for carbon-free energy from fusion, the nuclear process that powers stars.

Releasing energy through fusion reactions isn't unusual in the wider universe: the sun produces 4 billion kilograms' worth of pure energy from fusion reactions every single second. But, despite decades of hopes pinned on fusion as a clean and plentiful energy source on Earth, no one has ever shown it can release more energy than is needed to set it off – pretty fundamental for a power source. That is, until now.

What does it all mean? As ice and snow grip the UK, I hardly need say why energy is a good thing. It makes our lives better in a million and one ways. As a planet, we need a lot more of it. Nuclear fission and renewables are absolutely part of that story, but if the technology can be perfected, fusion offers carbon-free energy for everyone on the planet for thousands, probably millions, of years. It doesn't create long-lived radioactive waste, and there's no chance of meltdowns such as those at Chernobyl and Fukushima. Fusion would complement renewables by providing baseload energy, rain or shine, while taking up little precious land.

Of course, that doesn't mean fusion power that we can use is a reality yet. This is a single result on a single experiment. A commercially viable plant would need to produce 30 times energy out for energy in (30×), rather than the 1.54× seen in this experiment.

So this stunning achievement may not appear to bring us much closer to fusion power being available on the grid … at least, not directly. Indirectly, psychologically, the effect is akin to a trumpet to the ear: we now know fusion for energy is possible.

(*Arthur Turrell,* The Guardian, *13 December 2022*)

Task 4

In pairs, answer these questions.

1. Why is this scientific announcement so exciting, in the author's view?
2. List four advantages the article gives of fusion energy.
3. What are the challenges of using fusion for energy?
4. Create an interview with a scientist at the National Ignition Facility in the USA. Write at least five more questions and answers in your interview. Then present it as a role play. You could start the interview like this:

   Interviewer: You must be very excited about your achievement after 70 years without any success?

   Physicist: Of course. It's an amazing result. This experiment shows that dreams can come true. Carbon-free energy for the whole planet.

   Interviewer: Can you explain in simple terms exactly what happened in the experiment?

5. What are some of the factors that governments will need to consider before investing in fusion power?

Viewpoint

In some countries, people might have to choose between heating, air conditioning, water, or food. Opinions about whether energy should come from renewables or fossil fuels therefore differ. Families who struggle to pay high energy bills might care more about the affordability, whereas people with more income can choose to install solar panels on their house or have a wind turbine in their garden.

How sustainable is renewable energy?

In this section you will:

- consider how mining might affect the environment
- analyse the production and processing of materials needed for transition to renewable energy.

Causes and consequences

Cobalt is widely used in the production of goods such as batteries for smartphones, computers, and electric vehicles, for which demand is growing. Amnesty International has pointed out that producing these batteries relies on people working in unacceptable conditions that can affect their health. Amnesty International believes that phone manufacturers should have a responsibility to tell us if their supply chain uses such labour.

A line of enquiry

With the rise in demand for electronic devices that use rechargeable batteries, mining for the minerals and metals needed for the devices and batteries has increased globally. The global supply chain usually works in this way:

- countries that are rich in metals and minerals produce the goods
- mining companies process and refine the minerals
- the minerals are used by tech companies and car manufacturers and globally for mobile phones and electric vehicle (EV) batteries.

However, mining for these critical materials is a controversial topic. On the one hand, they are necessary to drive the development in technology required to reach net zero. On the other hand, mining can reduce biodiversity, produce greenhouse gas emissions, and contaminate water and soil.

▲ **Fig. 3.2** *Mining in Turkey*

▲ **Fig. 3.3** *A lithium battery pack for a car*

▲ **Fig. 3.4** *An EV car charging point*

Task 5

In pairs, answer this question.

1. Fill the gaps in the following dialogue between an EV driver (D) and an environmental activist (A).

   D: I bought the car because I believed that I can save money and the environment because a battery-only vehicle produces no _____.

   A: Yes, that's correct, but you have to think about how the battery is produced. What helps power the battery are minerals such as _____. Mining those minerals and the battery manufacturing process involves quite a lot of _____ _____.

   D: But we were told that we have to achieve _____ _____ by 2050. Surely, driving an EV is better for the _____ than driving a diesel car?

A: It's not that simple. Lithium mining is energy ____. Sometimes diesel ____ and carbon-emitting heavy ____ are involved.

D: As consumers we are driving the ____ for lithium mining because we think it's ____ energy.

A: Yes, lithium demand is expected to at least triple by 2025, which means more exploration and extraction globally. Only you can decide if this is something ____ or ____.

The green revolution and its dependency on mining materials

In order to switch to cleaner energy, governments will have to make big decisions about investing in renewables, and using more environmentally friendly materials as an alternative to fossil fuels.

An energy transition will involve energy efficiency, renewable energy generation, and mass electrification. Presently, about 80 per cent of the global population lives in countries that are net importers of fossil fuels.

Task 6

In pairs, study the two bar graphs and answer the following questions.

1. What contrast do the two bar graphs show? Which countries might control access to these resources in the future?

2. The economy of a country, medical and technological development, and renewable carbon-free energy all need minerals and metals for development. Should mining for these resources increase or decrease?

3. Producing 1 tonne of rare earth elements results in 2,000 tonnes of toxic waste, including 1 tonne of radioactive material. To what extent can mining for these elements be justified environmentally?

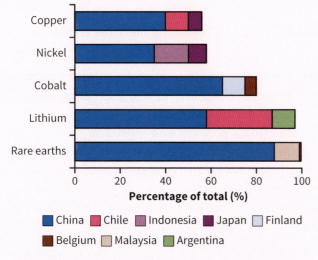

▲ **Fig. 3.5** Top **processors** of copper, nickel, cobalt, lithium, and rare earth elements

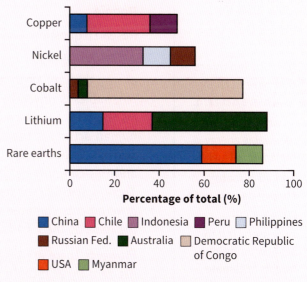

▲ **Fig. 3.6** Top **producers** of copper, nickel, cobalt, lithium, and rare earth elements

Moving towards assessment – Individual Report

Establishing a clear, global issue

In your **Individual Report** of 1,500 to 2,000 words, you should analyse a global issue, establishing the global nature of the issue and presenting relevant supporting information and explanations.

Skills focus – using climate change as a global issue

A student is attempting to include recent and relevant information that shows climate change is a global concern. They have created a mind map to decide which countries / regions they want to focus on in their report.

1. From what you have learned about climate change, anticipate and list the countries that would probably appear in a mind map.

2. Now reduce the number of countries so that you end up with two that you think are most useful for a thorough investigation and detailed research.

Sample student extracts

Three students have decided to write their Individual Reports on an issue related to climate change. Look at the paragraphs from each report which explain the issue as a global problem by focusing on a political perspective.

1. What are the strength and weaknesses of Ronnie's extract?

2. What could you add to Stefano's section to develop his writing?

3. How could Illyana develop her writing to have greater depth?

4. Who do you think has explained the global issue most clearly?

Proposed research questions

Look at the four research questions that have been suggested for Individual Reports on the topic of *Climate change, energy, and resources.*

Evaluate each one. How suitable are they as research questions? How could they be modified to ensure that they meet the expectations of a full report?

1. Describe ten things that have to change to achieve net zero.

2. To what extent can renewable energy replace fossil fuels?

3. Should climate change deniers be in government?

4. How useful is it to set new ambitious targets at climate summits when the Paris Agreement of 2015 has still not been achieved?

Ronnie

Research question: Can governments around the world achieve net zero by 2050?

As fossil fuel prices soar, the world is looking to develop renewable sources of energy that are clean and sustainable. The transformation from fossil fuels to renewables is driven by the rise in global temperatures and CO_2 emissions. As the UN Secretary-General stated during the climate conference in Egypt, human activity is the cause of the climate problem and must also be the solution. Globally, the temperature increase has to be limited to 1.5 degrees, and this can only be done by achieving global net zero emissions by 2050. There is scientific evidence that planet Earth is in an emergency room, and if governments continue to fail their targets, humanity will perish. The urgency of the issue at the COP27 climate conference could not be clearer.

However, there are disputes over how and if global governments can achieve net zero by 2050. In this essay, I will examine different viewpoints on to what extent this global problem is an urgent matter for all governments.

Stefano

Research question: Should developed nations be expected to pay for loss and damages caused by climate change?

Developing countries are feeling the effects of climate change. Droughts, floods, and rising sea levels pose a threat to many people in the global south. The developed world has realized that some countries are disproportionally hit by the climate crisis and need support. During COP27, a loss and damages fund was agreed to, which signalled a sign of hope that the world is coming together to solve the issue of climate change. However, the details of who should pay into the fund, and who should take out and for what, are left unanswered. A global transformation to a low-carbon economy is expected to require investments of at least US$4–6 trillion a year and the expectation that developed nations are coughing up the cash for developing nations is controversial. For example, during the conference, the USA and the EU disagreed over who should pay into the fund. And under a different president, the USA would perhaps not have agreed with the fund at all.

Illyana

Research question: Is deforestation really such a huge problem?

Clearing rainforests for agricultural use and to create more infrastructure for a growing global population is devastating and clearly bad news for CO_2 emissions and climate change. Trees capture greenhouse gases like CO_2, so the logical thing to do to combat climate change and achieve net zero is to plant more trees, not cut them down. Deforestation results in climate change and has negative consequences for plants, wildlife, and indigenous people. Indigenous people around the globe are particularly impacted by political decisions that allow or even encourage deforestation.

For instance, in recent years the environment in Brazil has suffered. Environmental agencies and the Indigenous Affairs Agency were dismantled, which resulted in more deforestation and a loss of indigenous lives. Deforestation in the Brazilian Amazon broke all records, and wildlife and native plants lost their habitat. However, the multinational food companies responsible for deforestation flourished. A spokesperson from one food company said, "There is a big demand for beef and the cattle has to be farmed. We provide what the world wants, more meat."

More recently, the Brazilian government has plans to reverse spiralling deforestation rates by encouraging environmental protections and a transition from ranching to farming on degraded pastureland. This would restore Brazil as a global player in the fight against climate change.

Assessment tip

Check the news to find a current global issue on the topic of *Climate change, energy, and resources*. Conferences and summits such as COP27 or COP15 are covered extensively in newspapers and on NGO websites, so use the media to help you to explain the significance of your global topic. Ronnie and Stefano have both chosen an issue that is recent and globally relevant, now and in the future. Both of their research questions relate to global targets linked to the UN and the sustainability goals.

Common misunderstanding

Your Individual Report should focus on one main global issue which you analyse from a variety of different perspectives. In her extract, Illyana focused on an in-depth analysis of the global issue in Brazil only, which is clearly linked to climate change. She explained how a country can be both for and against the globally agreed position, but she could have linked her comments to the UN net zero target to explain how this is a worldwide goal.

Moving towards assessment – Team Project

Adapting to climate change

Being able to cope better with climate change is just as important as trying to reduce the negative effects, because although the climate crisis is global, its impacts might be experienced in your home, community, or local area. But how can local communities adapt to excessive heat, drought, flooding, or rising sea levels? What influence and power do people in local areas have over the impacts of climate change?

Skills focus – collaborating in a team

A group of students plans to work together on the topic of adapting to climate change. They have already suggested four areas where adaptation might be necessary: agriculture, rising sea levels, rising temperatures, drought.

Work through the following issues.

1. Add more areas the team could consider as viable projects relevant to their local area or region. Which topics would not work in certain areas?

2. How should the team decide which topic to work on?

3. Conflict arises in a team as one student never completes their work on time and lets the others down. How would you try to resolve this problem?

4. Adapting to climate change could be compared to adapting to each other in a team. Who do you think should be responsible for calming emotions within a team and restoring communication?

5. Two team members voice strong opposing viewpoints. The other two members are very quiet and hardly talk. What problems can you predict for their team?

Proposed projects

Look at the following four ideas that have been suggested for a Team Project on the topic of *Climate change, energy, and resources*.

Evaluate each one. How suitable are they as projects? How could they be modified to become more appropriate and viable?

1. We will look at whether upgrading energy efficiency in houses is the best way for our community to adapt to changing weather patterns.

2. We will interview local families to see how much they have diversified their incoming energy sources.

3. To run a campaign against new nuclear plants, which are not in the best interest of people worldwide.

4. Should schools start having online classes during periods of heavy pollution or extremely hot weather?

Sample student reflections

Two students worked in separate teams on campaigns on the topic of *Climate change, energy, and resources*. Read what they wrote informally in their journals about their teamwork. Then answer the questions.

1. Of the two teams, which showed the better teamwork? Why do you think so?
2. What were the problems in Violet's team?
3. What could have been done to make Scott's team more successful?
4. What are the strengths in Violet's and Scott's teams?

Violet's team

Our school has a lot of single-glazed windows and, in the cold season, the wind makes our classroom really cold. So we decided that we needed to install double-glazed windows in school. At first, all team members agreed, but we had a very opinionated student in our group. He knew the answer to everything and dominated every discussion. He then decided that the way we wanted to raise money wouldn't work and suggested that we apply for a fund from the government. He had obviously looked into this and was very passionate about the political perspective, but the rest of us felt annoyed and demotivated by him. In the end, our group split in half. Two other students decided to write to the local government and the rest baked cakes. It wasn't the togetherness that I thought we should demonstrate as a team. In the end, there was no reply from the government and the cake sale didn't raise enough money to replace the windows either. If I could change one thing, I would have tried to get everybody to work together. I need to speak up more; otherwise strong teammates can just take over.

Scott's team

We set up a meeting on Zoom every week to discuss how far we had all got and what issues we faced in our research. Our team focused on the amount of water our school uses and we came up with a plan to install new flush systems in the toilets. We agreed that there should be a weekly Zoom meeting where we would discuss progress. Because we were friends, we knew the strengths and skills of each team member, so when it came to dividing the tasks, everybody got what they could do best. I ended up taking the role as a mediator because I like solving problems. At the beginning, two students wanted to be the leader, but in the end we decided we needed no leader at all and that worked very well. There were some initial disagreements as we wanted to address the window issue that Violet's group took, but after some discussion, we were happy with our focus.

Assessment tip

To work well in a team, you need to listen to others and not just push your own opinion. Violet's team struggled as there was a student with a strong character who did not listen to others. Violet doesn't criticize the student, but points out that this person was obviously passionate about the topic. Violet also suggests how she could have taken more of a negotiating role.

Common misunderstanding

Electing a leader is often one of the first things a team does. Although it can be a good idea, there are groups like Scott's where team members know each other very well and work well together without having a team leader. Don't assume that a leader can sort out all the problems in a team. It might be that someone with problem-solving or organizational skills benefits your team more than a leader.

Scan here to obtain the source material you need to carry out this examination practice work.

Question 4 in your **Written Exam** is a question based on all sources in the insert. Candidates answer by writing an extended response. Candidates are required to assess actions in response to the global issue and explain their judgements with reasons and evidence.

Q4. A government has decided to make contributions to a climate change disaster fund.

The following options are being considered:

- introduce a new environment tax for everyone in the country
- cancel the financial aid it usually provides to specific countries
- take an annual penalty tax from big multinational corporations with high pollution levels.

Which one of these actions would you recommend to the government, and why?

In your answer, you should:

- state your recommendation
- give reasons and evidence to support your choice
- use the material in the sources and / or any of your own ideas
- consider different arguments and perspectives.

Read the sample student answer, then answer the questions that follow.

> Rewrites the question. Every part of the answer needs to bring something of value.

> It would be a good idea to state clearly here which is the chosen option.

> Whenever possible and relevant, highlight taking and using material from the sources.

> Adding explanations for a viewpoint helps to establish a clear line of reasoning.

Jaqueline's response

When world leaders met at COP27, they agreed to set up a climate change loss and damages fund. It basically means countries that are disproportionately affected by climate change will be able to take money out of the pot to pay for damage to infrastructure and buildings. In the following, I will assess what the best way is to make contributions into such a fund.

I'd say that people in wealthier countries have a much higher carbon footprint than people in lower-income countries. The debate in Source 4 confirms that wealthier industrial countries created the problem in the first place and they should take responsibility for this. This means it would only be fair that people in developed countries such as the USA and in Europe paid more into the fund. I agree therefore with Onyiloko's ethical perspective. It seems wrong to me that people in developing countries who struggle with extreme weather due to climate change should be left to deal with this on their own. The world is interconnected and the right thing to do would be for governments in developed countries to help others.

How could a government raise money for a climate fund? The best way would be to introduce a new environment tax. In my country, the minister of industry and trade argued that there should be a green tariff on imports, which means that if countries have industries that produce goods with high carbon emissions, then those goods have to pay the extra green tariff. This is a carbon border adjustment mechanism and the tariff will be applied to iron and steel, cement, fertilizers, aluminium, electricity, hydrogen, and some chemicals. I think this is a good idea as it forces countries to produce goods in a cleaner way and the money that is raised could benefit the loss and damages fund. However, the disadvantage of increasing taxes for everyone is that many citizens even in wealthier countries already struggle to pay their bills. There is a high inflation in many countries and life has become very expensive. The writer in Source 3 explains how they cannot even afford to pay for cleaner energy, so we can see that from an economic perspective, many people would protest against paying more taxes. Perhaps a penalty tax for big polluting multinational companies would address the issue better from an economic perspective. On one hand, people in developed nations might argue that we should cancel the financial aid to certain countries altogether and pay the money to help our own citizens first. As Miguel in Source 4 explains, even wealthier countries have accumulated a huge national debt and cannot just pay millions into a disaster fund.

On the other hand, countries that are still developing their economies should also be treated fairly. It is unfortunate that most countries in the global south are impacted more drastically by climate change, as they are often poorer countries without infrastructure and health services. For example, some countries suffer from prolonged periods of drought, which can lead to food shortages and hunger. If flooding occurs, many people are forced to leave their homes and resettle. Low-income countries are also more vulnerable to illnesses that thrive in hotter climates or during flooding, which is very stressful for people. The money from the climate change disaster fund could provide better disaster management for people on low incomes. If governments in these countries could have access to more funding, they could make their countries more resilient, for example, by building flood defences or better drainage systems.

> Avoid asking questions. Instead make statements supported by evidence for a more logical and structurally sound response.

> Clearly considers an alternative perspective supported by evidence from the sources. A well-structured point.

> Target one of the actions (not all three) and build a solid debate around that choice.

> Clearly highlights a contrasting perspective.

> In concluding remarks, reinforce the line of reasoning already developed.

Engaging with Question 4

1. Is it clear which option Jaqueline chose to answer? Explain your answer.
2. Do you consider this response to be a balanced review of different perspectives?
3. In referring to the source material, how much do you think Jaqueline supported her arguments?
4. How would you change the way Jaqueline has answered this question in order to give a clearer response?
5. Does Jaqueline clearly explain her conclusion, and if so, do you think it is justified?

In this section you will:

- think about the nature of war
- learn about international humanitarian law
- consider what rules should guide different conflicts.

A line of enquiry

William Tecumseh Sherman, a general in the Union army during the American Civil War, stated, "I am tired and sick of war. Its glory is all moonshine. It is only those who have neither fired a shot, nor heard the shrieks and groans of the wounded who cry aloud for blood, for vengeance, for desolation. War is hell."

Think about what Sherman was saying. What images or stories about war does the quotation bring to your mind? Does the quotation seem to support the war as a way to achieve goals?

Thinking more broadly about war: do you think war is ever justified? The theory of *jus ad bellum* (just war) argues that there are times when war is just. The theory of *jus in bello* (justice in war) argues that there are both just and unjust ways to fight a war. Based on his quotation, do you think Sherman would agree that war can be just and fought justly?

Rules for war

International humanitarian law establishes rules for war.

- Military necessity: force should only be used to the extent that it is needed to accomplish military targets.
- Proportionality: force should not be excessive in relation to the goal sought.
- Distinction: combatants and non-combatants should be distinguished.
- Humanity: fighting armies should not aim to cause unnecessary suffering.

In small groups, complete Task 1, which analyses and reflects upon some of the rules of war.

Ever-changing world

International organizations such as the Red Cross, Red Crescent and the Red Crystal are *neutral* (they do not take sides) and *impartial* (they help people regardless of which side of a conflict they are on). Keeping these key characteristics allows these organizations to work in an area of conflict without the groups engaged in conflict worrying about what the organizations are doing. It also helps maintain a just war, as these organizations can help the wounded.

Task 1

1. Discuss whether you think wars should have rules. Discuss why rules might be necessary. Suggest as many reasons as you can.
2. Imagine your group has been asked to provide the United Nations with some rules for war. What rules would you suggest? Are all these rules equally important or could they be ranked in some way?
3. Consider how the world has changed between 1949 and the present. Do you think these changes necessitate new rules for war?

Rules during war

After the horrors of World War II, leaders from all over the world gathered in Geneva, Switzerland to discuss how to prevent a repeat of such cruelty against civilian populations. While there was agreement that avoiding all future wars would be ideal, world leaders decided to also make a set of rules, so that if conflict ever happened again, it would not repeat the violence against civilians seen during World War II.

The Geneva Convention sets out certain rules which much be followed when wars are fought:

1. Protect those who are not fighting, such as civilians, medical personnel, or aid workers.
2. Protect those who are no longer able to fight, such as injured soldiers or prisoners of war.
3. Do not target civilians.
4. Protect civilians and avoid harming their houses, food sources, water, etc.
5. Protect and care for the sick and wounded.
6. Do not attack hospitals, doctors, or those doing humanitarian or medical work.
7. Prohibit torture and degrading treatment of prisoners.
8. Provide prisoners with food and water. Allow them to communicate with their loved ones.
9. Limit the weapons and tactics that can be used in war, to avoid unnecessary suffering.
10. Forbid sexual violence.

Mindfulness

Take a moment to consider how you feel about personal conflict. Are there issues you would personally enter into conflict for, or do you avoid conflict at all costs? How you feel about conflict might be shaped by your personality and / or it could be shaped by how your family and culture view conflict. If you consider how your family views conflict, you might find that your views either mirror theirs or that your views are different.

Task 2

Deciding on an ethical course of action that respects these rules during a conflict can be challenging. With a partner, discuss what you would do if you were in charge of an army in each of the following scenarios.

1. Your soldiers are being shot at from a hospital. Would you shoot back into the hospital?
2. You have intelligence about a wanted terrorist who you believe will soon attack your civilians. However, any attack on this terrorist would result in the deaths of several children who live in the same house.

Perspectives

It could be argued that there need to be different rules for international conflicts and local conflicts. For example, if inhabitants of a city are violently protesting against the government, should the national army treat them as enemy soldiers to be fired upon? While the Geneva Convention addresses international conflict, the Universal Declaration of Human Rights provides guidance for how governments should treat their own populations.

Analysing conflict

In this section you will:

- consider current conflicts at different levels and how these are interlinked
- analyse the causes of conflict
- consider how different causes can interact to support further conflict.

A line of enquiry

If you read the news, conflict seems to be everywhere. You might note that not all conflict is international and classified as war. There can also be personal, local, national, and regional conflict.

▲ **Fig. 4.1** *Newspapers around the world discuss conflicts*

Task 3

Challenge yourselves to think about how local, national, and global conflicts might be interrelated. This means you should think about how local conflicts can result in national or international conflicts. Or think about how global conflicts can result in local disagreements. You can use historical examples you are aware of or discuss theoretical examples. Record your ideas in a table with headings: Local, National and Global, like the one shown. Use arrows to show the relationship between the conflicts.

Local	National	Global
Neighbours fight over the use of local woods for logging or as a nature reserve. →	A political party supports the views of those who want to log, and provides equipment. →	International environmental organizations get involved, conducting protests to demand that the logging stops.
A community group breaks into conflict as neighbours of different religions refuse to meet together.	← National religious groups start preaching in support of the country with the same beliefs.	← A war starts between neighbouring countries of different religions.

Causes of conflict

You might be thinking about how to prevent and / or stop conflict. To prevent conflict, we need to start by analysing it. To analyse an issue means to look at its parts, noting its causes and its consequences in order to understand the issue in depth. You should start by thinking about what causes conflict.

Climate change and conflict

By Vishva Bhatt

Increases in various climate-related disturbances such as floods, droughts, or fires further stress already vulnerable communities and threaten their livelihoods. Evidence links a rise in temperature to a rise in civil war. Researchers at Princeton University and the University of California, Berkeley found that a rise in average annual temperature by even 1° Celsius (1.8° Fahrenheit) leads to a 4.5% increase in civil war that year.

Experts point to Sudan's civil war as the first example of a modern climate change-induced conflict. The United Nations linked desertification and dwindling rainfall caused by rising temperatures to food and water insecurity. The insecurity then resulted in a rebellion that the Sudanese government reacted to with a campaign of violence. Famine plagued Sudan as rains dwindled and fertile land became arid. The lack of food paired with deep-rooted social and political tensions exacerbated the risk of conflict until the country broke out in civil war. Climate change heightened the competition for invaluable resources, further intensifying the pre-existing tensions between ethnic groups.

Research

If you only asked one side of a conflict what or who was the cause, it's very likely that you will get a one-sided view. This is why research is important. To understand a conflict, you need to understand both sides. In the Western Sahara conflict, Morocco does not recognize the Sahrawi Arab Democratic Republic, therefore its views on the causes for the conflict are different from those of the indigenous Sahrawi people.

Causes and consequences

Conflicts can have multiple causes. For example, if there is conflict between two cities because one is poor and the other is rich, the fact that inhabitants of the cities follow different religions might become a secondary cause for conflict. The Israeli / Palestinian conflict is an example of a conflict with multiple causes, including economic disparities and religious differences.

Task 4

1. In small groups, read the excerpt on climate change and conflict above. In your own words, explain how climate change might cause conflict.

2. What do the researchers note happens when average annual temperatures increase by even 1°C?

3. Was climate change the only reason for conflict in Sudan?

4. Do you think conflict would have erupted in Sudan if the effects of climate change had not been present?

Consequences of conflict

In this section you will:

- consider the consequences of conflict
- consider how conflict is changing in the 21st century.

A line of enquiry

Consequences are the effects or impacts something has. Conflicts have multiple effects. For example, personal conflicts can result in people feeling anxious, unsafe, and worried. Conflict can make a person tremble and sweat. It can disturb their sleep and lead them to change their lifestyle. Personal conflicts can have impacts that last for years.

When thinking about consequences, you have to consider not just immediate consequences, but also consequences that might only be visible in the longer term. Also, while some effects of a conflict might be expected, such as the death of those in combat, there can also be unexpected effects such as famine, migration, or technological developments.

Viewpoints

The history of wars is often written by the victors, so we might not hear about the consequences for the defeated. Going further, some voices are louder in a society than others, so the impact of war on adults, for example, might be heard about more than the impact on children. The impact on animals is rarely discussed. Animals have had multiple roles in battle, as transportation, messengers, and food.

Task 5

Burundi and Burkina Faso had short, minor conflicts up to 1990, with no visible effect on the economy. In the 1990s, however, their paths began to differ. The civil war in Burundi swiftly destroyed two decades of growth. Meanwhile, Burkina Faso had no conflict and benefited from strong global growth at the time. By 2008, Burkina Faso's average income was more than twice Burundi's.

The graphs compare the two countries over time. The line graph shows that the gross domestic product per capita (value of all goods and services divided by the population) grew in a similar way in both countries up to 1990. The bar graph shows when and how many deaths they experienced during conflict.

1. Look at the graph. What do the green bars represent?

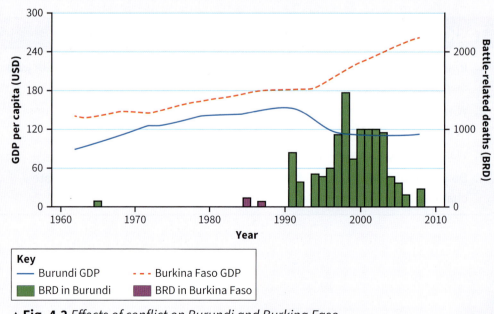

Key
— Burundi GDP   - - - Burkina Faso GDP
▇ BRD in Burundi   ▇ BRD in Burkina Faso

▲ **Fig. 4.2** *Effects of conflict on Burundi and Burkina Faso*

2. Which country is wealthier in 1980? In 2000?

3. Use the introduction to this task to argue that war can lead to more conflict due to poverty.

4. Consider other possible consequences of conflict. Copy and complete the following table with as many ideas as possible. Two examples have been provided for you. Note, some consequences might appear in more than one column.

Possible impacts of conflict			
Short term	**Long term**	**Expected**	**Unexpected**
Lack of access to food during war	*Destruction of farms and land, making growing food impossible*	*Lack of access to food*	*Chemical pollution of food reserves makes them poisonous*
Death of soldiers in armed conflict	*Effects on families (sadness, poverty)*	*Decrease of population, due to soldiers' deaths*	*Many disabled soldiers unable to work, traumatized, need care*

5. Review your table and circle the impacts that are personal consequences, draw a star next to national consequences, and underline global consequences. Some might fall in more than one perspective group.

6. Discuss what you think is the most significant impact of conflict. What criteria are you using to decide what is most significant? For example, are you considering the number of people impacted, the kind of impact, or how long the impact would last? You could, of course, use different criteria.

7. Now consider if conflict could have positive consequences. Try to think of an example of a conflict that has had a positive impact. Remember, you can consider a personal, local, or global conflict. Make sure you give specific examples or evidence to demonstrate the positive impact.

The changing nature of conflict

Conflict in the 21st century is not the same as it was in ancient times. In particular, technological advancements such as drones and social media have changed how conflict takes place. For example, think about how social media can spread information in seconds. This can affect how quickly a conflict starts and whether it spreads.

Task 6

1. Five students volunteer to take part in a role play. Each volunteer, with the help of your teacher, will represent a soldier in a different historical era. Each volunteer will describe the technology they used in battle without using the names of the technologies. The rest of the class will try to guess the era based on the technology described.

2. Describe technology used in conflict in the present. Contrast it with that used in previous eras.

3. Write a speech you could present to the United Nations about what rules for conflict are needed in an era of advanced technology. Keep your speech to one minute and try to deliver it without pausing. Present your speech to a partner and give each other feedback on how clear and logical your speech was.

Sustainability

The impact of conflict on the environment is something you might not have considered. Lead from bullets contaminates the ground and plants around a battle area. Landmines, another weapon of war, make land inaccessible to communities, and clearing them is often done by clearing vegetation with large machines, which can result in deforestation. Moreover, when the mines are detonated, hazardous chemicals are released into the environment.

Moving towards assessment – Individual Report

Researching your topic

In your **Individual Report** of 1,500 to 2,000 words, you will need to demonstrate that you can conduct research to understand a global issue that is currently relevant. In this case, you will look at how to select an issue within the topic of conflict and how to evaluate your sources.

Skills focus – finding suitable sources

For your Individual Report, you will need to demonstrate that you can learn about your issue by locating useful, valid sources. A useful source is one that gives you relevant information. A valid source is a source that gives correct and current information.

Look at the range of sources under consideration by a student and answer the questions that follow.

Individual Report issue: Can governments stop terrorism?

Potential sources

- A 2002 blog by the family of a teenager who was killed in an act of terrorism.
- The United Nations Counter-Terrorism Centre (UNCCT) Annual Report.
- A campaign video of a politician supporting stricter penalties for terrorists.
- A YouTube video by someone who says that people exaggerate the threat of terrorism.
- A report by a think tank on the threat of terrorism in different countries.
- News articles about recent terrorist attempts in your region.

---

1. Which sources provide a personal, local, regional, or national perspective?
2. Which sources provide a global perspective?
3. Which sources are likely to have quantitative data?

Proposed research questions

Look at the four research questions that have been suggested for Individual Reports on the topic of *Conflict and peace*.

Evaluate each one. How suitable are they as research questions? How could they be modified to ensure that they meet the expectations of a full report?

1. Should women be allowed to fight in combat?
2. What causes wars?
3. The only real reason for war is a fight over natural resources.
4. Is environmental conflict the most important conflict of the century?

Sample student evaluations

Read how three students evaluated the relevance and usefulness of some potential sources for their Individual Report. Look at the students' evaluations and answer the questions.

1. How many evaluative points does Luis make about his sources?
2. Why does Luis question whether some of his sources are biased? Do you think he presents enough evidence to make this claim?
3. How would you guide Cathena to improve her source evaluation?
4. What could Diego consider to evaluate the website he found?

Luis

To gain a global perspective on the extent of terrorism and how it threatens different countries, I looked at reports by global organizations including the UNCCT, and a report prepared by experts with a long reference list I can use to check data accuracy and to find other sources. The UN report provided a clear overview of global discussions on terrorism, with quantitative data that showed the size of the problem clearly. However, it lacked information on some smaller countries, leading me to change my national focus. For a national perspective, I looked at publications by our government and national think tanks. These noted that our government is working with regional allies to find terrorist leaders. All these sources appeared to support national actions without much criticism, making me question their bias. Blogs and YouTube videos by individuals on this topic were interesting, but I had to check that the information they provided was correct and did not simply present their opinions or assumptions. As I need to focus on the national perspective, not personal views, I did not use those sources.

Cathena

To understand how countries can co-operate to fight against terrorism, I looked for the anti-terrorism policies of several countries by navigating each government website. I also looked at newspapers discussing government actions against terrorism. Finally, I looked at declarations by global leaders on how terrorism should be addressed. These documents presented different points of views from various countries, but everyone agreed that terrorism must be stopped. I found a blog discussing how terrorism needs to be solved by ending poverty, which was an interesting perspective.

Diego

I think terrorists should have their passports taken away so they cannot travel to different countries. I did not find any sources that argued this position. The information I found looked at the impact of terrorism, which can destroy not just lives but also economies, as companies are worried about trading in countries where their money can be lost. I found a great website that noted that there are multiple reasons for terrorism and that these need to be addressed to stop terrorism.

Assessment tip

If you use sources with inaccurate or misleading information, your report might end with an inaccurate conclusion. For example, if Luis uses a YouTube video that makes unsubstantiated claims or provides inaccurate data, he might misunderstand the problem he is researching. This is why it is key to evaluate your sources to ensure the truthfulness and accuracy of how you present the issue.

Common misunderstanding

A person presenting their point of view is not biased – it is simply their point of view. A source is biased when it only presents one side of the argument and declines to engage with, or misrepresents, the other side. For example, if a student uses a source that blames local conflict on minorities, with no valid evidence, and refuses to acknowledge counter-arguments, the student would be using a biased source.

Resolving conflict

To help solve a conflict, you need to look at the conflict from different perspectives. If you don't understand why someone is offended, or how an event affected another group, it will be hard to find a useful solution. In an environmental conflict, such as deforestation, for example, the point of view of those who live in the forest will be different from those who live in distant places. Can you think of a situation where you felt another person did not agree with your views about the environment?

Skills focus – considering different perspectives relating to potential conflicts

For your Team Project, you need to work in a team that carries out an action to address a local issue. To identify a realistic and useful action, you need to clearly understand the issue you are addressing. It is important, therefore, to look at different perspectives on the issue. Each person in your team should help by researching a different perspective or aspect of the issue.

Look at the maps. What different perspectives does each source remind you to think about?

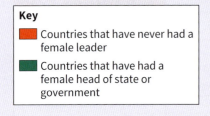

Key
- Countries that have never had a female leader
- Countries that have had a female head of state or government

▲ **Fig. 4.3** *Female leadership*

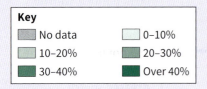

Key
- No data
- 0–10%
- 10–20%
- 20–30%
- 30–40%
- Over 40%

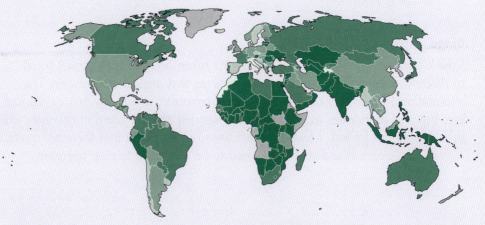

▲ **Fig. 4.4** *Global distribution of 13–15-year-old teenagers who reported being bullied at least once in the previous two months, 2015*

Sample student planning

Three groups wish to carry out a project to explore the issue of deforestation in their local region. Answer the following questions.

1. Each group has decided that they need two more members. Which group would you choose to join? Explain your reasons.
2. Ana's group are seeking a compromise. Is this an appropriate course of action for the group to take? Why or why not?
3. What are the strengths of the approach that Nageeb's team are suggesting?
4. Can you think of any additional viewpoints to bring in relating to a local issue of deforestation?

David

We have chosen to focus on the conflict between loggers and indigenous peoples as there is lots of news about this and we can interview some people. There are multiple perspectives to consider here: the loggers who sell wood to survive, the indigenous peoples whose homes are being destroyed by loggers, the politicians who seek to gain votes, and the buyers of the wood. We can also think about the international links – how people around the world buy the wood that is felled, even if it ruins the rainforest and causes global warming. Economics, politics, and sustainability are all part of this issue. A solution needs to address all of these.

Ana

We are looking at why loggers and indigenous peoples fight in the first place. It seems to be only about wood. And the land. I think they should just all get along. We will find ways to seek a compromise so that both groups are happy.

Nageeb

We are looking at why loggers and indigenous peoples are fighting. They have two clear perspectives: while loggers want to cut down trees, indigenous people want to continue living in their environment as they have done for many years. There are also the perspectives of those in the country who just want peace, and those who work driving the trucks needed to carry the trees. Our project will choose one of these perspectives and focus on addressing its problems.

Proposed projects

Look at the following four ideas that have been suggested for a Team Project on the topic of *Conflict and peace*.

Evaluate each one. How suitable are they as projects? How could they be modified to become more appropriate and viable?

1. What conflicts about identity exist in your community?
2. Do all community members feel they have a fair share of the local resources?
3. Why is there damaging and sometimes devastating conflict where you live?
4. Who is responsible for conflict management in the local region?

Assessment tip

Ensure you note what aspects and perspectives you considered in your Team Project, so you can note these in your Explanation of Planning and Research, and reflect on what you learned by considering different perspectives in your Reflective Paper. If you consider the perspective of indigenous peoples on the value of trees, for example, you might come to see the reason for a conflict in a completely new light.

Common misunderstanding

To understand a problem, you need to research it from multiple perspectives. However, your proposed action does not need to address every perspective you researched. For example, you might choose to help make people aware of the struggles of indigenous people losing their home to loggers, and not focus on the environmental impact of logging. Your course of action might focus on a small part of the problem or on the issues identified by one or a few perspectives.

Moving towards assessment – Written Exam

Scan here to obtain the source material you need to carry out this examination practice work.

> Question 1 in your **Written Exam** is a structured question based on several sources. There will be three or four parts to the question. Candidates are required to read the sources and analyse the information, arguments, and perspectives presented about the global issue.

Q1. Study Sources 1 and 2.

a. According to Source 1, what killed the greatest number of people in 2017?

b. From Source 2, identify two ways that technological advancements might affect conflict.

c. Using Source 1, explain why conflict is a personal issue.

d. Sources 1 and 2 discuss different types of conflict. Which type do you think world leaders should focus on solving first, and why?

Read the sample student answer, then answer the questions that follow.

> **Amelie's response**
>
> **a.** According to Source 1, in 2017, homicides killed the greatest number of people (almost half a million), ==more than war or terrorism.==
>
> **b.** Source 2 notes that artificial intelligence might be used to make different attacks more effective — making better decisions than humans, targeting more effectively. Second, new technology could make conflict deadlier, as demonstrated in the photograph in Source 2. For example, fighters could use drones to find their targets and deliver bombs to places where traditional fighting could not reach before.
>
> **c.** Conflict is a personal issue because it has causes and consequences at the personal level. ==Source 1 notes that almost half a million people were killed in homicides.== Homicide is personal issue, not caused by international conflict and not felt at the international level, but at the personal level. When a person is killed, their family is deeply affected. ==The source also notes that women and girls are in particular danger in their homes.== ==Again, this is a personal, private issue: gendered violence affects women and girls individually at the personal level. We could argue that women are endangered because of local or even global ideas on gender but, to the women affected by violence, it remains a personal issue. Organized crime is also mentioned. While the impact of this crime might also be felt at the national and even international level, it will be individuals at the personal level who make the choice or are forced to join crime gangs or face poverty or death.==

Goes beyond what the question asks for. Focus on what is asked for and no more.

Makes a direct connection to the source.

Further use of relevant material from the source demonstrates analysis.

In the relatively short time allowed, touch on an element and move on to include more. Don't repeat a point, unless you are sure it adds to your answer.

d. Technological advancements have changed conflict. New technology can help create more advanced weapons that can target more people, faster, in more dangerous ways. At the same time, however, research shows that "crime kills far more people than armed conflicts" (Source 1). Therefore, as a national leader, I would concentrate on solving crime as a way to stop conflict.

> Gives a clear answer to the question.

According to the source, in 2017, only 89,000 were killed in active armed conflict, which is less than a fifth of those killed by crime (Source 1). Crime has a greater impact than warfare in terms of deaths, therefore it demands the attention of governments.

> Begins to explore causes and consequences of a perspective.

Concentrating on preventing the development of advanced weapons while the population is killed by knives and guns makes no sense. We need to stop existing crime before worrying about crimes in the future. Crime creates insecurity and fear, damaging a society.

> Examines a possible counter-argument.

> Needs to be an explanation of how.

Crime, moreover, might allow the development of organizations that will use advanced technological weapons to obtain power and wealth. Crime also allows gangs to emerge, and they can then make use of new weapons. Source 2 notes that "Emerging technologies are lowering the barriers to the acquisition of biological weapons." This means that if crime is not controlled, criminals might become even more dangerous. Stopping crime, therefore, stops future threats to state peace.

> Tries to bring together the elements of the issue.

Because of its current impact – how many people it kills – and because it can result in the emergence of dangerous gangs and criminal networks, it is key for national leaders to concentrate on eradicating crime. This can be done by solving poverty, providing education, and ensuring a fair and efficient police force is set up.

> Concludes with a good summary of the argument.

Engaging with Question 1

Answer the following questions.

1. The first two parts of Question 1 usually test locating and interpreting specific details from the sources. Look again at the sources and devise questions you might ask others to test their understanding and your own of the source material.

2. How well do you think Amelie explains conflict as a personal issue?

3. Do you think Amelie justifies her choice of the type of conflict to resolve first? Does she use the source material appropriately?

In this section you will:

- consider the relationship between development, trade, and the giving and receiving of aid
- explore the relationship between free trade and Fairtrade
- discuss coffee, oil, and water in a free trade and Fairtrade context.

A line of enquiry

Development is not just an economic issue. You should also consider how people are affected by the ever-changing political landscape in different countries and how this impacts on daily life. As a result of policies towards trade, social development should be examined alongside economic development.

In an ideal world, every country would trade with each other, with the aim of sharing resources in global co-operation to supply people's needs and their desires. It really should be simple. However, in practice, global trade raises many issues and disagreements between countries, regions, and even continents about what should be traded, with whom, at what price, and under what terms and conditions.

Think about it from a national perspective. What do you know about your country's trade arrangements with other countries? Does it trade a lot or a little? Trading, aiding, and developing appear to be a triangle, with each interdependent on the others.

▲ **Fig. 5.1** *Benefits of Fairtrade*

Is free trade Fairtrade?

Fairtrade is a global organization that aims to ensure safe working conditions, fair terms for producers, and fair prices for all involved in production and sales.

Look at one interpretation of free trade. It's the opening speech made by Mr Renato Ruggiero, Director-General of the World Trade Organization (WTO), delivered in 1996 to the Argentinian Council on Foreign Relations.

It has been said that most policy makers look for the future in a rear-view mirror. Generals tend to fight the last war. Statesmen and diplomats, tasked with building tomorrow, usually start with a blueprint of the ancient regime. This temptation to look to the past is even stronger in today's globalizing economy, where all the landmarks seem new and where the ground under our feet is constantly shifting. It's also far more dangerous. We live in a world which is already launched on a path towards global free trade – it is a process which cannot be reversed or rolled back without unimaginable costs to our future growth and our future progress. The challenge now is to come to grips with a world of free trade and deeper integration, and to realize its immense benefits.

Task 1

In pairs, answer these questions.

1. Decide on your own definitions of free trade and Fairtrade. Compare them with another pair of students' definitions. How similar and different are they?

2. Do you agree with Ruggiero that policy makers look to the past? Give examples of those who do and those who do not.

3. What do you think he means by "unimaginable costs" to future growth and future progress?

4. Ruggiero stated that in 1996 the world was launched on a path to global free trade. Do you think he would be happy about the situation now? Has the world achieved the deeper integration he spoke of? Think about factors that have stood in the way of this that Ruggiero could not have predicted.

5. What message is the cartoon sending about Fairtrade? Does it make a reasonable point? Why or why not?

6. "Free trade and Fairtrade are both good ideas in principle but they can never really work well in practice." Discuss this statement.

Empathy

The aim of Fairtrade is to ensure safer and better working conditions, fair terms for trading for local farmers and producers, and, at the same time, fair prices for all involved in the production line and sales to consumers. What about empathy when it comes to buying the things you buy? Does your empathy stretch, for example, to purposefully seeking out Fairtrade sellers? Perhaps, given prices of goods, it's not so simple.

Bolivian Fairtrade coffee

Unión de Productores Agropecuarios (UPROAGRO) is an association of small-scale coffee growers located in northern Bolivia.

UPROAGRO has used the premium they receive from sales of Fairtrade certified coffee to start up several projects. These include:

- improvements to the infrastructure at the Tilata processing plant

- improvements to healthcare in the area

- providing a free breakfast to all children at local schools

- buying new equipment for the processing plants

- training for members of the co-operative in improving the productivity and quality of their coffee

- construction of a sanitation plant in the town of Tilata.

Sustainability

If we can obtain sustainable fuel from natural sources, then we should be able to live on a cleaner, greener, and more generous planet. But to what extent would this scenario affect trade? For example, to produce coffee and tea, we also need sustainable methods of cultivation, packaging, and delivery methods. Will we have to make judgements when some products we love are just not sustainable?

Task 2

In pairs, read about UPROAGRO and the projects it has started and then answer these questions.

1. From whichever perspective you look at Fairtrade organizations, they appear to be all good. Can you think of any viewpoints which do not agree?

2. Discuss the cost of oil. One of you argues that oil should be free to everyone globally, while the other argues that it's a regular product, just like coffee, which users must pay for.

3. Now hold another discussion, arguing about water. Given that humans die without it, shouldn't water be absolutely free, and shouldn't the entire process of providing it be Fairtrade?

Fast fashion

In this section you will:

- consider the advantages and disadvantages of fast fashion
- look at the components of slow fashion
- give a talk about the impact of cleaner and greener fashion on the established fashion industry.

A line of enquiry

The term "fast fashion" was first used about 30 years ago. It refers to clothing that is produced inexpensively, mimics fashion-house styles, and gets the clothes into the global marketplace to be sold cheaply. It allows retailers to offer a wide range of products and customers to increase their wardrobe at lower prices.

There are different perspectives about fast fashion. Read a viewpoint that is critical of it and some of the reasons why.

The dark side of fast fashion

According to an analysis by *Business Insider*, fashion production comprises 10 per cent of total global carbon emissions, as much as the European Union. It dries up water sources and pollutes rivers and streams, while 85 per cent of all textiles go to dumps each year. Even washing clothes releases 500,000 tons of microfibres into the ocean each year, the equivalent of 50 billion plastic bottles.

The Quantis International 2018 report found that the three main drivers of the industry's global pollution impacts are dyeing and finishing (36 per cent), yarn preparation (28 per cent), and fibre production (15 per cent). The report also established that fibre production has the largest impact on freshwater withdrawal (water diverted or withdrawn from a surface water or groundwater source) and ecosystem quality due to cotton cultivation, while the dyeing and finishing, yarn preparation, and fibre production stages have the highest impacts on resource depletion, due to the energy-intensive processes based on fossil fuel energy.

According to the UN Framework Convention on Climate Change, emissions from textile manufacturing alone are projected to skyrocket by 60 per cent by 2030.

Some advantages of fast fashion

The profits are excellent.

We can launch new trends quickly and shift high numbers to our global stores.

I can buy the latest gear and new styles. Why? Because they are affordable.

Our company's labour costs are low as we employ people who work for sensible pay.

As a global chain, we provide jobs for millions in places where they would otherwise be unemployed.

As a designer, I can make up a new garment in just a few weeks for a fast-fashion manufacturer.

With new technologies, fast fashion is getting faster. It's so exciting to be working at the high-tech end of modern fashion.

As a student, it's just practical to opt for fast fashion.

Task 3

In pairs, answer these questions.

1. How convinced are you of the dark side of fast fashion?

2. It's argued that fast fashion makes clothing disposable. This might be a factor in the UN's prediction of skyrocketing emissions by 2030. Do we make too many clothing items? What do you think happens to textile waste?

3. It can also be argued that pollution is inevitable if we live the way we do. Where do you think fast fashion ranks in the list of global pollution worries?

4. Do you think more people are becoming aware of fast fashion and the issues it raises?

5. Discuss each speech bubble comment. How valid are the viewpoints, arguments, or suggestions made?

6. Alternative viewpoints have developed in response to the growth of fast fashion. Copy and expand the table with some more information, perspectives, and ideas on these alternatives to fast fashion.

Ethical fashion	Eco fashion	Sustainable fashion
Data suggests 80% of fast-fashion workers are women aged 18–24; this is just not right and out of balance.	Also called green fashion. More clothes should be made of environmentally friendly materials.	It's simple – reduce the number of clothes people have.

7. What can people do to rebalance what seems to be happening in the fashion industry? Think of some examples from these perspectives, including your own: personal level, community level, professional, political, educational.

▲ Fig. 5.2

Cryptocurrency

In this section you will:

- explore the growth of cryptocurrency in Vietnam
- examine cryptocurrency from different viewpoints.

A line of enquiry

A major development in the 2020s is the growing use of digital currencies as an alternative to national currencies. Cryptocurrency is a digital payment system that doesn't rely on traditional banks. Anyone, anywhere in the world can send and receive payments. Cryptocurrency is stored in digital wallets and payments are recorded in a database which lists transactions.

How common is crypto?

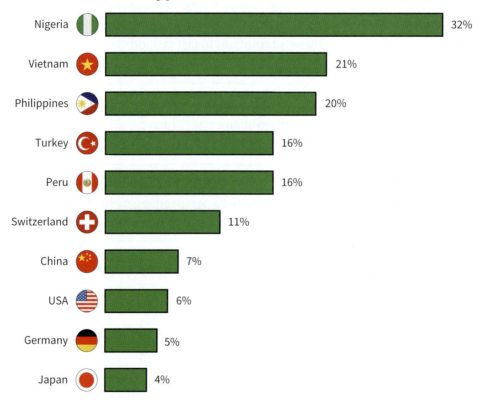

1,000–4,000 respondents per country

▲ **Fig. 5.3** *The percentage of respondents in selected countries who owned or used cryptocurrency in 2020*

According to the Crypto Adoption Index, in October 2021, Vietnam surpassed most countries in terms of the value of all cryptocurrency transactions, as well as payments made by individuals. Initially, cryptocurrency appeared to be a useful alternative when making overseas money transfers for those who were looking to avoid the hassle and costs associated with using banking services. In general, money transfers to and from another country have been representing a substantial share of Vietnam's GDP, which gave early cryptocurrency usage a good foothold in the country.

Another explanation for the popularity of cryptocurrency is that it is seen and used as an investment tool. The uncertainty brought about by the COVID-19 pandemic increased interest in investing in cryptocurrencies as a new income source for Vietnamese investors. Furthermore, the Vietnamese population has been known to embrace all things digital – the internet, smartphones, and digital payment formats, such as e-wallets and crypto assets.

Task 4

In pairs, answer these questions.

1. In your own words, what is the main reason that cryptocurrency was able to become established in Vietnam?

2. As it became established, it attracted attention from a specific group of users. Who were they?

3. "Embracing all things digital" is also given as a factor. Think about your own country or one you know well. To what extent does it embrace all things digital?

4. Are you surprised to see countries such as China, Germany, the USA and Japan as low crypto users? Why or why not?

5. Some of the popular cryptocurrencies are Bitcoin, Ethereum, Litecoin, and Ripple. Create a name for your own cryptocurrency and a reason for the name.

Perspectives

Cryptocurrency attracts a wide range of viewpoints covering a wide range of perspectives. For example, the local perception in Nigeria is likely to agree with the national perspective – that cryptocurrency is a practical, useful tool. But the local viewpoint in the USA might differ from the national perspective: a local investor in Bitcoin, for example, would be going against the mood of the national view.

Argument

What do you think about removing all national or regional currencies and replacing them with a single, global currency? Prior to money, humans traded items, such as animals or crops. That soon became a financial transaction, however. Could we stop using money? Or would it be simpler for all countries to adopt a single currency such as the US dollar?

Courses of action

In your **Individual Report** of 1,500 to 2,000 words, you should propose two courses of action for your chosen issue, give appropriate detail of how you would implement them, and evaluate their practicality and possible impact. You should then select a preferred option and justify your selection.

Skills focus – considering alternative courses of action

Look at some courses of action needed to help countries in South Asia. It's clear that when disaster strikes, a country needs swift help from whoever can help. Much of the help needed is from experienced emergency services and targeted financial support.

Proposed research questions

Look at the four research questions that have been suggested for Individual Reports on the topic of *Development, trade, and aid*.

Evaluate each one. How suitable are they as research questions? How could they be modified to ensure that they meet the expectations of a full report?

1. Development, trade, and aid have a triangular relationship – I will explain why.

2. The so-called Tiger economies of South East Asia are now more like kittens. What happened to soften them and do they need to dig in their claws more to compete again with the big cats of the USA, China, and India?

3. Cryptocurrency is the sensible and sustainable future for the global economy.

4. Free trade means never paying for anything.

Account 1
@UNICEFROSA • Follow

66% of Maldives could be under water if sea level rises by 1 metre.

As climate change worsens the scale, frequency and intensity of emergencies in #South Asia, we urge governments to double adaptation funding, to protect children by adapting the services on which they depend.

Account 1
@UNICEF_Pakistan • Follow

Yesterday @UNICEF launched the global Humanitarian Action for Children appeal to raise US$10.3 billion and provide 110 million children caught up in emergencies with assistance. Joining from Sindh, our colleague Zahida Jamali spoke about children's needs following #PakistanFloods.

Read the tweets and answer the questions.

1. Rising sea levels around the Maldives have a direct impact on children and their futures. How do you think this is impacting children's education?

2. The floods that affected Pakistan in 2022 were devastating. What factors do you think turned concerning events into a disaster and then a crisis?

3. Another perspective is that the Maldives and Pakistan both have strong and stable economies, and providing aid such as expertise and money is not the best approach. What are your thoughts on this?

4. What actions would you recommend as alternatives to raising funds or providing expertise?

Sample student extracts

Three students decided to write their Individual Reports on the issue of the financial aspect of disasters and crises. Their research question is:

"If governments were more efficient and provided funds to support local people after potential humanitarian disasters, would charity from others be needed?"

Read the extracts from their reports about courses of action and evaluate each using these questions.

1. While Mista raises interesting points, what is lacking in her approach?

2. What do you think of the courses of action Blu presents? How she has evidenced them?

3. What does Blu mean by "reactionary economics"?

4. Is it reasonable for Saskia to have included corruption, given the research question?

5. How could Saskia have improved her approach?

Mista

History shows that dependence is never an appropriate course of action. In the case of South Asia, where my case studies were carried out, the government had sufficient funds and, had they offered these sooner, the flooding wouldn't have been as bad. This would have saved probably 50 per cent of the schools that were damaged, simply by paying for flood barriers. Waiting for foreign aid is not an advisable course of action. A 1972 study of the refugee crisis in East Asia showed that waiting for foreign aid is not an advisable course of action.

Blu

Having researched two different perspectives — economic and humanitarian — I suggest two viable courses of action. In the first place, the government should have planned for this crisis as the evidence I gave clearly shows that it was inevitable. A swifter and stronger team being set up would have reduced the need for outside help and must be done in such cases in the future.

Secondly, once the crisis was apparent, the government should have been quicker to provide safe routes for the delivery of food, water, and equipment to those in the worst-hit regions. Interviews I included earlier show this was not the case.

My preferred action is the first one. Planning sensibly has to take precedence over reactionary economics.

Saskia

Corruption raises its ugly head yet again. It's commonplace in so many places, so it's not surprising that such disasters occur. Ministers are more interested in their own lives in the cities than in rural areas that don't add much to the economy. The only solution I can see is to clean up the government — a single action that resolves everything.

Assessment tip

Ensure that you make it very clear who is doing each course of action and how each can be done practically, so that a realistic proposal is put forward using the available human resources and other resources. For example, if Saskia was making the basis of her action to reduce corruption, she would need to be careful to make her action viable. Dealing with corruption in organizations can often take decades.

Common misunderstanding

Don't generalize courses of action. Remember that you have raised your own specific research question, so providing generalized actions does not deal directly with the issue. Mista mentions waiting for foreign aid, but doesn't give details of what this means or why countries would choose to do it. If it's a viable solution, Mista should develop it and use a country where this action might be sensible, perhaps looking at the advantages and disadvantages first.

Moving towards assessment – Team Project

Charitable aid

At a time when the divide between wealthier people and nations and those that are financially poorer is widening, global charitable aid is growing. Charities are trying to restore the balance and lessen the divide. They vary from huge global organizations to very small local operations. However, they all have one thing in common – they cannot make a profit. What is your opinion about charity? If charities cannot make a profit, they are surely not motivated by money. What are some advantages and disadvantages of charities? What is your opinion about charity?

Skills focus – reflecting on teamwork

It's likely that your teachers tell you that you are all part of one big community. Collaboration, working in a team, for example, on a community service project, may be the type of thing you often get involved in through school.

There are many different contexts where teamwork is vital for success. Each context measures success very differently. Choose a context from the grid and consider:

- the different roles that need to be played
- different aspects, perhaps depending on the background
- different viewpoints and perspectives
- some challenges and tensions that might occur
- some benefits and how success is likely to be measured by the team
- how and when the team might carry out its checkpoints and reflections.

Football team	Music band	Editorial team on a newspaper
Team of surgeons in a specialist hospital	Team of sales people in a shopping mall	Charity supporting local needs
Team of brokers working for a hedge fund in financial markets	Team of managers for a renewable energy company	Government ministers deciding how much to spend on the military

Sample student reflections

A large team completed its Team Project, working with a small local charity to support teenagers in developing entrepreneurial skills.

Read the extracts from three students' reflective reports where they wrote about the same incident. Then answer the questions.

1. Do you think Maxwell was correct to raise the problem as he perceived it? Are his objections valid?
2. Do you think the team had been fooled?
3. Do you have any empathy with Silva?

Proposed projects

Look at the following four ideas that have been suggested for a Team Project on the topic of *Development, trade, and aid*.

Evaluate each one. How suitable are they as projects? How could they be modified to become more appropriate and viable?

1. To work as a team for a global charity supporting people in need as disasters arise.
2. To be part of a global trade delegation speaking at a conference in a local town.
3. To run a project at school to warn of the dangers of cryptocurrency.
4. To raise awareness of a struggling local farmer who would benefit from a Fairtrade certificate.

4. Amma saw Maxwell's special meeting as a benefit. Do you agree? What about when Amma spoke to the 14-year-old?

5. How might each student continue their reflections on their teamwork?

Maxwell

At first, I agreed with the team that our focus on promoting local teenage business talent was a worthy cause. However, when we interviewed that 14-year-old at the charity centre who said he wanted to develop an energy-saving device that would only benefit wealthy people because the cost of installation exceeded £30,000, I had a big rethink.

I raised this with the team at a special meeting I called and, well, out of five of us, only three attended. Amma was on my side and she saw the situation we were in — we were using the charity's time and money to make rich people even richer! However, Silva didn't agree. She said that it was too late and we had already set the criteria — we couldn't complain if we've been fooled. That made me really frustrated. Let me explain about another very similar moment.

Silva

It was a challenge when Maxwell called the meeting. By that time in the project, everything was pretty much in place, so to make drastic changes would have messed things up. I personally couldn't see any benefits in what Maxwell was suggesting. I consulted the two other team members and they agreed with me and said they wouldn't attend Maxwell's meeting, as it was the third time he'd done this. Sometimes staying quiet in a team is the best approach.

Amma

Maxwell was right to raise this as a crunch point. What we should learn from this is to build in regular checking points where we can sort out any major issues before it's too late and the impacts are too big. It was a benefit that Maxwell raised the dilemma, and it showed we had been less effective as a team.

I spoke with the 14-year-old in confidence, and he told me that if no money was made it wouldn't be entrepreneurship, so it looks like we were at fault anyway. My personal actions here demonstrated that, if a problem is raised for the right reasons and responsibly, it adds value to the team. It's simply not possible for teams to engage 100 per cent all of the time.

Assessment tip

When you are reflecting on your teamwork, be sure to note specific examples where sharing the load would have helped. For example, you could give examples of where pooling the team's resources would have led to better use of skills. Maxwell tries to do this by calling the meeting but maybe goes about it the wrong way. Avoid being too general in reflecting on working as a team.

Common misunderstanding

The reflections should take into account the action that was undertaken. Avoid just listing occasions when individuals had differences; instead, evaluate these moments as weaknesses that could inform future collaboration. Maxwell was correct in trying to link his team's work to an expected outcome of supporting people who are not wealthy. It was good that three team members put forward their views in the context of the action, which was the interview at the charity centre.

Scan here to obtain the source material you need to carry out this examination practice work.

Question 3 in your **Written Exam** is a question based on a source that presents different arguments about the global issue. Candidates answer by writing an extended response. Candidates are required to analyse and evaluate the arguments, and make a reasoned judgement about the quality of the arguments.

Q3. Study Source 4.

Which argument do you find more convincing, Pippa's or Sam's?

Your answer should:

- consider both arguments
- evaluate their reasoning, evidence, and use of language
- support your judgement with their words and ideas.

Read the two sample student answers, then answer the questions that follow.

Sandy's response

The issue that both people are talking about is ==whether or not small countries should trade with larger ones.== When Pippa says she is worried that her small company will lose money if they keep on trying to get international work, what she is saying is ==that it's safer and easier to get contracts with companies in her own country.== This must be true as the two companies speak the same language and are close together in distance.

Pippa is scared about Covid-19 and ==what would happen if another similar pandemic came along.== She thinks her company would suffer and, as a result, her country would not be able to cope with the problems ==a pandemic raises such as supply of medical equipment.==

Investing at home is a good idea. It's a bit like when you are making sure you have everything you need in your house to make sure your family is fed and comfortable. Only then can you help others, with what you have left over.

==One thing I don't agree with is when Pippa says that countries shouldn't help each other if disaster strikes.== Let's face it — any country can have a crisis and when that happens we should all help.

Misinterprets the global issue; this is not accurate.

Makes an incorrect inference; Pippa does not say this.

Is there evidence of this in the text?

Tries to analyse what Pippa might be implying.

Is it clear what the final judgement is?

Ashad's response

Sam quotes persuasive evidence about what happened to his and Pippa's country in the past, in 1992, when a political policy led to closing doors on trading globally. This is detail that Pippa possibly wasn't aware about. However, if we look at why she cancelled the contract, we can see that it's for a different reason and is much more to do with nationalism and protecting her country.

Sam is making the point that balancing trade is also about sharing cultural and human values. If all countries did as Pippa suggests, there would probably be three or four powerful global trading regions that compete with each other mostly because of political differences. Smaller countries would just have to sign up with these and would lose their independent trading anyway.

Pippa's views can be seen as reasonable though. Putting her own country first, helping others where there is a spare supply of resources, and being less reliant on countries when a crisis or disaster occurs — it all sounds reasonable to me.

The language they both use reveals their viewpoints. Pippa talks about countries relying "way too much" on others, showing her frustration, but she uses "I'm afraid" in a way that shows she has some empathy with countries in need. The rhetorical question in the last thing she says and her use of "at home" and "similarly minded" show that she is not as global as Sam. Towards the end, Sam does start to show his colours with words such as "trust me", "I can tell you", and "after all". He comes across as the more knowledgeable.

In conclusion, I think Sam's reasoning and evidence are better targeted than Pippa's. Sam has prepared well and has focused his counter-argument on facts and consequences. Pippa is thinking closer to home, while Sam is thinking of more global perspectives. I do think Pippa has some valid points but Sam has made the more mature and sensible arguments.

Margin annotations:

> Uses source material well.

> Immediately shows skill of analysis.

> Is this good reasoning and based on evidence?

> This paragraph is very specific and uses almost 100 words on one theme.

> While the first point is an inference, the second point shows analysis skills.

Engaging with Question 3

1. What is the main fault with Sandy's response?

2. How much validity does Sandy's use of the comparison to a family household have in her response to the task?

3. What do you think about Sandy's final paragraph?

4. Ashad's response contains several strong evaluative points. Can you locate each one?

5. What do you think about the paragraph where Ashad focuses entirely on the language both people use?

6. How much do you agree with the conclusion that Ashad has arrived at?

> ### In this section you will:
>
> - explore how analogue differs from digital
> - speculate what the future might hold with quantum technology
> - learn more about algorithms and how they affect us.

▲ **Fig. 6.1** *Digital scales*

A line of enquiry

It is interesting to look at what "digital" actually means. A dictionary defines it as "data or signals expressed as a series of the digits 0 and 1". People will probably think of digital, however, as being associated with computers and electronics, and they would be right. What if you asked someone to tell you what digital means to them? What responses would you expect? What examples might they give?

Is digital always better? Will information in digital formats last for ever? Think about museums that still have writing by early humans on paper, clay, rocks – these are thousands of years old. Do you think we would be able to find the very first email compiled? Does the same logic apply to digital photographs? Can't they be more easily lost than original prints?

Quantum computers

▲ **Fig. 6.2** *Analogue scales*

The future is quantum! You don't need to understand the science of quantum physics, but have a look at the way it is being used in this decade and how it might lead to a post-digital world before very long.

Read the extracts from an article from NASA (National Aeronautics and Space Administration), then complete Task 1.

Google and NASA achieve quantum supremacy

Google, in partnership with NASA and Oak Ridge National Laboratory, has demonstrated the ability to compute in seconds what would take even the largest and most advanced supercomputers thousands of years, achieving a milestone known as quantum supremacy.

"Quantum computing is still in its infancy, but this transformative achievement rockets us forward," said Eugene Tu, center director at NASA's Ames Research Center in California's Silicon Valley. "Our missions in the decades to come to the Moon, Mars and beyond are all fueled by innovations like this one."

And here is what Eleanor Reiffel, a research scientist, added:

> "When I entered this field in 1996, I wasn't sure I'd be alive by the time we got to this point," said Rieffel. "Now, we can play around with quantum algorithms we couldn't run before. There are all these unknowns in quantum computing, and it's just incredibly exciting to enter the era where we can explore those unknowns and see what we find."

Task 1

The potential of quantum computing is likely to be a debate that takes us into the 2030s. In pairs, consider the implications and what a quantum world might look like.

1. What are some advantages of future computers being able to process in seconds what current computers take much longer to do?

2. What does Eugene Tu mean when he says future missions in space are fuelled by "innovations like this one"?

3. Look up the definition of "supremacy". It suggests a negative connotation. Do you think this is intended in the use of the term in the article title?

4. Eleanor Rieffel is excited to explore the unknown. Why is it important to explore the unknown?

5. NASA takes the position that speeding up the processing power of computers is a good thing and a benefit. Carry out a role play in which one of you is another NASA expert promoting these advances but your partner is arguing against them.

Algorithms

Not so long ago, "algorithm" was a jargon term only recognized by computer or digital experts. However, algorithms are so common today that you are likely to be impacted by at least one every single day. But what is an algorithm? And should we welcome them?

Task 2

1. Can you think of some examples or occasions where algorithms affect our daily lives?

2. What does this tell you about algorithms?

Perspectives

NASA is a national organization of the USA but it is regarded as the global leader in space exploration. It employs approximately 18,000 people directly and supports over 320,000 jobs across the USA. Its aims are also to benefit life on Earth, to run educational programmes for schools, and to promote diversity. Think about the perspective that NASA promotes. Is it national or international? Or is it truly global?

Sustainability

"Sustainable B2B digitalisation is a long-term process of symbiotic business-to-business relationships that result in non-digital companies becoming digital frontrunners. The companies which enable this process are often SMEs [small to medium-sized enterprises]. We call them 'digital enablers'."

(Dr Oliver Grün, president of the European Digital SME Alliance)

While Dr Grün's argument is for more businesses to digitize, he also implies that non-digital companies are not sustainable.

The digital divide

In this section you will:

- examine the digital divide from a UK perspective
- look at a case study from India relating to the urban and rural divide.

▲ **Fig. 6.3** *There's a real digital divide*

A line of enquiry

The Covid-19 pandemic showed the world how dependent it needed to be on digital technology. In many countries, people were forced to stay at home to ensure that they were safe from the coronavirus. This led to a complete rethink on how to go about two important aspects of society: work and education. As people around the world realized that they had to learn and work from home, online dependency grew. However, this also stretched the digital divide, with some people being left behind.

Read the article and complete Task 3.

Digital inclusion is a social issue

Millions of people in the UK don't have the basic digital skills they need to thrive in today's world. How much are they missing out on?

A lack of digital skills and access can have a huge negative impact on a person's life, leading to poorer health outcomes and a lower life expectancy, increased loneliness and social isolation, less access to jobs and education.

It can mean paying more for essentials, financial exclusion, an increased risk of experiencing poverty. People who are digitally excluded also lack a voice and visibility in the modern world, as government services and democracy increasingly move online.

What's more, it's those already at a disadvantage – through age, education, income, disability, or unemployment – who are most likely to be missing out, further widening the social inequality gap.

What's the impact of the digital divide?

- 3.7 billion people are digitally excluded worldwide (International Telecommunication Union (ITU), 2020)
- 10 million people in the UK lack the very basic foundation skills needed for our digital world (Lloyds Bank Essential Digital Skills survey, 2021)
- 6.9 million people in the UK will remain digitally excluded if nothing is done to help them (Centre for Economics and Business Research, 2018).

(From Good Things Foundation website)

Task 3

In pairs, answer these questions.

1. What does the article above tell you about the digital divide?

2. Does it surprise you that a country as developed as the United Kingdom is experiencing a digital divide in the 2020s?

3. What does the writer mean by saying that people who are digitally excluded "lack visibility"?

4. Which people are likely to be most affected by the digital divide?

▶

▶

5. Find out the population of the Earth in 2020. What percentage does the ITU suggest is digitally excluded? Does this statistic surprise you?

6. Form a group of four. You are going to give a brief talk on the digital provision in your area. You should all contribute, but nominate a team leader to deliver the talk to the class.

A case study – India's digital divide

The transcript below is from a speech delivered by the chief executive officer (CEO) of a digital enabling company based in the city of Bangalore – a city often referred to as India's Silicon Valley. The speech was given to the Indian government to raise awareness and prioritize a way forward.

Read the transcript, then answer the questions that follow.

I read in a 2019 report from the Telecom Regulatory Authority of India, the TRAI, that in its urban population, India had achieved just under 98 per cent of what we call internet density. As you may know, about 35 per cent of Indian people live in towns and cities. Contrast this to the figures for internet density in rural areas and it was barely 25 per cent.

Internet density is a measure of access to the internet. Overall, in our country, that stood at 48 per cent in 2019. That translates to the fact that for every one person who has the internet, there is one who does not.

I also noted that only about 15 per cent of internet users were women.

It is now nearly 2023 and while the situation is better, we still have a long way to go. Digital empowerment is vital to push India further up the global economic ladder. It disappoints me to hear that even now there are some local village communities that are restricting access to the internet for women and children.

I want us to connect people all across our nation, and that's why we are announcing extra funds for last-mile connectivity in rural areas.

Reflect

What about your own experience in the digital world? Do you feel you have good access to digital tools and the internet? Have you ever felt digitally excluded? If so, provide some examples as evidence. Maybe you can prepare an anecdote or two which tell the story of your own encounters with the digital world.

Task 4

The CEO's viewpoint has the national interest in mind. However, there seems to be a different viewpoint in some rural areas. The community leaders there present their own local perspectives.

1. What different perspectives and different viewpoints does the transcript present?

2. Could these perspectives and viewpoints be aligned?

3. How might local and national perspectives clash in other ways relating to digital provision?

Mindfulness

Can digital technologies such as smartphones, tablets, and laptop computers assist in achieving mindfulness? If so, how? Surely this is ironic – as these are the very devices that are also responsible for a high degree of human stress.

Fake news

In this section you will:

- engage with fake news by creating a fake news story
- learn about some of the tools used by creators and spreaders of fake news
- recognize and respond to the harm that fake news can cause.

A line of enquiry

It is easy to access a huge amount of information online in a matter of seconds. It is not so easy, however, to determine whether the information is reliable. This can be harmful to people who trust that the information is true but find out later that it has been distorted in some way or is completely untrue. Fake news is an example of the distortion of information.

Fake news

News or stories on the internet that are not true. They may be in the form of disinformation or misinformation.

Disinformation

False information that's created and shared to deliberately cause harm.

Misinformation

Generally used to refer to misleading information created or disseminated without a deliberate intent to cause harm.

Task 5

You are going to create a fake news report. In small groups, use the plan below to formulate your fake news.

- What is the topic of your news story? Decide on a catchy headline that attracts people to read your news story.
- You will need to think of information that is not reliable or not true. Is this going to be disinformation or misinformation? Or perhaps both?
- Design your news story as a web page or as a social media post to make it look authentic.
- Your news could be an advertisement. The aim will be to sell a product. The product is real, but the news to support it is not.
- Watch your language! Try to make it seem as if this is established news, so that readers feel they are finding out something that many people already know. Clever use of language achieves this.
- Present your fake facts as very believable ones.

Share your fake news with the other groups. Have a class discussion about how effective (how fake) they all are!

How harmful is fake news?

Some of the mechanisms that the creators of fake news use are very well established.

Clickbait

Posts, articles, and videos in social media, or websites that offer free items or make false claims to get as many people as possible to click on the article. The clickbaits might be funny, emotional, or catch your attention in another way.

Deepfakes

Facial movement technology of a well-known person in a video. For example, deepfaking a famous sports star to sell a product, or a leader to convey a fake message as if it were true.

Phishing

Fake communications via the internet that pretend to come from a reputable organization in order to gain someone's personal information.

Hoax

Disinformation that spreads because of its amazing and unbelievable topic and claims.

BOTs

Automated web robots that create fake social media profiles that are then used to spread fake news.

Satire

Articles using satirical or humourous content to fool people into thinking the content is real.

Task 6

It's clear from these mechanisms that the creators of fake news intend to mislead or even harm people. In small groups, consider each of these quotations and provide a response to each.

1. "There are only two intentions of fake news: one is to force people to be parted from their money; the other is to make people change their opinion of something."

2. "More than 50 per cent of children depend on social media for their source of news but only 33 per cent of children believe that news on the internet is true."

3. "Teachers state that only about 2 per cent of children have the literacy skills to tell the difference between real and fake news."

4. "Children are getting wiser to the problems of fake news."

5. "The trust that children have in the news, particularly in political news, is becoming less and less."

6. "It's easy to teach children some basic rules so that they can tell what is true or fake on social media and on websites."

Causes and consequences

You have examined some of the consequences of fake news, such as people losing their money, the effects on children's confidence and mental health, and people being persuaded to support something radical. But what of the causes of fake news? What triggers fake news to come about? Think about different reasons for misinformation. Why isn't all reported news accurate and factual?

Empathy

While being exposed to fake news enables many people to see it for what it is – unreliable, misleading, and potentially dangerous – there are some groups of people who, for one reason or another, are not able to recognize fake news. How have their needs been ignored? What about their rights to access news that is clear, plain, and true? How might this be achieved?

Moving towards assessment – Individual Report

Presenting different perspectives

In your **Individual Report** of 1,500 to 2,000 words, you should research, explore, and present different perspectives. There should be a global perspective and, additionally, a local, and / or national perspective. This means that to compile a good report you should present two or more different perspectives that are relevant to the issue in your research question.

Skills focus – covering a range of perspectives

Do these outline plans meet the requirement for a report on the digital world to cover appropriate perspectives?

Outline plans	Yes	No	Partly
1. I will consider three perspectives; two local and one global.			
2. The two perspectives I will cover are the digital divide and how it relates to the lack of spacecraft being built in Cambodia.			
3. I plan to consider six perspectives; three for and three against.			
4. My local perspective is also a global perspective so I only need the one.			
5. I am looking at the perspective of the world having no digital technology in the industrial era compared to the current digitally enabled world.			
6. Locally, the main issue of the relatively low availability of Wi-Fi connectivity will be contrasted with the relatively high access globally.			

Proposed research questions

Look at the four research questions that have been suggested for Individual Reports on the topic of *Digital world*.

Evaluate each one. How suitable are they as research questions? How could they be modified to ensure that they meet the expectations of a full report?

1. What is the digital divide?
2. To what extent does the USA have the most developed digital tools globally?
3. Everywhere has problems with digital technologies – locally and globally.
4. Should we all follow the example of China and restrict online access and social media content?

Sample student first drafts

Three students have decided to write their Individual Reports on the issue of the reliability of social media to report news in an accurate, fair, and responsible manner.

Look at the extracts from each student's draft opening page and answer the questions.

1. What is the fundamental problem with the approach that Jake has taken?
2. What is a strength of Jake's work?
3. Do you think Jasmin's report will be balanced?
4. Jasmin has approached the main issue in a reasonable way. But what element is she missing?
5. What do you think about the location choices in Jade's report?
6. Is "opposite" the correct word for Jade to use?

Jake

There is only one perspective that carries enough weight here and that is that yes, of course, social media should report things as they really are, covering only the facts of the matter. How could there be any alternative viewpoints? I will focus on how social media should ensure that they meet the needs of their users who are disadvantaged, such as those who find it difficult to establish whether what they read is accurate, for example, from the perspective of people who are partially sighted as they are often neglected in this area.

Jasmin

I am using a local social media influencer as a main source in my report. She has many years of experience in the region and has provided me with an in-depth perspective on how she has covered local issues in an accurate and empathic way and has always been open to scrutiny to ensure that her posts are accurate and standards are maintained. If global populist social media operated under the same principles then we would not have any misleading news. However, to make sure I have a balanced report, I will also focus the second half of my work on a local character, who has been reporting local news in a very inaccurate way, mainly to attract attention to herself, and causing protests in our area.

Jade

According to my first source, which is based in Russia, the Russian state government social media channels only ever show one side of an issue. Predictably, it's the side that conveys the point of view of the national government. Contrast this with where my second source is from – a local Dallas-based media channel's research centre here in the USA – and it will be shown that there are two opposite views being presented. News is only reliable when it sets out in its charter to responsibly report a counterview.

Assessment tip

Remember to focus on a single issue as you construct your research question. Think of a clear global perspective on the issue. For example, progress in digital enhancement is being made much faster in highly developed countries. Then think of the position in your country, or more locally, and ensure that a different perspective is present. You could contrast the global position to the relatively low broadband speeds in your area.

Common misunderstanding

It's important to begin analysing perspectives and not spend too much time describing them. In the case in the Assessment tip above, you might choose the digital capacity of Singapore, which is very high. You don't need to describe examples of this in any detail. For example, you could consider how digital facial recognition is used across the city in places such as banks and government offices. You will gain more marks if you analyse, for example, why Singapore has invested so much in extensive facial recognition.

Is digital surveillance going too far?

There are probably more ways of following a person's daily activities than ever before in the history of humankind. Every time you step out of your house, you are almost certainly subjected to some kind of surveillance or close observation. "Surveillance" suggests a military context and it is often associated with the work of government agencies and spying. How, then, does it relate to you, your friends, and your family?

1. Look at the two photographs. How usual, or normal, is it for you to see similar recording devices in your local area and elsewhere in your country?
2. How does each image make you feel?
3. Where would you like to see more digital surveillance devices being placed?
4. And where would you like to see some removed?

Proposed projects

Look at the following four ideas that have been suggested for a Team Project on the topic of *Digital world*.

Evaluate each one. How suitable are they as projects? How could they be modified to become more appropriate and viable?

1. The global growth of the digital world.
2. The rationale for digital surveillance devices in schools.
3. Should we be spending so much money on developing digital technology?
4. Resetting the digital divide is the aim of our local community project.

▲ **Fig. 6.4** *Closed-circuit television cameras*

▲ **Fig. 6.5** *Drone with a mounted camera*

Skills focus – obtaining suitable data and evidence

How likely are each of the following activities to be productive for a Team Project focused on surveillance using digital tools?

1. Providing video evidence to demonstrate the growing problem of traffic congestion in the local town.
2. Interviewing the staff at the town's railway or bus station for a survey about safety.
3. Having a meeting with the local police about how they go about policing the weekend's major football game.
4. Going on a short tour with a local council leader to look at how the town's parks are kept clean and pleasant for everybody to use.

Sample student planning

A team of three students has decided to collaborate on a project which explores the current differences in access to digital technology in their small town. In some parts of town, people are well served by digital technology, but in other parts of town there is a clear divide. They have identified three different aspects that each of them wishes to investigate. Examine their comments and answer these questions.

1. Which perspective is each of the three students presenting?
2. Would it be better if Ashma decided to spend a few days with a family with low access to digital technology?
3. How might Tamir and Reeta end up covering some of the same ground?
4. Consider the three aspects that the team will cover. Is there currently a good balance? Which perspectives might they have missed out?

> **Tamir**
>
> I will follow up the interest shown by a potential investor. They have $1 million to invest to develop digital communication technology and increase access for local people. The investment company wants to involve local people in the design and development stages, so that they can connect more people.

> **Ashma**
>
> I will spend a few days with a family who live in a wealthier part of town and show the wide range of digital tools that the family can access and use on a daily basis. This will work as an example of one side of the issue and will help to demonstrate the divide.

> **Reeta**
>
> I would like to focus on the need for government intervention and the proposal of a large grant from the local government, targeted at the poorer communities in town. We could ask the town mayor to give a speech to highlight the issue, raising awareness in the town.

Assessment tip

It's not sufficient to provide just information about a topic, even if it goes into some depth, without identifying a perspective. For instance, spending too much time on describing the range of digital technologies available in a town and how different they are from each other (for example, satellite internet access versus overhead cables) might lead you to spend less time on the different viewpoints held about the bigger issue.

Common misunderstanding

It's important to have an aim that can realistically be met. For example, Tamir, Ashma, and Reeta are debating how money can be raised to pay for digital technology in a disadvantaged part of town. It may work, money might be found, but your Team Project does not have to solve the issue. It is just as good to raise awareness that there is a divide in the town.

Moving towards assessment – Written Exam

Scan here to obtain the source material you need to carry out this examination practice work.

> Question 3 in your **Written Exam** is a question based on a source that presents different arguments about the global issue. Candidates answer by writing an extended response. Candidates are required to analyse and evaluate the arguments, and make a reasoned judgement about the quality of the arguments.

Q3. Study Source 4.

Which argument do you find more convincing, Abbey's or Krishna's?

Your answer should:

- consider both arguments
- evaluate their reasoning, evidence, and use of language
- support your judgement with their words and ideas.

Read the sample student answer, then answer the questions that follow.

Michael's response

I think that Krishna is better as he uses evidence from Germany. He also has a useful fact that some workers work six hours non-stop and this cannot be good for your health. Krishna places the argument in a global perspective also, by saying that he connects with people in various countries. He doesn't seem to have any bias either, whereas Abbey has a vested interest, which is that she has taken her job because she wants to work from home.

Abbey's reasoning is based on her own personal struggles. Her evidence is from her doctor. However, there may be another reason why she has the headaches. Abbey doesn't say what she answered in detail about her general health. It could be that she is socializing too much, staying out very late, and not sleeping well. We have to infer that it's only her long hours with the digital devices. As Krishna's evidence suggests, Abbey could have been having one of those "continuously working for six-hour periods".

▶

Uses source material appropriately, as an indirect quotation. Also makes a useful, reasoned point about health.

Develops a personal viewpoint. It may be evaluated for elements of bias or vested interest.

Begins to develop clear comparison between perspectives.

Shows awareness that Abbey has a personal perspective and is motivated by self-interest.

We can ignore where Michael says that Krishna is "better" as there is a balanced conclusion here. It's good to see some empathy with Abbey's perspective.

The **different tone they use** shows their different viewpoints. Abbey says she is angry and frustrated, while Krishna uses "comfortable" to describe how people need to be in the modern digital world.

Krishna argues that in jobs like theirs, he and Abbey should enjoy digital multitasking and **he gives details to explain**. Overall, **my conclusion is that Krishna's argument is more convincing, although he could have had more sympathy** with Abbey's medical worries.

Very sophisticated analysis and evaluation of specific language use.

It would have been good to have an example here.

Engaging with Question 3

1. Analyse the arguments presented by both Abbey and Krishna in Source 4, then copy and complete the tables below.

Abbey	
Strengths	**Weaknesses**
Justifies her stance with medical evidence.	

Krishna	
Strengths	**Weaknesses**
	Doesn't consider that modern life might not need to be digitally dependent.

2. What additional evidence could Abbey have used to strengthen her argument?

3. Comment on the structure of Michael's response.

4. How much of Michael's response is evaluation? Does he evaluate more than he analyses?

In this section you will:

- conduct a survey to get feedback on your ideas on education
- debate ideas about education.

A line of enquiry

The ancient Greek philosopher Plato argued that mathematics should be a fundamental part of education, as well as poetry and physical exercise. In West Africa, storytelling was a key part of education. In the 19th century, middle-class girls in Europe were taught skills such as needlework and etiquette that would, it was argued, help them to become good wives.

The education you receive is not the same as the education students received 200 or 300 years ago. What young people should learn has been the source of much debate for centuries, and continues to be.

Changing education

Today, many would argue that young people should be taught coding to programme computers.

▲ Fig. 7.1

Task 1

If you were in charge of designing the perfect school, what would your school look like? What would you put in the curriculum? Would you let students learn only what they wanted to? Would you change how the school is run? Maybe start classes at noon? Try and be as creative as possible – this is your chance to imagine your ideal school.

In pairs, work through the following.

1. What do you think education in the future might look like? Think of a future classroom environment.

2. Create a questionnaire to survey your classmates' opinions on your school and any positive changes that are needed to make it a better school for the future. Remember, the more focused your questions, the better the feedback you will receive.

3. Exchange questionnaires with another pair. Answer their questionnaire to help them improve their school for the future. Consider the feedback you have received. Use it to improve your ideas for your school.

Debating education

There are many different perspectives on education. Two different perspectives are given below.

Joe Marks, Head of Free Tree School, New Zealand

I think schools should be shaped around each child's interests. There is no point in trying to teach maths to a child who does not want to learn it. Instead, focus on art, or the sciences, or literature. Whatever the child likes. This means their education will match their interests and they will be engaged and enjoy learning. There will be fewer distractions in class and happy, participating children. "Don't these children need to learn other skills?" opponents might ask. Of course, and they will, when they find that they need them to expand their interests. Artists needing to measure paint, for example, will need to learn maths. Scientists wanting to explain their ideas will learn to write.

Afad Sayed, Head of New World Academy, Egypt

To succeed in the future, there are some things we all need: we need to be able to communicate, we need to be able to understand data, and we need to know how to stay healthy. For this reason, I think all schools should teach language, maths, and physical education. Young people might not enjoy some of these lessons, but they will come to appreciate them when they grow older and understand their benefits.

Task 2

In small groups, work through the following.

1. Look at the perspectives on education presented by the head teachers of two different schools. Decide which you think presents a better argument and why.
2. Think of a counter-argument for each of the perspectives.

Viewpoints

Consider these viewpoints about why schools exist. Economically, parents need a safe place for their children to be while they work. At the same time, children need to be prepared to be productive citizens, supporting the economy. Culturally, schools can provide education to help support the civic values of a society. Psychologically, schools can give children the support they need to grow up healthy.

Evidence

According to the United Nations, in 2020 about 25 per cent of primary schools around the world did not have access to electricity, drinking water, or toilets. Only about 50 per cent of schools had access to modern technology (ICT) and only about 50 per cent were accessible to students with disabilities. Perhaps discussions about the future of education need to start by considering inequalities in the present.

The value of education

In this section you will:

- research national and global education inequalities
- discuss local and global barriers to education, and possible solutions.

A line of enquiry

Everyone gains from education. A more educated world means people live longer, healthier lives. It means a world with less conflict and poverty.

- "Each year of education reduces the risk of conflict by about 20 per cent." (World Bank, 1999)
- "420 million people would be lifted out of poverty if they completed a secondary education." (UNESCO, 2017)
- "Children of literate mothers are 50 per cent more likely to live past the age of five." (UNESCO, 2010).
- "A single year of primary school can increase the wages women can earn by 10–20 per cent, and a secondary education means an increase of between 15 and 25 per cent." (Psacharopoulos and Patrinos, 2004)

Access to education

Despite the importance of education, many children around the world struggle to access safe, good-quality education.

Reflect

Imagine what your life would be like if you had no access to education. You might be unable to read this textbook. Letters would look like incomprehensible symbols, randomly placed on a page. Imagine how challenging it would be to go to a new place and find directions or a job if you had no education. Perhaps you would think differently about the world if you couldn't read or understand how things work.

Task 3

In pairs, consider the value of the data and the research that can be found by responding to each of these questions.

1. What is the percentage of school-age children around the world who are not in primary school? Is the number equal for boys and girls?

2. What is the percentage of school-age teenagers around the world who are not in secondary school?

3. How many school-age children in your country are not in primary school? Are there differences between boys and girls?

4. Are there other differences between those who do and do not go to school? Consider religion, ethnic identity, or geographic location.

5. How much does your government spend on education per person? How does that compare to what is spent in other countries?

6. How much do large economies like the USA, the UK, and China spend on education?

Barriers to education

Children struggle to access education for many reasons. In some places, there are no schools or they are too far away. In some cases, accessing education can even be dangerous. For example, getting an education almost cost Malala Yousafzai her life. Malala was 15 years old when she was shot by the Taliban for attending school. Despite this attempt on her life, Malala has continued her education and has worked hard to ensure other girls can attend school.

Task 4

Read Roseline's story. In pairs, answer the questions.

1. Describe what has caused Roseline to stop going to school.
2. Imagine you could write to Roseline and her parents about their decision to take her out of school. What would you tell them? Could you offer some solutions? Write a letter with your thoughts.

Sustainability

Education is a powerful tool for sustainability. As we become better educated about our world, we understand the impact our actions have on the environment and can act more quickly and more efficiently to protect our planet. For example, when we realised that certain substances damage the Earth's ozone layers, countries signed the Montreal Treaty to stop using these substances.

Roseline's story

My name is Roseline and I am 13 years old now. I live in Haiti and am one of six siblings.

My mother wanted us all to go to school and I used to go when I was younger. The school is only a couple of miles from our house. The education is free but my family still had to pay for books, pencils, and paper. There are lots of us so that is expensive and my parents began to argue about whether I should continue going to school after my twelfth birthday. My dad thought it was better for me to stay at home and help with the younger children. My mom was very upset. But as I started to mature, even my mom agreed it was not sensible for me to attend school anymore because the school is outside and there is no bathroom for girls. Then the Covid-19 pandemic happened and more kids stopped going to school.

I miss school. I had fun on the walk there and liked reading and learning new ideas. I am still good at reading but there is not much to read at home. I try to read some of my brothers' books, but they don't usually let me.

▲ **Fig. 7.2** *Elementary school is compulsory in Haiti for children aged 6–11 years*

Different perspectives on education

> **In this section you will:**
>
> - consider the arguments for and against bilingual education
> - find counter-arguments to different perspectives on education.

A line of enquiry

Education does not need to end when you are a certain age. You can keep learning all your life. When you think of education for all, you can think about the perspective of adults who want access to further education, for example, to train for new jobs.

There are also cultural perspectives on education. For instance, in a multilingual country, parents might want their children to be educated in their home language. However, the national government might want all students to learn a common language. Or it might decide that education needs to be bilingual or multilingual.

Read the text about education in South Africa, then answer the questions that follow.

Bilingual education in South Africa

In South Africa, there are twelve official languages, including South African sign language. The constitution allows that any of these languages may be used as a medium of instruction in schools. But only English and, in a minority of schools, Afrikaans are used and resourced beyond Grade 3.

Only 9 per cent of the population speak English as a home language and the majority of these speakers are white.

Basic Education Minister Angie Motshekga announced in March 2022 that indigenous African languages will be used as languages of instruction beyond Grade 3.

In 2019, Grade 6 learners involved in a bilingual pilot scored on average 28 percentage points higher in natural science and technology than their English-only counterparts.

▲ **Fig. 7.3** *Young pupils in a South African school*

[However,] successful implementation depends on preparing teachers for bilingual education.

Bilingual education is possible for all South Africa's children. With a multi-pronged approach to implementation … bilingual models will contribute to the goal of decolonising the country's schooling system.

Task 5

In pairs, answer the following questions.

1. How many official languages are spoken in South Africa?
2. What percentage of the population speaks English? Why do you think this number is so low?
3. Why do you think students in the pilot study did better than those learning only in English?
4. Do you think education in South Africa should be provided in multiple languages? Explain your answer.
5. Is education provided in more than one language in your country? Why or why not?
6. Discuss one of the following questions.
    - How would you feel entering a school where your language was not spoken?
    - How would you feel entering a school where few people shared your traditions?

▲ **Fig. 7.4**

Research

To decolonize education means to change the content and structure of education so it is no longer for the benefit of the colonizer but for the benefit of those previously colonized. This includes acknowledging the value of the indigenous languages, knowledge, and history of those who were colonized. Decolonizing education might include reading texts from local and diverse authors and learning more about the literary achievements of those who were colonized.

Argument

One way to find a counter-argument is to consider a different perspective. For example, if someone argues that school days should be longer, you could provide a counter-argument on how this would affect teachers, parents, siblings, janitorial staff, bus drivers, etc. For a parent, a longer school day might mean they have fewer hours to enjoy being with their children. For teachers, longer hours might mean needing more childcare for their own children.

Analysing a global perspective

For your **Individual Report** of 1,500 to 2,000 words, you should consider the issue from global and local / national perspectives. A global perspective is one that affects people around the world. In the case of education the United Nations Educational, Scientific and Cultural Organization (UNESCO) offers a global perspective.

Skills focus – establishing global perspectives on education

Look at the topics in the left-hand column of the table. Match them with appropriate perspectives in the right-hand column, which use sources that provide a global perspective.

Topics	Perspectives
1. Should governments provide special funding for indigenous children's education?	a. An interview with a local director of the International Action of Disability and Development Organization
2. Should adapting schools to support children with disabilities be mandatory?	b. A report from the United Nations on the state of education for all
3. Can education through television be expanded to make education accessible to all?	c. A report from an NGO trying to set up libraries in East Africa
4. Can education be made more accessible around the world by using only printed sources?	d. A report from an NGO working on digitalised global literacy

Sample student analyses

Three students have decided to write their Individual Reports on issues related to diversity and educational access. Read their analyses and answer the following questions.

1. What is each student's global issue?
2. What source(s), if any, does each student use to support the global perspective?
3. How could Jackson improve his work by adding a global perspective?
4. What global data does Omar use to demonstrate a global perspective?
5. How does Omar analyse the global perspective? How does he use it to build an argument?
6. Do you think Hai's strategy of discussing her personal perspective is appropriate?

Proposed research questions

Look at the four research questions that have been suggested for Individual Reports on the topic of *Education for all*.

Evaluate each one. How suitable are they as research questions? How could they be modified to ensure that they meet the expectations of a full report?

1. All education is good and that is how the human race has evolved.
2. To what extent is education unnecessary?
3. Should parents be able to choose not to send their children to school?
4. Who should pay for education?

Omar

Research question: Why should governments provide special funding for education for children with disabilities?

Disabilities affect people around the world. According to the World Bank, 1 billion people, or 15 per cent of the world's population, have some sort of disability (World Bank, 2022). This is a significant proportion of humanity that deserves access to quality education. Educational institutions, therefore, should make provisions for people with disabilities. At the moment, this is not happening. According to Humanity and Inclusion (2020), 50 per cent of children with disabilities in low- and middle-income countries are not in school. If we want to promote education for all, then education for children with disabilities, which is a global concern, needs to be prioritized.

Hai

Research question: Why schools need to change to support neurodiverse students.

Neurodiverse students include those with ADHD, ASD, and other diverse conditions. These are students who need special support in order to access and succeed in education (Wilson, 2015). Around the world, 15–20 per cent of people are neurodiverse (CDC, 2022). I have ADHD and I have struggled throughout school. A survey of our community shows that about 25 per cent of students in our schools also have ADHD (Survey, 2022). The school has limited support for these students and the government does not give the school any funding for them (Interview). Around the world, there are an increasing number of programmes to help neurodiverse students and these should be brought to our school. In the USA, for example, those diagnosed with one of thirteen recognized learning disabilities are entitled to free public education through the Individuals with Disabilities Education Act (IDEA). In other countries, however, neurodiversity is not fully understood and neurodiverse children are seen as bad students, rather than students needing help. This is a point made by a professor of education in his blog (2021).

Jackson

Research question: Why is education for adults important?

I think education for adults is important because adults need to be constantly learning to adapt to changes in the market. If you, for example, know the software language C++ but never learn Python, there are some jobs you will not be able to access. Adults need to update their education to get new jobs and avoid losing their job if their skills are not up to date. My aunt struggles to get a job because she did not study after school.

Assessment tip

Make sure your global perspective is clear and supported by evidence. Jackson does not give a specific global perspective. For example, he could have looked at the need for adult workforces to learn new skills as technology develops. A global organization, such as the World Economic Forum, might serve as a source that provides such a global perspective.

Common misunderstanding

Presenting the perspective of a few countries is not the same as presenting a single global perspective. Hai, for example, isolates the USA appropriately, but then confuses matters by adding other countries. She should look for global organizations that discuss how education for neurodiverse children around the world is lacking. A global perspective is a point of view voiced by an organization or person that has a global focus, such as the UN Secretary General.

Moving towards assessment – Team Project

Educational inequality

Look at the photographs and answer the questions.

1. Are there schools in your country that look like either of the photographs?
2. How would you feel as a student in each of these schools?
3. What challenges do you think each group of students faces on their educational journey?

▲ **Fig. 7.5** *A school with limited resources*   ▲ **Fig. 7.6** *A school with the latest technology*

Skills focus – reflecting on group work

Look at the table and imagine you have carried out a Team Project investigating access to higher education in the local region.

Team tasks	What went well	What didn't go well	What the team could have done differently
Working together to create a plan			
Collecting data on access to education			
Discussing different perspectives			
Working together on the project			
Evaluating the project's success			
Other aspects			

Sample student reflections

Three students participated in different projects seeking to increase educational equality. Look at their reflections on teamwork and answer the following questions.

1. How does Iliana discuss teammates' work? Do you think she provides enough information?

2. Do you think Iliana or Zahir was more thoughtful about how they could have been better teammates? Why?

3. What are some weaknesses of Juan's report?

4. Which student do you think has learned the most from the experience? Explain your answer.

Iliana

My team decided to build a game to teach children from a poor neighbourhood to read. I was never in full agreement with this project, so I found it hard to be enthusiastic and put enough energy into it. This was a mistake on my part as it affected my teammates' moods. When we took the game to the children and I saw their smiles, I realized that I was wrong and that my teammates had led me to do something amazing. In future, I plan to be more open to ideas that are not mine and to keep a good attitude during work. I will also try and voice my opinion better so I feel heard. I think my teammates did a good job, to be honest. We all worked hard to get information and build the game, so I think we deserve credit for that.

Zahir

My team split the work so that each of us was responsible for finding barriers to education on different continents. From there, we were supposed to find inspiration for a local project. The focus was all wrong, however, and looking at continents made us lose time, so we then had to rush a project which raised funds for a local education charity. In future, I think it is important for teams to think about their goal before they rush out to do things. Time management is also important. We didn't discuss our project until it was almost too late and then had to rush it. In future, I will try to set up a timeline to avoid this.

Juan

Our team decided to have each person doing a separate task and then bring it all together. This was not the best plan because we did not realize what was wrong until we all came together. David was in charge of contacting influencers who could help us raise awareness about local education issues, but he didn't do that. So our project failed at the end because of that.

Assessment tip

We can all improve how we work with others by explaining ourselves more clearly and by being better listeners. Your reflection should look at both what your teammates did in their specific roles and how you all interacted as team members. A good reflection will have specific examples of areas where your team not only did well but also struggled.

Common misunderstanding

A reflection asks "Why?" If you simply list what each person in your team was supposed to do, who failed and/or who did well, you are not asking "Why?" For example, why did David in Juan's team not complete his task? Perhaps he didn't understand it or he felt overwhelmed. Maybe he needed a partner to support him in the task.

Moving towards assessment – Written Exam

Scan here to obtain the source material you need to carry out this examination practice work.

> Question 4 in your **Written Exam** is a question based on all sources in the insert. Candidates answer by writing an extended response. Candidates are required to assess actions in response to the global issue and explain their judgements with reasons and evidence.

Q4. A government has decided to revise its education policy.

The following actions are being considered:

- make school mandatory every day of the week
- provide optional after-school programmes for children who are struggling
- focus on technology: computers and internet access for all schools.

Which **one** of these policies would you recommend to the government, and why?

In your answer, you should:

- state your advice recommendation
- give reasons and evidence to support your choice
- use the material in the sources and / or any of your own ideas
- consider different arguments and perspectives.

Read the sample student answer, then answer the questions that follow.

Clearly states the chosen option from the start.

Good use of Source 1 to give a specific example and highlight different perspectives.

Tries to explain exactly how suggested policy will help address different inequalities.

Repetition in this paragraph damages clarity of the argument.

Susanna's response

As an advisor to the Ministry of Education, I would suggest providing after-school programmes for children who are struggling. We need to ensure that all children have access to education. However, at the moment access is not equal. We need to consider the barriers to education and put programmes and policies in place that address these.

To start with, we know the Covid-19 pandemic had a severe impact on access to education. Children without access to computers and the internet were left entirely without education during the pandemic. They are behind in their studies and need extra support. Research shows that this particularly affects girls, minority students, and those living in rural areas. After-school programmes could concentrate on these areas (Source 1). After-school programmes can help to close the gaps created by the pandemic and also those that existed even before that, by concentrating help and resources on students who are struggling, particularly girls, minorities and children from rural backgrounds. After-school clubs can be designed to address specific inequalities: clubs for girls, clubs for minorities, clubs for those with no internet.

Some might question why we would focus on after-school activities when some schools are struggling to provide even basic security to their students. Some schools, for example, lack electricity, drinking water, and sanitation (Source 2). While it is true that expenditure on these basics is also urgently needed, spending only on these would not necessarily address education gaps or make education available to all. For example, a school might be given new computers, electricity, and water, but it might still not attract girls if they are not made to feel safe there. After-school programmes focused on girls can address this, making girls feel safe and investing in their education so their families also become invested in it.

After-school programmes can also be designed to support local cultural diversity. Some children who are struggling with school might speak other languages and struggle with the national language or English. After-school programmes in their own language could help them overcome their educational gaps and also support cultural diversity and appreciation (Source 3).

Ultimately, school should be about preparing us all for the future. We cannot afford to leave some children on the side. One way to ensure all children are involved is to create after-school activities that attract them. Once children come to see school as a safe and fun place to be, they will want to return to learn. Making school attendance mandatory will not address the needs of those who need extra help. After-school clubs allow the focus to be narrowed. They are not about having everybody in school more, they are about supporting those who need help. Giving all schools computers will not help when children are struggling to read or just to feel part of the school.

In short, I argue that given limited funding, schools should invest their funds in after-school clubs as the best way to solve educational inequalities. This makes sense considering the perspective of girls, children from rural areas, ethnic minorities, and other children who need extra support to overcome gaps. Other policies are also good but will not necessarily help to solve inequalities within a school. After-school clubs allow each school to address the inequalities it faces. Thus, it is a national policy with a local understanding.

> Considers a counter-argument.

> Provides a reasoned argument.

> Further use of reasoning supports an additional perspective.

> Focuses on the question being answered.

> The conclusion needs to demonstrate that other perspectives have been considered, but this final judgement has been made based on the previous reasoning.

Engaging with Question 4

1. Do you think Susanna considered all the perspectives in her chosen topic in a balanced way?

2. What pieces of evidence did Susanna use to support her judgement?

3. Create a list of points that illustrate Susanna's argument. Do you think the structure is clear, relevant, and logical? How might Susanna further develop her lines of reasoning?

A line of enquiry

Employment is not only about being employed. How do we classify people who work for themselves (self-employed)? Or who own their own small companies? Or the CEOs of large companies, who probably have profit shares? Are they employed in the same way as most employees?

What about unemployment? What does it mean and what does it imply? For example, many people who work do not receive payment. And what about retirement? Does that imply no more work?

One of the key social factors in how people are described is posed by the questions, "What do you do?", "What career have you chosen?" and "What work do you do?" Other people might ask you, "What are you going to do with your life after compulsory education?"

Career highs

Each of these nine people are enjoying successful careers. Each has given a one-line response to the question, "What do you really like about your job?"

"Helping millions of people, of course."
(CEO of a global charity)

"The intensity and passion of an Olympic final."
(Professional volleyball player)

"Seeing the smiling faces of students who have just received their exam results."
(Teacher)

"That piece of code that tells me we are onto a winner."
(Big Tech programmer)

"Sometimes it takes me years to solve an equation."
(Theoretical physicist)

"It's that moment, often late at night, when I'm the only one who can help."
(Nurse)

"The big headlines, when millions of people are watching me and waiting to hear what I say."
(News broadcaster)

"That's easy. To see a sunrise from 38,000 feet of altitude."
(Airline pilot)

"To see pristine water, on a cool autumn day, and to see the river alive with freshwater fish."
(River environmentalist)

Task 1

In pairs, look at the range of jobs and the statements made by each person.

1. Why do you think each of these people does their job? What is their motivation?

2. Are they telling us the full story? How might each person respond if asked, "What sometimes irritates you about your job?"

3. To what extent do we judge people by the jobs they do? Is it more precise to say "the positions they hold"?

4. Can you think of different viewpoints people might have about the nine jobs? For example, *"I agree with what George Bernard Shaw wrote – those who can, do, those who can't, teach."*

5. Think of three more jobs people can do to attain a "career high". Write a one-line response for each person to the question, "What do you really like about your job?" Join with another pair and challenge each other to "name that job".

Unconventional jobs

Think about jobs that fulfil some of these criteria.

- I would do this job even if they didn't pay me.
- This would be my dream job.
- If I did this, it wouldn't feel like working.
- It's too good to be true, surely.
- Well, somebody has to do these so-called jobs. I just need to be in the right place at the right time.

Chocolate taster

This could be your dream job – getting paid to eat chocolate all day as a part-time chocolate taster. It could be the ideal job for a student if you're hoping to balance studying at university with paid work. All you'll need is a passion for the sweet stuff and a good grasp of the English language.

Cool hunter

Most of us would like to think we're really cool, but are you cut out for this unusual job? How much do you know about trends in popular culture? If you seriously know your stuff and can predict what the latest fads will be, you could be a trend-spotter. You can earn good money by writing reports on the next big trends and selling them to interested businesses.

Sustainability

Think about what is meant by a sustainable job. Is it a job that sustains a healthy planet, viewed from a global perspective? Or should sustainable employment be viewed from a personal perspective – a job intended for the whole of an employee's lifetime, so it sustains them and those close to them?

Task 2

In pairs, read about these two specialized jobs.

1. Are you interested in or could you do either of these two jobs?

2. What do you think are the highs and lows of each job?

3. Who might be excluded from each of these jobs? Give details and reasons.

4. Are these jobs sustainable? Why or why not?

5. Write a job advert for another unconventional job. Be sure to include a summary of the job, the qualifications needed, the required skills, related experience, and how to apply.

Labour underutilization

In this section you will:

- explore factors that affect employment and unemployment
- illustrate the global labour force in graphical form.

A line of enquiry

These bar charts show the unemployment percentages for some of the nations in the world. For example, in South Africa, almost 30 per cent of the available workforce is unemployed. By contrast, in Qatar, 99.9 per cent of the workforce is employed. (Note that the scale is different in each chart.)

In pairs, examine the two graphs and answer the following questions.

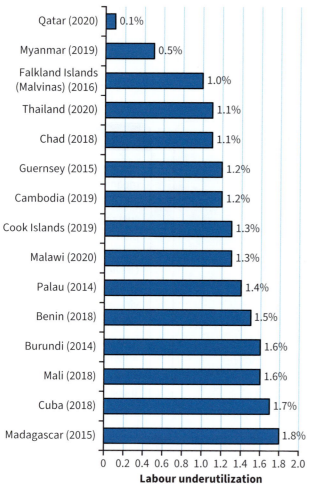

▲ **Fig. 8.1** *Countries with the lowest rates of labour underutilization*

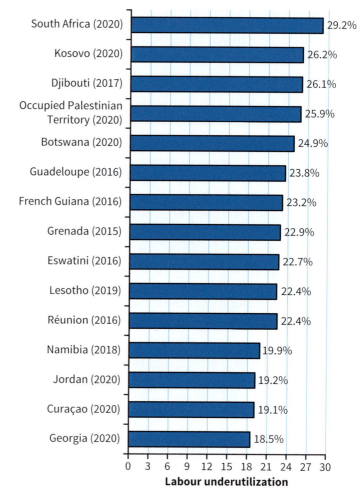

▲ **Fig. 8.2** *Countries with the highest rates of labour underutilization*

Task 3

1. Why do you think the term "labour underutilization" is preferred to "unemployment"?

2. Copy and complete the table. Write some more reasons for employment and unemployment. Aim for ten factors on both sides.

Reasons for high employment	Reasons for high unemployment
A strong Big Tech industrial base	Famine

3. Scan the 30 countries covered in the graphs. Is there anything in this data set that surprises you? Explain why.

4. If your country is not on the graphs, estimate the percentage of unemployed people. If it is on the list, choose a country you know well and estimate its percentage. Research the percentage of unemployed people in your chosen country. Was your estimate close?

5. Create a graph on regional shares of the global labour force from the data below. Choose the most appropriate type of graph. Interpret the data. What do you notice about the distribution of the global labour force?

Regional shares of the global labour force, 2022

Arab States (1.8%)

Northern Africa (2%)

Central and West Asia (2.2%)

Eastern Europe (4%)

North America (5%)

Northern, Southern and Western Europe (6%)

Latin America and the Caribbean (9%)

South-East Asia and the Pacific (10%)

Sub-Saharan Africa (13%)

South Asia (20%)

East Asia (27%)

Other (5%)

Perspectives

Employment and unemployment can be looked at from various perspectives. On a global level, it would be a good thing if the entire population of eligible working people were employed. At a national level, a country with full employment is in a stronger position than one with low employment. At a local level, employment rates may be very different from the national picture. At a personal level, unemployment is almost never good.

Causes and consequences

Are the causes of unemployment related to the causes of employment? For example, if the closure of a local factory causes unemployment (resulting in local people losing their jobs and the local area becoming deprived), then a cause of employment is the opening of a local factory. Think about what might have caused a situation, for example, where a country has a high number of highly qualified graduates who are not employed.

Part of the union

In this section you will:

- consider the advantages and disadvantages of joining a union
- explore the work of a centre in Mexico set up to protect and promote workers' rights.

A line of enquiry

What could a worker, or group of workers, do if they feel they are not receiving their full rights? They might consider joining a workers' union.

HOW HARD IS YOUR UNION WORKING FOR YOU?

Today's workplace presents an increasing number of challenges. The Workers' Union understands that changes in the workplace, new technologies, and evolving shift patterns have affected the way that companies recruit, retain, and develop their staff. It's not easy out there, and that means hard-pressed workers need a strong, responsive organization that holds employers to account.

The Workers' Union is here to do just that. Our motto is simple: protecting your rights leads to a stronger, fairer, more productive workplace. So, become a member of our family and help us fight for a better future for working people.

FOUR REASONS TO JOIN THE WORKERS' UNION:

- Unlike traditional unions, we are not affiliated to any political party. We exist to represent the interests of our members – nothing more, nothing less.
- We keep things simple. By listening and responding to our members, we focus on the issues that matter.
- Whether you've experienced bullying, harassment, injury, intimidation, or discrimination, we have experts that can help.
- There are no different grades of membership. Everyone who joins us pays the same flat fee, with no hidden costs and no extras.

Viewpoints

The issue of workers' rights attracts many viewpoints. One human rights viewpoint is that nobody should ever suffer discrimination at work or when applying for a job. From an economic viewpoint, governments might argue that paying a national minimum wage could harm the national economy. Or a private, successful company might argue that paying high salaries is simply a reflection of high profits.

Task 4

In small groups, answer the following questions.

1. Look at the advert. Why do you think anyone would choose not to join a union? It seems like an obvious thing to do.

2. In a workers' union, who is included? Who might be excluded?

3. How relevant would the benefits offered by the workers' union be to your school, do you think? Does your school already have a students' union? If so, what are the benefits? If not, what do you think about starting one?

4. In your group, write a song lyric, draw a cartoon, or tell a few jokes about unions. You can choose whichever perspective you want.

The power of the unions

Read this article (in US English) about the opening of a new centre to protect workers' rights in Mexico.

Research

Independent trade unions might be an interesting theme to research. For example, in 2022, other newly formed unions in Mexico also won victories over powerful rivals. And US manufacturer General Motors agreed an 8.5 per cent wage increase with a new, independent union at its pick-up truck plant in Silao, Mexico.

A new Labor Center in Mexico will advise workers about their rights and how to mobilize and organize unions and collectively bargain. The Labor Center, at the Autonomous University of Querétaro in central Mexico, is supported by the Solidarity Center and the UCLA Labor Center.

"The aim is to strengthen and promote the full recognition of labor rights, freedom of association and organization, and the democratic participation of workers through research, linkage, and accompaniment," said Labor Center Director Dr Javier Salinas García. Salinas spoke at a recent Solidarity Center event in Mexico to announce the opening.

The Labor Center comes three years after Mexico's government announced a series of comprehensive labor reforms to establish a democratic unionization process, address corruption in the labor adjudication system, and eradicate employer protection (charro) unions prevalent in the country.

" WE HAD THE UNION MEETING HERE BECAUSE I FELT THIS WAS THE MOST APPROPRIATE PLACE TO PRESENT MANAGEMENT'S CONTRACT OFFER. "

▲ Fig. 8.3

Task 5

In small groups, answer the following questions.

1. According to the centre director, why was there a need to set up this new centre in Mexico?

2. Can you find a national perspective? What is it?

3. Pretend you are interviewing Dr Garcia. Ask questions from different perspectives about the way forward for unions in Mexico, and globally.

Structuring your Individual Report

In your **Individual Report** of 1,500 to 2,000 words, you should ensure that the structure is easy to follow. Imagine that someone else is reading it. Would they be able to follow the flow of your report from start to finish? Do your evidence, analysis, and evaluations all help to answer your research question in your conclusion? If so, you have a clear and cohesive report.

Skills focus – structuring a report for a specific audience

Imagine you have just started your first job, working in a team as a recruiter of doctors for a hospital. Your team has the following set of guidelines.

To identify candidates for positions as doctors in a hospital specializing in heart conditions:

Criterion 1: Candidates apply with their curriculum vitae, two relevant testimonials from senior colleagues, and verification of their medical qualifications. These three aspects must be cleared before a doctor can be contacted.

Identify strong candidates you wish to call to a Stage 1 interview.

You can only interview 20 per cent of applicants who have met Criterion 1. Provide a rationale for your selection of interviewees.

Conduct Stage 1 interviews of 60 minutes.

Criterion 2: Establish three strengths and one area of concern that arose during the interview.

Make a recommendation to your team leader about whether to conduct a Stage 2 interview.

Your target is to choose suitable applicants to put forward to a Stage 2 interview. The recommendation must be in the format of a brief written report.

Write two reports of around 100 words each – one for a strong candidate and one for a weaker candidate who has not made Stage 2.

Proposed research questions

Look at the four research questions that have been suggested for Individual Reports on the topic of *Employment*.

Evaluate each one. How suitable are they as research questions? How could they be modified to ensure that they meet the expectations of a full report?

1. To what extent is unemployment brought on by an individual's lack of purpose?
2. Employment and unemployment are two sides of the same coin.
3. The only way to have great job prospects is to work for a globally successful company.
4. Are the jobs of the future related mainly to technology and Big Tech?

Sample student first draft

A student has decided to write their Individual Report with this title:

Does vocational education prepare people for work better than academic-based education?

Read the topic sentences David has drafted for his report, then answer the following questions.

1. David's approach is reasonable in parts, but it seems jumbled up. Reorganize his topic sentences to make more sense, and to provide a better flow.

2. How else could you improve David's draft?

3. There are some aspects of David's draft on which a teacher is likely to want to give feedback. Predict what his teacher might say.

David

The main perspective chosen is the level of qualifications that people hold in the realm of educational technology.

The main cause of this is that educational technology is a new area and not enough places offer courses or apprenticeships — this is also the main consequence.

To decide on which issue this report will delve into, we will consider unemployment and the factors that make it worse, the number of graduates that have technology-based qualifications, and the government's policies towards employment.

As a case study, we can look at the global position where, in developed countries, it's clear technology is greater, but in LEDCs technology is lower.

Even though I have considered other aspects, I remain with the view that it is obviously better to train than to teach.

In Finland, educational standards are probably the best in the world, with almost all Finnish students going to university to study traditional academic subjects such as languages, sciences, and maths.

A course of action is to bring in someone like Elon Musk who is a technical expert and a successful employer.

Common misunderstanding

David's Individual Report could have been a lot stronger if he had not made the common error of trying to cover too much. He could have focused on his third theme, about the impact of an increased number of graduates with technology degrees, as this is often discussed in terms of modernizing global and national workforces.

Assessment tip

David shows that he has some control over the structure of his report. If control is lost, the focus on the research question can become blurred and stray from the main issue. For example, if David had included a section on how billionaires achieved success despite not having a vocational or academic background, this would lose focus on the research question. Stay focused on one main issue.

Moving towards assessment – Team Project

Local business and multinationals

The issue of providing local jobs for local people is a global concern. In an ideal world, there would be a balance between regional businesses that provide local jobs and international companies that offer products and facilities to benefit local people. Many international companies also offer jobs to local people, such as operating local franchises.

However, this is not an ideal world and there is sometimes friction at the local level. Can you think of any reasons why local people would object to multinational companies having a strong presence in their area?

Skills focus – working to a team's strengths

A team of four town planners is considering the proposal of an international company to open two branches of its well-known fast-food restaurant chain in the town. The food is not often eaten by local people and is not available through other restaurant chains.

1. Think about the roles of the four planners. Each planner will investigate a different aspect of the proposal. First, each planner must declare their specialist area with details about their availability and any personal or professional restrictions that will affect their contribution.

2. Set out these roles in the first planning meeting. Note the challenges each might face and any disagreements that might arise.

A teacher's evaluation of sample teams' reflections

Three teams have completed their projects, which were all focused on resolving issues related to rising local unemployment. Their aim was to explore why unemployment was rising and what could be done about it.

Read the excerpts from notes made by the teacher on how well each team worked together during the planning stages and when carrying out the action. Then answer these questions.

1. Why is it fair to conclude that Beth's team achieved partial success in its collaboration? Give reasons.

2. Why do you think Peter's research was not used? Did this seem to cause a problem?

3. Is it sensible in a Team Project to nominate a team leader, as Beth was? Why or why not?

4. Is it fair for the teacher to conclude that Tahlia and Ali would have worked better as a team of three? Why or why not?

Proposed projects

Look at the following four ideas that have been suggested for a Team Project on the topic of *Employment*.

Evaluate each one. How suitable are they as projects? How could they be modified to become more appropriate and viable?

1. To research global trends in unemployment and form a team of four international experts to discuss the issues that arise.

2. To form a picket line in front of a local factory, with each team member protesting about how the factory is losing jobs due to multinational companies.

3. To make a video of local people who have views on how more jobs can be created in their local area.

4. To explore the psychology of work and the 'happy factor' of a workforce.

5. Would you have tried to convince Tahlia and Ali to expand their team? If so, what other roles could have featured?

6. How did Jason's team make things difficult for themselves? Give some reasons.

7. What are some of the strong elements of Jason's team's performance? Do these illustrate collaboration?

8. Which team would you have enjoyed being part of? Why?

Beth's team

Beth did a tremendous job in bringing the team together to achieve some success at the end. She played the role of lead presenter in establishing the causes and consequences of high unemployment. She worked well with Tobias, who supplied useful statistics, which Beth used in her slideshow presentation. Simon failed to engage, however, stating that *he* was the expert in maths as he is studying AS Level statistics. Peter's skills at researching global trends in unemployment could have been used better, as his research never made it to the presentation. It was not made clear why.

Tahlia's team

Tahlia and Ali chose to work in a team of two and set their aim to reflect this. They focused on only two perspectives but ensured that these were very different and dealt directly with the main local issue. Tahlia played the role of the university expert, brought in to investigate why unemployment had risen so rapidly. Ali played the role of a local trade union leader offering solutions to the region's employers. However, a third role – to play a local person who has just been made unemployed – would have added value to the ten-minute recording of the interview. That aside, Tahlia and Ali shared their work equally and the result was a smoothly presented video to raise awareness and offer solutions.

Jason's team

There were five members in Jason's team. Observing how they went about their planning was difficult as there was no occasion when all five were present. Jason didn't seem too concerned as he said he was managing via remote meetings and "catch ups", mainly in the evenings. Rachel seemed to be Jason's deputy, but she often disagreed with Stephen about who did what and deadlines. Jason decided that deadlines needed to be fluid to ensure equality in the team, which helped to resolve arguments between Stephen and Rachel. Paul was passive during the planning as he was the busiest team member during the action. Mark was allocated the role of the angry demonstrator and played that role very well.

Assessment tip

Your teacher will use a range of methods to assess how well your team collaborated, for example, examining how you documented evidence of planning, regularly observing how you worked together, and assessing how smoothly you carried out your action. You need to show evidence of collaboration at different stages of the project, though Jason's team seemed to be ignorant of this.

Common misunderstanding

It is permissible to have a team of only two members. If you choose a team of two, you probably cannot cover the full range of aspects and / or perspectives that feed into the issue you are investigating. Note how Tahlia and Ali show awareness of this and plan to cover two significant aspects. In Beth's team, might Simon and Peter have been better to do a Team Project as a team of two?

Scan here to obtain the source material you need to carry out this examination practice work.

Question 2 in your **Written Exam** is a structured question based on a source that describes some research or evidence about the global issue. There will be two parts to the question. Candidates are required to evaluate the research or evidence, and suggest ways to research or test a claim related to the global issue.

Q2. Study Source 3.

a. "Successful global companies all show the same qualities of leadership." Evaluate the strengths and weaknesses of the research outlined in Source 3.

b. "Most employees would perform better if the company made them feel inspired." Explain how this claim could be tested. You should consider the research methods and evidence that could be used.

Read the two sample student answers, then answer the questions that follow.

Asim's response to Question 2a

a. No specific research is given. Most of what is said by the company boss is their own views, such as where they say at the end that they have charm and that employees respond to this and work harder. This seems unreliable to me, unless we can see the results of questionnaires or something that demonstrates it. At the moment, my father is struggling with his job. He is not a manager and his company is not doing well. But my dad says the leadership is doing the best they can and it's the global recession that is causing the company to lose profits.

I think it's Elon Musk and his SpaceX mission that are being referred to. I do admire Mr Musk for some things but I don't think it's fair to use him as a normal person. He seems to have charisma, but he also makes a lot of his staff unemployed. To make the argument stronger they should have used a normal manager and evidence of how they are inspirational.

I worry about the data. It's not clear which data tells us about failing companies except for personal accounts, so surely these are unreliable data? There must be examples of companies that fail for lots of different reasons.

And it does matter which country you live in. In my country, we use a different model for running companies. So what they say is not global. To be honest, I can't see any strengths in this perspective at all.

Annotations:

Research is given but is mainly qualitative.

Attempts to evaluate the research and give rationale to support it.

Attempts evaluation but only partially achieved with the example.

Personal accounts can be reliable data.

A useful way to end and Asim consistently tries to evaluate rather than just describe.

This is not assertion as it probes and stretches the point made in the source.

Not a strong way to conclude, and the source does contain some strengths.

Omari's response to Question 2b

b. This is an interesting assertion as, in an ideal world, it could hold firm. However, we need to test this claim using a wide range of research methods as, at first, it looks like a subjective point of view. For example, we shouldn't just take the argument of a successful CEO who tells us that, as a result of his charm, the workforce is happy and therefore works hard. ==There are likely to be many factors involved in a global company's success.==

==I would start by looking at how success is measured. Is it by profit margins, by the company's global reputation in the media, or by how much the company gives back to humanity== (such as space programmes to secure the future of this planet)? The best way to find out is to use ==a combination of case studies of successful global companies and detailed data based on their input. We can create pie charts==, for example, to show the key factors clearly.

I would be interested to use the global "Happy country index" to see if that matches successful economies. ==If the argument is that inspiration equals productivity, then surely happiness equals inspiration?==

I would ==request company profile documents — such as mission statements and aims —== from a range of countries.

How about interviewing a CEO who is boring? That might help to provide evidence of the claim. We could ask them what inspiration means to them and the role they feel it should play on a day-to-day basis in the company.

Psychological research is also needed. I suggest looking at the history of people like Sigmund Freud and finding out more about mental conditions.

> A very competent opening paragraph that hints at a response which will design useful research.

> Justifies his research design here.

> A reasonable methodology and way to capture evidence based on the global issue and by using Source 3.

> A direct response to statements made in Source 3, and suggests relevant research.

> It's useful research but it would be good to know about the specific evidence that could be found.

Engaging with Question 2

1. Responses to Question 2a should balance the strengths and weaknesses of the research that underpins the argument. What has Asim failed to do in his response? Give some examples.

2. Is it appropriate for Asim to mention his father in this context? Explain your choice.

3. Responses to Question 2b should test the claim using relevant research methods to obtain useful evidence. Do you feel that Omari is doing this in his last two paragraphs?

4. Can you think of additional research methods that would provide useful evidence that Omari has not mentioned?

In this section you will:

- imagine a better future with a cleaner environment
- consider what might be an acceptable level of pollution.

A line of enquiry

Living organisms need oxygen to survive, yet the air we breathe is often taken for granted. An adult breathes 12–20 times a minute – around 25,000 breaths a day, inhaling approximately 10,000 litres of air.

Air pollution is one of the biggest threats to our health and many large cities are heavily polluted. Air pollution is one of the main contributory factors to respiratory diseases such as asthma and lung cancer, so the air we breathe sometimes makes us ill.

Many countries have policies to cut carbon dioxide emissions to net zero by 2050, or earlier if possible. Things can change fast, however, as humans can be very creative and ingenious. Perhaps in the next 25 years, science and humanity will combine to find ways to make the Earth much cleaner, and a great place for everyone?

Our green and clean future

Think about how green and clean the future could be. In pairs, look at Figure 9.1.

▲ **Fig. 9.1**

Quote

"Today we're dumping 70 million tons of global-warming pollution into the environment, and tomorrow we will dump more, and there is no effective worldwide response. Until we start sharply reducing global warming pollution, I will feel that I have failed."
(Al Gore, 2007)

Task 1

1. Describe what you see in the photograph. How convinced by it are you?

2. Fill in the gaps of speech that a concerned politician is making about the state of her local city.

   "It's fine to talk about sustainable development but look outside and you will see the ____ in our urban areas. Policymakers should be ____ about the future. We should find solutions for ____ waste, ____ pollution, and climate ____. It seems that years of ____ are impossible to change."

3. Here is a report that a journalist wrote about her newly regenerated city. Fill in the gaps in her report.

   "In my local park, we have ____ turbines, a variety of trees and grass which are ____, and air that is ____. The park is in the centre of our city and was classified as a ____ zone five years ago. It just shows what can be achieved with a strong ____ and people who ____ for the environment."

4. Match each keyword on the left with the correct definition.

Species	The rich variety of life on Earth, including the communities they form and the habitats in which they live
Conservation	A group of living things that can mate with one another but not with those of other groups
Habitat	The place where an animal lives and provides it with food, water, and shelter
Biodiversity	The reintroduction of a plant or animal species into a habitat from which it has disappeared to increase biodiversity and restore the health of an ecosystem
Ecosystem	Keep safe or preserve something in nature
Rewilding	A large community of living organisms (plants, animals, and microbes) all working together in a particular area
Restoration	The act of returning a landscape or ecosystem to its former condition or place
Protect	Protecting and looking after Earth's biodiversity, its health, and our natural resources for current and future generations

5. Some people suggest that it is too late and we cannot change our consumerist lifestyle. Others argue that developing countries have the right to make progress without being restricted by environmental rules. What might you say to them?

6. Are you pessimistic or optimistic about the future? Describe to a partner your image of what the future will look like.

7. What do you think about the concept of allowing pollution to continue with some mitigation but focusing on investing in technology to combat it?

Argument

In November 2022, Greta Thunberg and more than 600 other young climate activists began the process of suing the Swedish government because of its insufficient action on climate change. They wanted the court to rule that the country's climate policies have violated its citizens' human rights. This is despite the fact that Sweden pledged to reach net zero by 2045 and 100 per cent renewable energy.

Sustainability

A healthy and sustainable environment is good for the economy because eco-conscious consumers will want to spend their money on products and services from companies which prioritise a low-impact, low-damage policy on the planet. For example, businesses can promote that they use renewable energy, they can offer to plant trees for major purchases, and support wildlife projects. Their success is based on reflecting their customer base, and customers will part more happily with their money when they feel good.

Everything on Earth is interconnected

In this section you will:

- understand the impact of environmental disasters
- develop ideas for making a positive contribution to the environment
- create a brochure and itinerary for an eco-holiday in your country.

Reflect

At the UN Biodiversity Conference (COP15) in 2022, UN Secretary General Antonio Guterres said that it is time to create a peace pact with nature. Seeing all living organisms as equally important and avoiding thinking just about humanity is crucial for restoring the balance on Earth. Think about your role in saving nature. Are you actively making peace with nature?

A line of enquiry

Whenever there is an environmental disaster, the media shows photographs of the effects on wildlife, humans, and infrastructure. For example, an oil spill kills millions of seabirds, a wildfire threathens life and consumes vegetation and buildings.

In addition to loss of wildlife, communities are affected if the environment is affected, businesses are ruined, and tourists stay away. Fewer tourists leads to job losses, for example, in the fishing industry, restaurants, hotels, and souvenir shops. This economic downturn and loss of earnings then affects families. People may have to find jobs elsewhere and even have to move away. As a result, the entire ecosystem is disturbed and will take years to recover.

If we can learn how to protect wildlife and keep the land, air, and water free from pollutants, this will also have a positive effect on us as humans. How could this work in practice?

In pairs, look at the photographs and work through Task 2 to explore the possibilities.

▲ Fig. 9.2

▲ Fig. 9.3

▲ Fig. 9.4

Task 2

1. In pairs, identify the environmental issue in each photograph and how humans have responded to it.

2. Thinking about the effects that environmental disasters have on countries, which area of life do you think is impacted the most:

   a. ecosystems

   c. the economy

   b. people's health

   d. tourism?

3. Imagine the government in your country has $1 billion to invest. Where do you think it would be most useful to invest the money:

    a. schools and education

    b. hospitals and medical care

    c. renewable energies and new technologies

    d. infrastructure and housing

    e. environmental projects and wildlife protection

    f. food and new jobs for poor families?

4. Who do you think should pay for mitigating the effects of environmental disasters and dealing with the after-effects? Explain your choice:

    a. the government of the country in which the disaster occurs

    b. the business that caused the environmental disaster

    c. private businesses and national government together

    d. an international body set up to deal with environmental disasters

    e. wealthy nations and developing countries which caused climate change

    f. emergency donations through charities.

5. What would you be most prepared to do to in order to save the planet:

    a. become vegan

    b. use only public transport

    c. give $50 a month to an environmental charity for life

    d. join a local community group to pick litter once a week

    e. join a climate action group, go on protest marches, and / or plant trees

    f. never buy any more new clothes?

Ecotourism

As tour operators all over the world struggle to revive their businesses after the flight and travel restrictions during the Covid-19 pandemic, a new form of tourism is continuing to emerge. Ecotourism and nature-based holidays attract customers who are more conscious of the negative environmental impacts humans have on the planet.

Task 3

1. In small groups, discuss the idea of ecotourism. Would this type of holiday be one you could enjoy? Why or why not?

2. In your group, create a brochure that advertises an all-inclusive eco-holiday in your country.

- Give your holiday a catchy slogan to attract bookings.
- Decide where the holiday is going to be and what the area has to offer.
- Design a title page for your brochure. Include pictures and drawings.
- Include a day-to-day itinerary for the tourists.
- Think about meal options and optional excursions or activities.

Ever-changing world

Ecotourism is defined by the International Ecotourism Society as "responsible travel to natural areas that conserves the environment, sustains the wellbeing of the local people, and involves interpretation and education". Conserving the environment, respecting the culture of local people, and educating tourists are some of the main aims of ecotourism. Ecotourism was worth $180 billion in 2019 before the Covid-19 pandemic hit the global tourist industry. By 2027, it is predicted that ecotourism will be worth $333 billion globally, thus nearly doubling in value.

Threat of extinction

In this section you will:

- discuss the impact of humans on the animal world
- develop a perspective on conservation through rewilding.

A line of enquiry

As humans, our populations grow and we hunt, farm, industrialize, build bigger cities, and destroy natural habitats. Habitat loss means that biodiversity decreases. Combine all this with climate change and you have the perfect conditions for whole species to become extinct. Environmentalists, conservationists, indigenous people, and scientists have warned that if we don't make drastic changes to our way of life, we will destroy wildlife to the point where ecosystems won't recover.

▲ **Fig. 9.5** *"These, my son, are the tracks of a very dangerous animal we should always try to avoid…"*

Task 4

In pairs, look at the cartoon and answer the questions.

1. What is the cartoon trying to express about the relationship between humans and wild animals?

2. Discuss the different ways humans are using animals. Decide which are, in your opinion, acceptable uses and which should be banned:

   - hunting foxes, deer, rabbits, birds
   - keeping wild animals in zoos
   - testing cosmetics on animals
   - eating meat
   - wearing fur coats or hats
   - using animals in entertainments, such as the circus
   - using animals such as horses for work
   - keeping wild animals as pets
   - using animals, such as greyhounds or horses, in sports
   - farming animals for meat
   - trading ivory
   - using animals for medicinal purposes.

▲ **Fig. 9.6** *Bear habitat in Italy is being rewilded*

Rewilding

There is increasing awareness that the biodiversity crisis is urgent. Breeding projects have been supported globally and members of the World Association of Zoos and Aquariums spend nearly $350 million a year on conservation projects in the wild. One of the most recent developments in conservation includes rewilding large areas of land to attract wolves, bears, beavers, and bison.

Read the different opinions about rewilding and answer the questions in Task 5.

Wild Park Spormaggiore's view

The Wild Park Spormaggiore is located in the village of Albarè-Plan della Fontana, outside Spormaggiore. It was founded in 1994 with the aim of allowing captive bears to live in their natural surroundings. Today, various animals have their homes in the park, every one of them in a separated zone each adapted to make a natural environment. During a visit to the park you can watch bears, foxes, lynx, eagle owls, feral cats, and wolves surrounded by the beautiful natural landscape of the Trentino.

A farmer's view

Hans Witte, a farmer who lives in the village of Fiedland, around 35 km south-west of the rewilded site, explains that 20 hectares of his land have become unusable due to beaver digging. He also says there is a wolfpack living in his area, which has attacked his neighbour's livestock. "That makes you feel extremely uncomfortable," he says. "The way I see it, a wolf that does that has to be destroyed. And I think the same thing about beavers."

He expresses exasperation at authorities and conservationists, adding that he believes they should have kept the animals on protected land. "Now we have them everywhere and no one is taking care of the situation . . . The landowners have to bear all of the consequences and are not compensated properly." On top of this, Witte says there was recently an elk in his neighbourhood that had wandered across from Poland, and he is worried about the threat posed to humans. "[Elk and bison] are a huge danger to cars and other vehicles," he says. "They are not normal wild animals for us here."

A local nature guide's view

"The future for this region is in nature tourism," one local nature guide, Gunter Hoffmann, tells me when I meet him in the main square of Anklam, the nearest large town. "When people see that the animals can benefit them, things will change. But I think it will take a new generation." Nature safaris are becoming increasingly popular in this part of Germany. In other eastern German states, such as Saxony, dedicated wolf tours are also becoming commonplace.

Task 5

In pairs, answer the following questions.

1. Are these three viewpoints for or against rewilding?
2. List the different reasons given both for and against rewilding.
3. Discuss your own views about rewilding. Include reasons and examples for your opinions.
4. What are the benefits and drawbacks of rewilding from economic, environmental, political, scientific, and agricultural perspectives? Which perspective has the strongest benefits? Show your ideas in a table.

   One environmental benefit could be: "Greater biodiversity; more animals, plants, more natural". A drawback could be: "Reintroducing animals into the wild causes problems such as invasive species."

Moving towards assessment – Individual Report

Environmental issues

In your **Individual Report** of 1,500 to 2000 words, you should propose two courses of action for your chosen issue, give appropriate detail of how you would implement each one, and then evaluate their practicality and possible impact. You should then select a preferred course of action and justify your selection.

Skills focus – analysing impacts

Read through these media headlines on environmental issues.

> **Extinction Rebellion activist faces $50,000 fine for smashing bank window to protest against dying ecosystems**
>
> **Former Brazilian president declares Brazil's right to cut down the Amazon rainforest as it belongs to Brazil**
>
> **Climate activists in Italy glue themselves to Botticelli painting**
>
> **France's Interior Minister calls those who oppose giant water reserves for agricultural irrigation "eco-terrorists"**
>
> **Animal Rebellion occupies top chef's three-star Michelin restaurant in London**
>
> **TikTok star, 24-year-old Franziska Trautmann, helps restore eroding coastlines with glass sand**
>
> **#FridaysForFuture school strike sees millions of students globally miss their lessons**
>
> **Humans should protect the planet not just for their own sake but for each animal and plant, as they are equally important**

1. What are the effects of the actions in the headlines? Evaluate how useful they are for protecting the environment. Which actions have more than one effect?

2. Which actions do you think are the most and the least useful for protecting the environment? Give reasons for your answer.

Sample student extracts

Four students have written their Individual Reports on the issue of protecting the environment. Read each one and answer these questions.

1. How many developed courses of action has each student included?

2. Which student evaluates how the course of action could work and what impact it might have?

3. Which students have included their personal preference and argued for it to be the best course of action for protecting the environment?

Madhi

Having examined two courses of action aimed at avoiding a mass extinction of wildlife at the local level, I looked at education and schools. Schools educate students to be more aware and to understand how endangered animals and plants could be saved. Having lessons in biology and life sciences would give young people an awareness of what species are endangered and what you could do to change this. These lessons would be very helpful as they would get many young people involved in protecting native wildlife such as bees and hedgehogs.

Tran

Many NGOs and charities advertise their causes on social media. I looked at Greenpeace and the World Wide Fund for Nature. It was easy and quick to look up their causes on the internet. People who join these groups get actively involved, and that has both strengths and weaknesses, as it takes up some time and you have to be convinced that what is done is not against the law. On the other hand, I think that taking part in a peaceful demonstration or putting leaflets through people's letterboxes are very exciting actions. It makes you feel part of a good cause and it certainly raises awareness.

Alessandra

I haven't found a solution to the problem and I don't think anyone has. People do what they can but it's big industries that pollute rivers and land. I do my share by recycling and I gave money to Friends of the Earth once, so I don't feel guilty about the environment. We need to spread more awareness, and I think if I had an option, I would rather give money to an animal charity than become vegan.

Irina

After comparing data from different wildlife charities and international bodies such as the United Nations, I believe that in order to save the environment, many sacrifices will have to be made. The most reasonable and efficient way would be to ban single-use plastic. By making it illegal, companies that still produce it and individuals who use it could be fined and the money used to restore and protect the environment.

Furthermore, any vehicles that are not electric must be stopped with immediate effect and public transport should be free, subsidized by the government to make it more popular to use. I understand that this would cause chaos and a collapse of car industries, but it is a strong course of action as it results in advancing our net zero goal and would show governments are serious about it. I prefer a dramatic action to just discussing and target setting. We've had enough of this.

Assessment tip

You can choose to include a dramatic idea for your course of action, like Irina has done. She is thinking about taking most cars off the road and making public transport free. That's clearly a controversial action as it has serious impacts. Car manufacturers would suffer, but CO_2 emissions would be reduced significantly. Such a course of action is difficult to put into practice but, from an environmental point of view, it is probably effective.

Common misunderstanding

There are no easy answers to global issues. Alessandra states that she hasn't found a solution. However, she could have developed some previously researched ideas, such as modernizing recycling processes or the impact of a meat-free diet on the environment. This would have offered her a viable course of action. Showing the strengths and weaknesses of actions and then choosing your own preference is the best approach to take.

Moving towards assessment – Team Project

Marine life and conservation

The issue of the plastic in our rivers and oceans is of global concern. It is estimated that around 100,000 marine mammals die every year due to being entangled, injured, or contaminated by plastics. An estimated 8 million tons of plastic are swept into our seas and oceans every single year.

▲ **Fig. 9.7** *A sea turtle mistakes a plastic bag for a jellyfish*

Proposed projects

Look at the following four ideas that have been suggested for a Team Project on the topic of *Environment, pollution, and conservation*.

Evaluate each one. How suitable are they as projects? How could they be modified to become more appropriate and viable?

1. Is rewilding the answer to the loss of biodiversity in our area?

2. What can be done practically to set our school on a path towards being net zero?

3. A campaign to force businesses to stop selling or using single-use plastic.

4. What can be done to show that there is no need to protect the global environment as nature always wins?

---

31 October; full moon

It's Halloween in Costa Rica and I have witnessed how hundreds of baby sea turtles hatch from their eggs. From March to November, sea turtles come ashore to lay eggs and, around 60 days later, the eggs hatch.

You may wonder what sea turtles eat. Unfortunately, they eat a lot of plastic. That's why we are here – to clean up the beaches. Usually, my day starts with breakfast at 7am. Then I help out to clean the beach of any plastic that arrives from the cruise ships and tourists. You won't believe how much plastic people throw away – and it ends up in our oceans.

Research suggests that 52 per cent of the world's turtles have eaten plastic waste, because a floating plastic bag can look like jellyfish, algae, or other species that make up a large part of the sea turtles' diets.

The most amazing thing here are the night shifts when I patrol the beaches, count the eggs in nests, tag turtles, or spot nesting turtles. Tonight was the most amazing nightshift I have done so far. I felt like David Attenborough when I filmed these little baby turtles hatching their nests in the moonlight. This programme has left a big impact on my life and I want to study marine biology when I return home.

Skills focus – completing an action

Read the blog entry written by a student volunteering on a sea turtle conservation programme in Costa Rica.

1. Is the conservation project likely to have a positive influence on the marine life? Why or why not?

2. How was the student able to evidence what they did? Give two examples.

3. If you could take part in such a programme, would you volunteer? Why or why not?

Sample student reflections

A team of three students worked on a campaign to attract more wildlife to their school and local area. Read through what they thought about their actions. Then answer these questions.

1. Analyse the three actions. Which action do you like best? Why?

2. Why was Brandon's group not entirely successful in the end? How could they have improved this?

3. What could be done to make Svetlana's team even more successful?

4. Evaluate the action Bettina's team proposed? What are the strengths and weaknesses of fundraising for charity?

Brandon

Our group thought it would be a good idea to raise awareness and educate primary school students. We wanted to do this by offering them a workshop to build insect hotels and bird boxes, which they could then take home to put up in their gardens. We felt this would make a big difference as parents would see what their children had learned and the kids would see a reminder every day in their gardens. In the end we could only build the bird boxes and not the insect hotels, but the children still enjoyed the workshop and we had lots of fun.

Svetlana

Our idea was to create a wild garden at school. We found that people like to visit gardens, so we mapped out some areas in our school that were not used. We then wrote to the head teacher for permission to sow wildflower seeds. She agreed and now our school looks very different. You can see flowers and bees everywhere. It's colourful, inspiring and, best of all, it was our idea. We think it was a great idea and easy to implement, but it had a great effect on the environment.

Bettina

Our group decided to raise money for a local charity that advises people on how to create bee-friendly gardens. Unfortunately, our group was very disorganized and I ended up having to do everything on my own because my team members had forgotten to bake cupcakes for our fundraising day. We ended up giving away the cakes without doing the fundraising. It was embarrassing.

Assessment tip

In December 2022, representatives from 196 countries met at the UN Biodiversity Conference (COP15) to set new targets to protect the environment on Earth. Global events such as these impact on your local community. If a team of students were able to travel to the conference to conduct interviews with different UN representatives, it would be a very useful action.

Common misunderstanding

Many students want to raise money for charity as their action. Fundraising is always a good idea, but direct actions such as Brandon's workshop or Svetlana's wildflower garden are also very effective. Often the results of direct actions are clearly visible to others such as parents, teachers, and other students, so it will be easy for you to evidence your action.

Scan here to obtain the source material you need to carry out this examination practice work.

Question 2 in your **Written Exam** is a structured question based on a source that describes some research or evidence about the global issue. There will be two parts to the question. Candidates are required to evaluate the research or evidence, and suggest ways to research or test a claim related to the global issue.

Q2. Study Source 3.

a. Identify the strengths and weaknesses of the research outlined in Source 3.

b. "Most people care for the environment and want to protect wildlife."

Explain how this claim could be tested. You should consider the research methods and evidence that could be used.

Read the two sample student answers, then answer the questions that follow.

Sabrina's response to Question 2a

a. Her research is very strong. ==All the statistics she has mentioned are fine. So I think her evidence is very solid.== It's difficult for a high school student to read all these academic articles, so I think ==knowing that a real person is promoting ethical fashion makes you think more about the issue of fast fashion and the environment.== It's very influential.

> Does not engage with the statistics.

> Is this relevant to whether the actual research is strong or weak?

> Makes an assertive statement, but it is better to support it with detailed explanation and reasons.

Elsa's response to Question 2b

b. To begin with, it is possible to conduct personal interviews with open-ended questions, but this research method would have to be conducted on a large scale, otherwise it could not be representative. Some charities and environmental groups do primary research and collect this kind of data. ==I once answered a questionnaire in the high street about what I do to protect wildlife==, so it is possible to collect data from thousands of people and then to conclude that they mostly care for the environment.

Secondly, the qualitative method of observations would be suitable to prove this statement to be true. ==For example, I could go into primary and secondary schools and observe== the life science lessons or one

> If reworded, this would support an understanding of primary research. Always look to build with every statement.

> Gives an explanation and some development.

could observe volunteer groups at a beach clean or wildlife conservation centre to get an impression of how people interact with their environment. This is called participant observation and the researcher observes the group for a set period of time.

Finally, in my view, the best research method for finding out if people genuinely care for the environment is to do case study research. For example, you could follow an environmental protest group and an environmental volunteer group for a period of time because it is the behaviour of direct actions related to the environment that you are interested in. You can then make a generalization from your observation and either prove or disprove the correctness of the claim. You will have to include some sort of quantitative research as the number of people involved in such groups needs to be seen in relation to the general population, who might not get involved in any kind of environmental activism.

In conclusion, I think the claim unfortunately will be disproved as there are many people who do not actively get involved when it comes to the protection of the Earth.

> **Example of good structural framework, which helps a reader follow the reasoning.**

> **Gives another example with development, justifying her research methodology.**

> **Always focus on answering the question asked. Avoid commenting on the statement itself.**

Engaging with Question 2

1. Suggest two elements you would add to improve Sabrina's answer?
2. Suggest what Elsa might add to the evaluation of her first research method to make it clearer?
3. Do you think Elsa's examples are explained sufficiently to understand their advantages?
4. Can you suggest some other research methods that Elsa could have used?
5. How could Elsa have explained her final choice in a simpler way?

In this section you will:

- engage with some of the advantages and disadvantages of globalization
- analyse the impact of globalization on companies.

A line of enquiry

Globalization is the interconnectedness and interdependence of businesses, trade, culture, the economy, and politics around the world. In the past 50 years, for example, many US and European companies have been producing and / or selling their products in other countries. This economic globalization is caused by the desire to explore new markets in order to sell more products.

What do you think about globalization? Is it just the expansion of capitalism or are there other benefits? Who do you think are the winners and losers of globalization?

Two sides of the same coin

For many businesses, globalization has brought benefits. More competition also means cheaper goods and services for consumers. On the other hand, there is a concern that smaller local businesses lose out to big global players.

Empathy

Some children grow up in several countries, speak more than one language, and may be more culturally aware than others. But where do they call "home"? In our globalized world, identity is more complex than just showing a passport or national ID card. For many children, home is everywhere and nowhere. Leaving friends behind and starting somewhere totally new can be daunting. Next time you see someone new in school, think about how different their life might have been to your own. Or indeed, how similar.

▲ **Fig. 10.1** *Conglomo Industries Board Meeting*

"Whenever I get discouraged, I just say to myself, 'Sure, my company exploits indigenous people around the world, plunders natural resources and leaves economic, cultural and environmental desolation in its wake, but that's not what defines me as a person!' It works like magic every time!"

Task 1

In pairs, answer these questions.

1. What main message is the cartoon sending?

2. Conglomo Industries in the cartoon appears to be a conglomerate. The word "conglomerate" can also be used as a verb meaning to gather things into a centre. What do you think is the company's central message to customers and clients? Try to write the company's mission statement.

3. The owner also uses the words "exploit", "plunder", and "desolation". This suggests nobody benefits from the company's work. Do you think this is the case? Why?

4. Imagine you are going to make a PowerPoint presentation, as an employee, about expanding the company's global business. Copy and complete the table, then add two more slides.

Slides	Opportunities	Threats
Setting up another branch abroad		
Employing staff from different countries		
Supplying local and regional markets with exotic fruit and vegetables		
Increasing the company's shipping fleet and containers		
Early signs of rich mineral resources in land we want to buy		Plundering natural resources

Evidence

Protectionism is when a country protects its own domestic interests against foreign competition. Taxing imports can reduce the dependency on imported products and encourage people to buy local products. For example, the EU Common Agricultural Policy aims to protect the income of EU farmers and for EU countries to tax products from non-EU countries.

Quote

"Where globalization means, as it so often does, that the rich and powerful now have new means to further enrich and empower themselves at the cost of the poorer and weaker, we have a responsibility to protest in the name of universal freedom." *(Nelson Mandela)*

"This is a very exciting time in the world of information. It's not just that the personal computer has come along as a great tool. The whole pace of business is moving faster. Globalization is forcing companies to do things in new ways." *(Bill Gates)*

Cultural globalization

In this section you will:

- understand what cultural globalization is
- express a personal view on cultural globalization.

A line of enquiry

Cultural globalization is when elements of a local culture, such as ideas, values, and foods, are quickly transmitted across national borders and around the outside world. We can see this in everyday life as we interact with elements of other cultures – in what we read, watch, and listen to, and in what we eat and drink, for example. Is a global culture emerging as a result of this?

▲ **Fig. 10.2** *Hip hop and rap music are part of a global youth culture*

▲ **Fig. 10.3** *Learning English is popular because it is understood around the world, including on the internet*

▲ **Fig. 10.4** *Many traditional local and national dishes are now enjoyed in other countries*

▲ **Fig. 10.5** *Technology allows people to connect and communicate across the globe*

Account 1
@myworldyourworld

I don't see how cultural globalization can be a bad thing. We are all more connected. I can text my girlfriend in Italy any time and I can download my favourite music from Turkey. I watched the World Cup in Qatar. It has never been easier to learn about different cultures around the world.

Account 2
@rwethelastlivingsouls

I say boo to cultural globalization. It seems all teenagers now look the same and do the same thing. It's like a big global fan club and I want out. It makes me anxious to constantly use social media and I like to be different. I prefer listening to classical music and I think we should learn other languages, not just English.

Account 3
@Cheshirecatphilosophy

Of course globalization needs to be more inclusive of local cultures. I don't think it's right to have Starbucks in the Amazon or Burger King at the foot of the Himalayas. That would destroy something. But, for most young people, globalization is just about being connected with others around the world and sharing messages online. That's a good thing.

Task 2

In pairs, look at the photographs and answer these questions.

1. What cultural trends do the photographs suggest? What trends and behaviours do you think teenagers around the world have in common? Where do they differ?

2. How does global culture relate to your local culture? Can global and local cultures exist alongside each other or are they mutually exclusive?

3. Do you think the spread of global food corporations has caused a decline in local food traditions?

4. An online culture forum has started a debate about whether cultural globalization is a good thing or not. Read the comments above, which were made by some teenagers, then write your own comment.

Viewpoint

In his book *Runaway World* (1999), Anthony Giddens evaluates the increasing impact of globalization. He argues that one consequence of globalization is detraditionalization – where people question their traditional beliefs and ways of life because they are now more aware of alternative ways. Therefore, cultures are less stable and less predictable than before globalization.

Mindfulness

Food can connect us with friends and family but, for some, it poses a problem linked to body image. Try this exercise in mindful eating. Place a raisin in your hands. Take time to notice the weight, colour, texture, and how it smells. Don't eat it yet. Where did the raisin come from? Consider the long journey from grape to raisin. Be mindful of the fact that ingredients from different countries are combined to make the food we love.

Globalization and the internet

A line of enquiry

Globalization can be measured on the basis of international flows of trade, capital, information, and people. While business, financial transactions, and tourism all suffered during the Covid-19 pandemic, the flow of information continued to grow. So, is the internet all we have left of globalization? The pandemic has certainly made people question whether globalization as we know it is over and what the future of globalization might look like.

Analyse the data in the graph to start to see what role the internet plays in globalization.

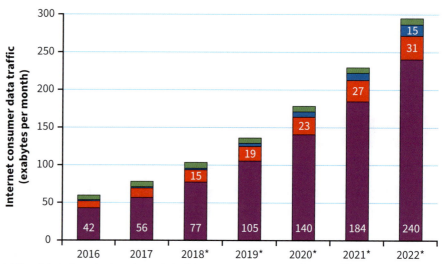

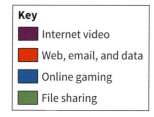

Key
- Internet video
- Web, email, and data
- Online gaming
- File sharing

▲ **Fig. 10.6** *Graph showing global internet consumer data traffic, 2017–22*
(years are projections)*

Task 3

In pairs, study the graph and answer these questions.

1. What trend does the graph illustrate?
2. Which type of internet usage has increased the most? Which has increased the least?
3. Why do you think video usage increased so much?
4. Based on the trend, make predictions for the next five years. Give your reasons.
5. What does a mobile phone mean for many people? What does your mobile mean to you, if you have one?
6. Evaluate the following statement: "The internet is the heart of globalization. As long as the internet increases, globalization increases."

Starlink technology

In May 2019, SpaceX, a private spaceflight company, launched its first 60 satellites into the sky. By November 2022, the company had 3,236 operational satellites in low Earth orbit and hopes to eventually increase its satellite network, known as Starlink, to 42,000 units. A Starlink satellite has a lifespan of approximately five years, so how sustainable is the SpaceX operation? Opinion is divided. While some scientists and astronomers are concerned, others think this is the solution to the digital divide.

▲ **Fig. 10.7**

Read the different viewpoints below to help develop your own perspective on using satellite technology for broadband provision.

A Unreliable broadband in our rural area means students cannot connect with school to do homework or follow up on lessons.

B I bought my son a telescope for his birthday. I want him to see the Moon and the planets, not robots floating in the sky.

C Collisions between satellites in space are definitely going to happen.

D What will happen to satellites after they expire or when companies go bankrupt?

G Broadband from satellites is very expensive. Only the biggest companies can afford this.

H Every location on Earth can be connected by 2024.

E Heavy rain, wind, and snow can affect satellite internet connections and result in lower internet speeds.

F Who controls the sky? We don't have laws that decide which companies can control access to information on Mars.

I Satellites have special sunshades to deflect the Sun's light.

Task 4

In pairs, complete this task.

1. Make a for and against table indicating which of the above viewpoints are for and which are against using satellites for internet connectivity.

Perspectives

According to some research, the global technology market lost $3 trillion in 2022. The world's five biggest technology tycoons lost about $85 billion as a result of investors selling shares to invest in more traditional stocks such as gold. From a Big Tech perspective, globalization could therefore be considered to be in danger, no longer a viable business venture.

Sustainability

A McKinsey global survey showed that transforming businesses to be sustainable is important for 90 per cent of executives. However, only 60 per cent of companies focus on sustainability in their strategy and only 25 per cent incorporate it into their business model. SpaceX has promised its investors a safe and sustainable environment as it goes about its business of orbital and solar system missions.

Proposed research questions

Look at the four research questions that have been suggested for Individual Reports on the topic of *Globalization*.

Evaluate each one. How suitable are they as research questions? How could they be modified to ensure that they meet the expectations of a full report?

1. Why is a middle way between protectionism and free-flowing globalization the answer to a fairer global world?

2. Describe how international organizations such as NATO, the UN, and the IMF push a globalization agenda.

3. Does the internet play a role in increasing the interdependence of the whole world?

4. What is the next step up from globalization? Do you think more companies will operate on a universal scale, beyond Earth? Who do you think the main players will be?

Different perspectives on globalization

In your **Individual Report** of 1,500 to 2,000 words, you should reflect on how your own perspective has been impacted by research, learning, and other people's perspectives.

Skills focus – changing attitudes towards globalization

In 2020, an online survey in 15 emerging markets and developed economies showed that public opinion on globalization changed between 2018 and 2020. The graph shows the change in percentage terms between 2018 and 2020 in those who thought globalization is a force for good (light blue) and those who thought it is a force for bad (dark blue).

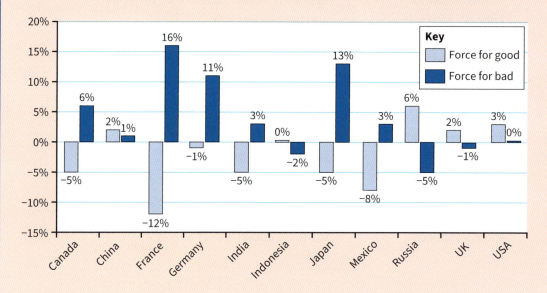

▲ **Fig. 10.8** *Graph showing changes in attitude towards globalization in various countries, 2018 and 2020*

1. In which countries did people change their view in favour of globalization being a force for good? Why do you think this was the case? Do you think this view might have changed again after the Covid-19 pandemic? Explain your reasoning.

2. Do you think change is positive or negative? If you change your view while doing research is that good or bad? Give reasons for your answer.

3. A student originally concluded that globalization is something very positive. However, after finding this graph, they changed their view and used the graph as one of their sources. How would this change of view affect the writing of their report?

Sample student reflections

Three students reflected in their Individual Reports on how the different pespectives they researched impacted on their own viewpoint. Their research question was: "Is globalization a force for good or for bad in the world?"

Read through the reflections, than answer these questions.

1. Why did Jamie think globalization is something positive?
2. Describe how Monica's perspective has changed.
3. Explain the problem with Noah's approach.
4. Who do you think has learned the most from their research? Why?

Jamie

In my mind, globalization had always been something positive. I grew up with the internet and I enjoyed being able to play games with people around the world. My family went on holidays to many parts of the world and I loved getting to know different cultures and foods. So when I read the article about winners and losers in a globalized world and how big businesses push capitalism, I began to think more deeply about those who are disadvantaged in our global system. I learned to be more aware of the problems globalization brings.

Monica

I never thought that so many developing countries encouraged companies from the USA to set up their businesses in their country. I thought that globalization meant the exploitation of workers and the expansion of US ideas, but the blogs that I found on the internet are all about how the economy in developing countries has grown because of investment from US firms. I cannot say that this totally convinced me, because I also found an article that showed how indigenous languages disappear and local culture gets repressed by a more dominant global culture. All in all, my research made me more sensitive to how I express my own views. I have become more careful about generalizing, for example. There are good and bad things about globalization and we need to respect and listen to everybody.

Noah

As a young person, I cannot imagine a world without global connections or dependencies on other countries. My trainers were made in Indonesia, my mobile phone was made in China, and the music I listen to is made in the UK. However, last year, I experienced personally what it means when this global chain stops functioning. My parents bought a new television during the pandemic, but the shop apologized for the long delay in delivery, saying that they had supply issues, so we were without a television for almost two months. This experience taught me how vulnerable globalization is, and I think that it is important for national governments to make sure there are many different options available, so people can choose where to buy from, both locally and globally.

Assessment tip

Analyse your own perspective so that you know your own opinion about an issue before researching other people's perspectives. For example, after researching different viewpoints, Jamie was able to compare them with his own viewpoint and reflect on how his research had impacted on his perspective.

Common misunderstanding

Your report should reflect other perspectives. This does not mean you should only refer to academic articles, as personal experiences can be a good place to start to reflect on different perspectives. For example, Monia's own perspective changed through reading online blogs which supported globalization as a force for good in many developing countries. Other perspectives can come from primary research through interviews, videos, chats, and surveys.

Moving towards assessment – Team Project

The local community as part of the global village

As you walk through your local town, you may notice people from different parts of the world. There may be people speaking a different language or businesses that offer foreign products. You may also have international students studying at your school. All these people connect part of their world with yours. Therefore, a good idea for a Team Project could be to investigate whether the world has become a single global community where global, national, and local values have become intertwined.

Skills focus – evaluating the use of a survey as the action of a project

A group of students wanted to find out how global their local community really was. They made a questionnaire and asked 200 people in their local area to fill it in. Read this summary of their results.

Survey questions	Survey results		Team notes
Which countries have you been to on holiday?	Many countries: most go to France, Spain, USA		• Difficult question to evaluate • Better to give options
How often do you go to restaurants that offer international cuisine?	Once a week: 111 Once a month: 34 Twice a month: 9 Once every two months: 22	Three times a year: 8 Twice a year: 6 Never: 10	• Time scale missing in the question • How to summarize findings?
Can you speak another language?	Yes: 164 No: 36		• Would we want to know what language? • Follow-up question?
How often do you watch or read news from around the world?	A lot: 20 Not much: 89 Sometimes: 55	Every day: 21 Don't know: 10 Left blank: 5	• Reasons needed • Needs multiple choice

Study the survey results and read the team notes, then answer these questions.

1. What are the strengths and weaknesses of questioning people in the community?

2. What should the team have done better to make this survey a success?

3. Has the action of doing a survey resulted in finding out how global the local community is? Why or why not?

4. These students chose to do a survey for their action. If you had decided to carry out primary research on the same research question, what action would you have preferred?

Sample student reflections

Two students produced a questionnaire in which they asked local business owners about their dealings with global suppliers and products. The question they wanted to research was, "How has the pandemic affected local people's view of globalization?" In their Reflective Paper, the students should have evaluated how successfully their survey tackled this aspect of globalization in their area.

Read their reflections, then answer these questions.

1. Which student do you think is best at evaluating the action?
2. Identify the strengths and weaknesses of Amira's evaluation.
3. Analyse Isaac's reflection. How could he have developed his evaluation further?

Amira

I found writing the survey questions extremely difficult. The questions had to be neutral and I had the task of writing most of them. That was very hard. Many local business owners struggled after the immediate effects of the pandemic and this impacted on their view about globalization. So the questions had to be sensitive and not lead to a specific view. I spent so much time discussing and rewriting the questions that I lost my patience in the end. It was very stressful because I had such a big responsibility. I think we should have divided this task better.

Isaac

After we had agreed on our survey questions, we went into town to ask business owners how much they dealt with people and products from other countries. I felt quite nervous asking these questions. Obviously, I could feel that some people had no time, but most were really helpful and, in the end, I got more relaxed and comfortable with interviewing people. The main problem for me was to remember what they said. I just could not take notes quickly enough. It was easy with a yes/no question, but when they said more and explained, I couldn't write it all down. Then I had a brilliant idea and I asked if I could record their answers on my phone. That was really helpful for Amira, who analysed the answers in the end.

Proposed projects

Look at the following four ideas that have been suggested for a Team Project on the topic of *Globalization*.

Evaluate each one. How suitable are they as projects? How could they be modified to become more appropriate and viable?

1. Our school will develop a partnership with a school in another country.
2. To interview some students who are taking a gap year abroad and ask what benefits they expect.
3. To explore whether our local businesses can manage without a global network of suppliers.
4. What could our country do better to promote multiculturalism?

Assessment tip

Surveys make good actions in Team Projects and provide plenty of ideas to evaluate. An action such as a survey consists of many different parts. For example, Amira wrote the questions and analysed the answers, whereas Isaac asked the questions and recorded answers. There could also be other actions such as summarizing the results or presenting the findings to an audience. Be clear about the part you are reflecting on.

Common misunderstanding

It's important to have a positive outcome from an action for a Team Project. For example, Isaac explains how he felt when asking questions and writing down the answers. Although this is an evaluation, it does not evaluate how successful the survey was in finding the answer to the research question. He should have included the strengths of using a survey.

Moving towards assessment – Written Exam

Scan here to obtain the source material you need to carry out this examination practice work.

> Question 1 in your **Written Exam** is a structured question based on several sources. There will be three or four parts to the question. Candidates are required to read the sources and analyse the information, arguments, and perspectives presented about the global issue.

Q1. Study Sources 1 and 2.

a. According to Source 1, in which country are students predicted to study mostly online?

b. i. Identify two challenges that refer to the digital divide in Source 2.

ii. Explain how online education helps people on low incomes.

c. Describe the perspective that online education is the learning of the future.

d. Sources 1 and 2 suggest that there are advantages and disadvantages of online learning. Which advantage and which disadvantage do you think is the most significant? Explain why.

Read the sample student answer, then answer the questions that follow.

Gabriella's response

a. Chile

b. i. Not everyone has a computer; it's hard to work properly in a house.

ii. The digital divide is between young and old people. Young people like to use computers and they know everything about the internet and technology, but old people don't. ==Online education is cheap.== You only really need a small computer these days or a tablet. Some homework can be done on a phone, ==though that can be stressful== due to the small screen size.

c. Online education has advantages and disadvantages. There is the health perspective and that is mainly against online education because you can get ill from being online too long. Some students get depressed because they are bullied online.

==Then there is the technological perspective and from that view online education is good.== It is more convenient and environmentally friendly and cheaper. Technology has developed and education ==can now be more flexible.== You can learn in many different ways — online lessons or reading articles from online libraries. Outside of school hours ==you can upload your homework or revise from the slideshow that the teacher has sent.==

Pick out and use relevant source material, and add a little explanation.

Make sure you focus on what is being asked in the question.

Pick out and highlight alternative perspectives where relevant, even those that support other arguments.

Tunes into the requirement of the question and helps to justify the answer.

Uses examples to support the answer.

Describes how it might help in the future. The explanation is suitably linked to the question.

d. In my view there are many good points of online teaching but also a few problematic things. To start with, online teaching is cheaper than in-person classes. You don't have to pay any travel costs and that is making it more eco-friendly, too. I like studying from home. It just feels more comfortable to use your laptop in your own bedroom and follow the lessons. The only thing is, I find it difficult to concentrate for long and taking notes during the lesson is also not easy. In class, the teacher always checks your notes but they cannot do that online.

Moreover, as an international student you could just enrol onto your course at university and then follow the lessons from your country. You don't need a visa, ==so that's another benefit==. Source 1 says that 97 per cent of college students have switched to online learning during the pandemic. That's a lot.

> Stay focused on the detail of the question you are actually being asked.

The most important benefit is that online studying is so much more convenient. You can follow the lesson at your own pace — I sometimes cannot make early morning classes, so I can watch the lesson later on in the day.

> Include very clear signposts to show you have understood what is required. Keep it simple.

==The biggest problem== with online learning is that some families have only one computer and several kids, so how are they supposed to follow the different classes? ==My friend lives in a village and they have really slow broadband, which means that she sometimes cannot follow the live lessons or download the videos==. That is an issue, but overall there are more advantages than disadvantages with studying online.

> Make a more general point of this to demonstrate you understand it can have a wider effect.

Engaging with Question 1

1. Modify the answer to Question **1b i** in order to link it more closely to the source material.

2. In Question **1b ii**, evaluate Gabriella's explanation about the issue of online education for low-income people.

3. Do you think Gabriella deals with considering the future of online learning in a balanced way? Explain your answer.

4. In answering Question **1d**, Gabrielle uses her own knowledge and experience. Do you think this is relevant to the task?

5. Analyse Gabriella's response to Question **1d**. What issues does she raise?

In this section you will:

- consider how local and global health issues can interact
- analyse how health and wellbeing are linked to other issues such as poverty and education.

Education

1.6 billior
students out
of school

▲ Fig. 11.1

Environment

Less than 30%
investment in clean
energy

▲ Fig. 11.2

Poverty

**More than
251 million**
people pushed into
poverty by 2030

▲ Fig. 11.3 *Impacts of the Covid-19 pandemic on education, climate, and poverty*

A line of enquiry

In 2022, gene therapy was able to cure 13-year-old Alyssa of what was previously considered incurable leukaemia. We live in a time of great scientific advancement, with new knowledge to treat illnesses. However, being healthy is not just about finding cures and treatments for illnesses. It is also about maintaining a healthy lifestyle. What do people do to keep their minds and bodies healthy?

Health and wellbeing affect all parts of our lives. Imagine you could solve any health problem in the world. What would you focus on? For example, would you help people improve their eating habits and general lifestyle? Or would you focus on finding cures for diseases such as leukaemia? If you could make people live for 200 years, do you think this would be a positive thing?

Why does health matter?

Why is health and wellbeing an important topic to explore? To start to answer this, think about the impact of ill health at different levels. You can think about health from personal, local, national, and global perspectives to understand its importance. The Covid-19 pandemic made some of these impacts very clear.

Task 1

With a partner, answer the following questions.

1. According to the information in Figures 11.1, 11.2, and 11.3, what was the impact of the Covid-19 pandemic on poverty and the environment?

2. Figure 11.3 states that the pandemic pushed more than 251 million people into poverty. How do you think a health pandemic resulted in greater poverty?

3. Copy and expand the table to help you think about the impacts of poor health from different perspectives.

Personal impacts of poor health	How does a person's health affect their community?	How does the health of a community affect a country?	How does a country's health affect the world?
Impact on what jobs a person can do	Community members need to care for ill people	Cost of healthcare increases for country	Diseases can spread around the world

How does health impact other issues?

Health and wellbeing impact all other aspects of our life. Health affects, and is affected by, the economy, politics, beliefs, the environment, and more. A good way to visually explore different perspectives on these issues and the connections between them is to use mind maps.

Task 2

In small groups:

1. List as many areas that affect health as possible. Try to think beyond the obvious and consider other areas that might impact on health, such as television, cleaning products, food additives.

2. Create a mind map to explore the connections between human health and the different areas you have listed.

   Below is one example, but your mind map will look different depending on your chosen areas and how you think they connect to health.

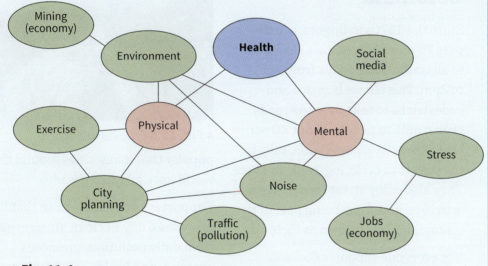

▲ Fig. 11.4

3. Your group is going to explain to the government how health affects many more areas of life than might be expected. Create a two-minute presentation explaining some of the links you have explored in your mind map.

Ever-changing world

Understanding of health and wellbeing has grown and changed as scientific knowledge has developed. For example, 17th-century doctors mistakenly thought bubonic plague spread through bad smells, so they wore masks filled with scented plants to stay safe. Hand washing to stop spreading disease was controversial in parts of Europe until the 19th century.

Getting your country fit

In this section you will:

- learn about Sustainable Development Goal 3, good health and wellbeing

- analyse, interpret, and use quantitative data and sources.

A line of enquiry

In 2015, the United Nations (UN) adopted the Sustainable Development Goals (SDG), 17 goals that nation states agreed to work to achieve by 2030. The goals form a plan for a healthier, fairer, and more sustainable world. Goal 3 focuses on health and wellbeing, and aims to ensure healthy lives and promote wellbeing for all.

Ciclovía, Bogotá, Colombia

Since the 1970s in Bogotá, a little over 75 miles of roads are closed off to all traffic on Sundays from 7am to 2pm. This allows bicycles and pedestrians to take over the roads. Over a million people, about 20 per cent of the city's population, take to the streets to cycle, jog, walk, or skate. They also enjoy street food, join group activities, and enjoy being part of the community. It is known as Ciclovía.

Not everyone supports Ciclovía. Some businesses have complained that it reduces their profits, and others say it prevents them from making important journeys. Despite these complaints, Ciclovía has been so

▲ **Fig. 11.5** *Ciclovía in Bogotá*

popular that many cities around the world have adopted the idea.

Supporters of Ciclovía note that it provides a day of clean air, a respite from daily pollution, promotes exercise, and builds community spirit. It also provides a safe place for women in particular to cycle, which has changed cycling culture to make it more inclusive.

Task 3

Imagine you are in charge of creating a programme to ensure your country meets SDG 3. In small groups, answer the following questions.

1. What can you learn from the example of Ciclovía?

2. What are the advantages and disadvantages of Ciclovía? Copy and expand the tables to help you think through these.

Advantages	Who is affected
• A day with less traffic pollution • •	• Those who live in the Ciclovía zone • •

Disadvantages	Who is affected
• Difficulty travelling to appointments • •	• Perhaps those with medical issues • •

3. Consider some aspects of health your programme could focus on. List the health objectives below in order of priority. Discuss which you think is more important and why:
   - diets with plenty of vegetables and fruit
   - plenty of exercise
   - plenty of rest
   - not smoking
   - good emotional health
   - good eye care
   - more blood donations.

4. Decide how you are going to design and promote your programme to meet the needs of the specific group of people you have made a priority.

Causes and consequences

Because of globalization, germs, viruses, and diseases can spread faster than ever before. War, natural disasters, and poverty can also create health crises that become pandemics. For example, Pakistan suffered historic floods in 2022, which allowed dengue- and malaria-carrying mosquitos to multiply. There was concern not just for the local communities affected, but also about how these diseases might spread beyond Pakistan's borders.

Researching health statistics

It is interesting to understand the state of a country's health. Is the population in generally good or poor health? For example, if you want to help people to stop smoking, you need to know how many people smoke, how often, and why.

To learn about health and wellbeing in a country, you need to research current, accurate, and reliable data. Quantitative data can provide a measurement of how a country is addressing a particular health issue.

Task 4

1. In pairs, research the following information about your own country. Make sure you keep notes of your sources and check the data is current, accurate, and reliable.
   a. What is the age expectancy for men and for women?
   b. What is the leading cause of death?
   c. What is the rate of malnutrition? Is this rate different in different regions?
   d. What percentage of the population smokes? What health consequences does smoking have?
2. Choose another country, in a different continent. Research and answer the same questions for that country.

Evidence

Evidence shows that, on the whole, the world is getting healthier. In the last 100 years, child mortality has decreased tenfold. According to Our World in Data, 95.4 per cent of all children around the world now survive the first 15 years of life, a considerable change from the past. Until relatively recently, only about half of chidren survived so long.

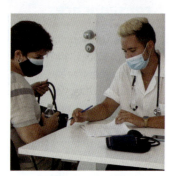

▲ **Fig. 11.6** *Preventative healthcare in Havana, Cuba*

Health policies

A line of enquiry

To keep populations healthy, local and national governments have to design health policies. Ideally, health policies focus on both preventative and curative medicine. Preventative medicine aims to prevent people from becoming ill. Curative medicine aims to heal people once they have become unwell.

Prevention better than cure

Cuba's health service is one of the best in the world, outperforming not only other low- and medium-income countries, but also some higher income countries. Cuba spends $431 per head per year on healthcare compared with the $8,554 average spent in the USA. Yet Cuba has lower infant mortality and similar life expectancy.

World Health Organization Director General Margaret Chan thinks that other countries could learn a great deal by following the preventative nature of Cuba's healthcare model. This preventative care is based around primary healthcare provided by local family doctors.

The Cuban government views healthcare as a fundamental human right, so it is free and available to all of its population of 11 million people. Cuba has 90,000 doctors – that's one for every 125 citizens. The USA has one doctor per 400 and the UK one per 370 citizens.

Task 5

In pairs, answer the following questions.

1. How much money does Cuba spend on healthcare per person? What about the USA? What do you think about the contrast?

2. What is the Cuban government's policy towards healthcare, and what do you think about it?

3. How do you think different levels of access to healthcare impacts personal and community health and wellbeing?

4. Think about the following policies:
   - providing people with clean water
   - checking people's blood pressure
   - using vaccines
   - prescribing antibiotics.

   Which do you think are preventative? Which do you think are curative?

5. Discuss whether you think government policies should focus more on preventative or curative medicine. Give at least two reasons to support your position and two examples to illustrate your reasons.

Different perspectives on health

Different cultures have different ways of thinking about health and healing. Cultural beliefs affect when we should eat cold or hot food, how to handle dead bodies, and what to use for personal hygiene, for example. Some cultural beliefs can be harmful to health, but others simply reflect a different understanding of health and how to support wellbeing.

▲ **Fig. 11.7** *A healing ceremony in Bolivia to assist a person suffering with arthritis*

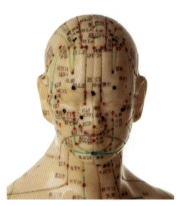

▲ **Fig. 11.8** *Acupuncture is believed to have originated in China and is still practised there and in many other places around the world today*

Task 6

In small groups:

1. Discuss different perspectives relating to the following beliefs.
    - Someone who has died should be looked after for several days before being buried, in order to allow their soul to pass to the afterlife.
    - A river holds healing waters and the community habitually drinks the water and bathes in it. However, the river is increasingly polluted by manufacturing waste.
    - Mental health is caused by spiritual beings and therefore cannot be treated by doctors.

2. Discuss the following statement: "To best serve patients and save lives, governments should ignore local ideas about health."

3. Imagine you are in charge of your country's limited health budget. You can only afford two programmes:
    - vaccination programmes
    - a programme to reduce the use of sugar
    - education programmes about health
    - free food in all primary schools
    - improving the sewerage and water systems
    - organizing exercise programmes
    - any other programme, decided by your group.

    Which two would you fund and why?

Mindfulness

Take a moment to think about your own health and wellbeing. What do you already do to keep yourself healthy? Is there anything else you could do to improve your health? Are you getting enough rest? Do you eat healthy and nutritious food? Do you spend enough time outside? Do you find ways to relax with families and friends?

Causes and consequences

Individual choices about health can have serious consequences for other people too. For example, smoking is a personal choice that will damage a person's health. However, smokers also spread carcinogenic smoke to children and others who do not choose to smoke. This is called a negative externality. There can also be positive externalities such as the increased energy you can devote to family life if you eat healthy food or exercise.

Addressing health and wellbeing issues

In your **Individual Report** of 1,500 to 2,000 words, you need to choose a course of action to address the global issue your research question is focused on. First, you need to look carefully at two different courses of action, and then after considering local/national and global perspectives, you need to decide which of the two actions you prefer and why. Which course of action might be most effective and realistic for each research question?

Skills focus – proposing a relevant course of action

Match each research question below with two possible courses of action.

Research questions	Courses of action
A. Should governments make vaccines mandatory?	**1.** Government television runs daily exercise shows every morning and evening.
B. Why should governments take local cultures into consideration in their health policies?	**2.** A committee of cultural leaders is set up to discuss health concerns with the government.
C. Should daily exercise be enforced by the government?	**3.** Vaccines are mandatory to obtain employment.
	4. Local communities vote on community health proposals.
	5. Government structures cities to increase public green spaces and safe walking paths.
	6. Vaccine clinics are set up for all school children.

Proposed research questions

Look at the four research questions that have been suggested for Individual Reports on the topic of *Health and wellbeing*.

Evaluate each one. How suitable are they as research questions? How could they be modified to ensure that they meet the expectations of a full report?

1. Can mindfulness be taught?
2. What effect are influencers having on teenage mental health?
3. Should education about mental health be mandatory?
4. Which disease in the world needs a cure most urgently?

Sample student extracts

Two students have decided to write their Individual Reports on the issue of mental health. Look at these extracts from their reports where they discuss possible courses of action and argue for one to be followed.

1. What is the main weakness of Mirabel's strategy?
2. How does Lucia evaluate the impacts of the courses of action she discusses?
3. Do you think Lucia effectively justifies her chosen course of action?

Lucia

Research question: Why should governments focus on their population's mental health?

Guterres, a UN official, has stated that mental health must become a global priority. He further noted that countries should concentrate on solving the root causes of mental health problems such as violence and abuse (UN 2022). This, however, seems a broad and undefined course of action. It is also a course of action that will not be immediately successful, as violence and abuse might take years to address in a society. On the other hand, Zimbabwe has decided to focus on loneliness and mental health, putting in place "friendship benches" where those who need friends and those who are happy to befriend new people can meet. While I agree with the need to look at the root causes of mental health, it is important to start small to start making a difference sooner rather than later. Zimbabwe's approach can have great impact at limited cost and, therefore, proves a powerful course of action. People suffering from loneliness need support now, not once they can afford it or have left abusive relationships or violence. To address mental health, small, low-cost, and highly effective projects, like friendship benches or free phone lines to speak with trained counsellors, should be prioritized.

Mirabel

Research question: Why are teens struggling with their mental health?

The WHO estimates that one in seven young people suffer from mental health issues. It has developed a guide on child and adolescent mental and behavioural disorders to help medical professionals recognize and help with the mental health of young people. The WHO is also working with educators to help them understand the importance of mental health in schools. In Indonesia, a small NGO working with teens has set up support systems for those struggling with their mental health. They have listed phone numbers young people can call to speak with trained counsellors. Teens can also join community groups that participate in weekly walks and gardening to get people outside and support those struggling with loneliness.

Assessment tip

When choosing between two courses of action, you can consider their impacts. If one course of action has immediate impact, such as Zimbabwe's friendship seats, you might choose this over an action with impacts that will not be felt for a longer time. Or you could consider whether a course of action might have unintended consequences. Some courses of action might also be more practical or realistic. Explain clearly why you chose your action.

Common misunderstanding

Listing multiple courses of action without evaluating them, as Mirabel has done, is not an effective strategy. If you are just listing courses of action, you are probably not giving enough information about them to explain why one action is preferable to others. For your report, you only need to discuss two courses of action and to argue why one of these is better at solving your issue than the other.

Moving towards assessment – Team Project

Can we be healthier by changing our diets?

People's eating habits have dramatically changed as our world has changed. In some countries, longer hours at work, longer commuting times, and access to processed food have led to people eating more fast food and cooking less at home. In many places, people consume more calories than they need, often from food with few vitamins or minerals. Changing how people think about their diet can help improve their health.

If you took photographs of the meals you eat and the activities you do in a week, what would be in them? How could you change your life to eat better and exercise more?

Skills focus – planning and explaining a Team Project

1. A team of students is planning their Team Project to encourage their classmates to eat healthier local food. Decide on the order in which they should do these tasks:

Create a poster showing healthy food options.

Decide what their Team Project will focus on.

Create posters to advertise a food fair.

Interview participants at the food fair.

Decide how they will measure the success of their project.

Count how many people come to the food fair.

Research what classmates usually eat and what local food is healthy.

Meet local food vendors who can attend the food fair.

Find a space to host the food fair.

Check if permits are needed to host a food fair.

2. The team is now working on its Explanation of Research and Planning. Which of these tasks should be on the plan:
   - list of all the research sources
   - clear statement of their action
   - list of the food chosen for their fair
   - statement of what their chosen issue is and what action they will take to address it
   - notes on who did not do the jobs they were assigned to
   - list of the different parts needed to complete the project
   - discussion of how the team could have been more successful
   - explanation of the measurement for success
   - explanation of how the team will demonstrate their action
   - photographs of the team planning their project?

Proposed projects

Look at the following four ideas that have been suggested for a Team Project on the topic of *Health and wellbeing*.

Evaluate each one. How suitable are they as projects? How could they be modified to become more appropriate and viable?

1. Create an app where people can track their health habits.
2. Organize a community dance to get local people moving for their health.
3. Make all food in the school canteen vegan.
4. Track each team member's food and exercise for a week.

Sample student planning

A team of students is working on their Explanation of Research and Planning. Look at their document and answer these questions.

1. How does Dimitri's team plan to evidence their action?
2. Advise Dimitri's team on the way they have set out their research and planning.
   a. Might it have been better if they had used a table? If so, which headings should they use?
   b. What could be added to their plan?
3. Would you like to join Dimitri's team? Why or why not?

Dimitri's team

Focus: Looking at health and specifically child malnutrition.

Issue: Why people eat less traditional food: processed food is seen as easier and cooler.

Perspectives researched:

- Jonah looked at overall children's health in our country, looking at government, the UN, and national NGO websites.
- Maria looked at differences between boys and girls.
- Eduardo looked at children in different areas of the country.
- Chidinma looked at programmes trying to make a difference in this area.

Action: We found that as people eat less traditional food and more processed food, they eat less nutritious food. We decided to create YouTube videos to make traditional food exciting again and publicize fliers for local childcare facilities.

Research: Maria, Jonah, and Eduardo researched traditional recipes and their nutrition.

Plan of action: Jonah and Maria will choose traditional recipes. Eduardo and Chidinma will get the ingredients. Maria will film. Jonah and Maria will edit. Everyone will put up posters to advertise our videos.

Measure of success: We will track how many people watch our YouTube videos.

Common misunderstanding

A project plan should provide an overall vision, not just a quick list of what you did and when. It needs to state clearly what your topic and issue are, and show that you undertook research to decide on a plan of action. In Dimitri's example, research made the team realize that a project action focusing on traditional foods could be particularly effective in addressing poor eating habits.

Scan here to obtain the source material you need to carry out this examination practice work.

Question 2 in your **Written Exam** is a structured question based on a source that describes some research or evidence about the global issue. There will be two parts to the question. Candidates are required to evaluate the research or evidence and suggest ways to research or test a claim related to the global issue.

Q2. Study Source 3.

a. "Social media can have a great impact on the health of young people."
Identify the strengths and weaknesses of the research outlined in Source 3.

b. "Positive role models improve your health."
Explain how this claim could be tested. You should consider the research methods and evidence that could be used.

Read the two sample student answers, then answer the questions that follow.

Mary's response to Question 2a

a. The writer explains her position and why she did the research that she did. ==It seems to me that she understood that sometimes things we see online are not always positive.== There has been a lot of publicity worldwide about harmful content online and the writer was obviously aware of this, probably through school, and decided she wanted to do something different. Good for her, I say! ==She mentions asking for advice from friends and a teacher; this shows that she was proactive in her research and not just doing more online stuff. I do think her tone is a little bit angry.== She talks about "real people" and "not filtered and computer-enhanced avatars". This seems quite emotional and might suggest that she is on a bit of a mission to prove something. I think this might cloud her judgement a bit. ==Also, she doesn't really say where she got her statistics from so they lack some credibility, although she does add a timeframe to one of them.==

==Overall, I think the writer does focus on why she is doing the research and does support quite a few of her statements with some justification, but I think the whole thing seems a little unbalanced. There are plenty of good online sites that already promote healthy living, but she kind of brushes them aside in favour of this newer wave she has found.==

Clearly understands why the research is being done.

Highlights primary research directly related to the topic.

Good evaluation of the language used. However, don't over-read how things are said; look for reinforcement.

Think about the validity of a source if the origin is not clearly signposted.

A solid conclusion with further explanation of the final judgement which suggests alternative perspectives might have been considered more.

Min's response to Question 2b

b. ==This is quite a tough assertion to assess. In reality, it could be true, but there are so many other factors to consider when looking at improving health. How do we single out positive role models for one?== As a consequence, we need to test this claim ==using a wide range of research methods.== It would not be sufficient just to do a ==questionnaire survey as people rarely answer these honestly.== I would start with looking for a comparison between physical and mental health. Data from medical journals would help to make that link, and this comparison may vary from country to country, men to women, and adults to children. The variables are numerous, so we would need to narrow down a sample to test before we decide what we are testing for. Otherwise, the results would be so varied as to be virtually meaningless.

We could ask people if they have a clear positive role model they look to for inspiration — a sports star or actor, perhaps, or even a member of their own family. ==My dad is my hero and I follow his example.== Once we have a sample of people who do identify a role model, we could compare their health with individuals of a similar age and social and economic status, to see if there is a noticeable difference. This would be putting together comparative case studies of groups or individuals to spot trends in the data.

==However, I do think this would be a very difficult assertion to pin down and, if I were to investigate this topic, I would probably change the research question to make it more meaningful to answer.==

> Suggests the possibility of using different methods. Cover these and it leads to a good explanation of the overall research method.

> Needs to be more formal, as appropriate for assessing a research topic.

> A good opening explanation of difficulties gives the opportunity to explain how to overcome them.

> A critical evaluation of a method which could give more explanation of why.

> Repeats the problem and offers a possible alternative solution.

Engaging with Question 2

1. Responses to Question **2a** should balance the strengths and weaknesses of the research that underpins the argument. Do you feel that Mary achieved this?

2. Mary considered the tone angry. Do you agree? Justify your answer.

3. Responses to Question **2b** should test the claim using relevant research methods to obtain useful evidence. Do you think that Min was able to supply sufficient insight as to how she might do this? Explain your answer.

4. Can you think of additional research methods that would provide useful evidence that Min has not mentioned?

A line of enquiry

We would probably prefer most countries around the world to have the same, or very similar, laws to keep people safe and provide justice. But legal systems vary significantly from country to country. Why might this be so? Do different cultures require different sets of laws?

What about the impact of a country's history? How much does the nature of crime committed in a country's past influence its legal system? For example, some of the laws in England can be dated back several hundred years. Should laws be regularly updated?

Justice seems simple to define. Everyone would want to be treated fairly and equally by the law no matter what our social and cultural background is. However, the path to justice can be difficult sometimes.

International law

What is meant by international law? Is it an agreed set of principles that all countries should adhere to? Think about if you travel to another country – you need to observe its laws, so does international law enter into your mind at all?

Read about Interpol and look at the logo in Figure 12.1, then answer the questions in Task 1.

Today's crimes are increasingly international. It is crucial that there is co-ordination among ==all the different players== in maintaining a global security architecture.

Since Interpol is a global organization, it can provide this platform for co-operation; we enable police to work directly with their counterparts, ==even between countries which do not have diplomatic relations==.

We also provide a ==voice for police on the world stage==, engaging with governments at the highest level to encourage this co-operation and use of our services.

All our actions are politically neutral and taken within the limits of existing laws in different countries.

▲ Fig. 12.1

Interpol's crime programmes

We provide a range of policing expertise and capabilities to our member countries, supporting three main crime programmes:

Counter-terrorism

Assisting member countries to prevent and disrupt terrorist activities through the identification of individuals, networks, and affiliates.

Organized and emerging crime

Targeting and disrupting international criminal networks; identifying, analysing, and responding to criminal threats.

Cybercrime

Making cyberspace safe for all by supporting member countries to prevent and investigate cyberattacks.

Task 1

1. In small groups, discuss what you think international law and national law are. Can you give an example of both?

2. What do OIPC and IPCO stand for on the Interpol logo? What do you think about other aspects of the logo?

3. Do you think Interpol is able to overrule a country's national laws? What evidence do you have?

4. Look at the three highlighted phrases. What overall message is being sent? Pick out three key words that communicate each message and replace them with words of a similar meaning. Is the message the same?

5. One of Interpol's programmes tackles cybercrime. In your group, nominate someone to take part in a "hot seat" activity. That person will play the role of Interpol president.

   a. In your group, try to predict the questions that another group will ask the president about cybercrime.

   b. Prepare some questions for the president in another group.

National crime profiles

Interpol has 195 member countries – a large percentage of countries in the world. One of its policies is to support countries by sharing data about crimes and criminals.

Task 2

1. In pairs, take a few minutes to research whether your country is a member of Interpol. Where is the Interpol National Central Bureau (NCB) office based?

2. Look at the most common crimes in your country as reported by the NCB. Is this what you expected?

Viewpoints

A crime can be seen from a range of viewpoints. For example, with illegal migration, when nationals from one country enter another country without making the appropriate legal application, there are the perspectives of the migrant, who feels they need to relocate; the police in both countries, who have to enforce the law; the taxpayer in the receiving country. Crime is not straightforward.

Causes and consequences

When studying the theme of *Law and criminality*, it is useful to identify causes and consequences. For example, a car is stolen in Finland by an organized Russian gang. It is driven into Russia, avoiding border patrols, where it is sold with forged documents from Germany to a buyer who believes it is a legal import. The Russian police arrest the new owner because its registered plates are suspicious.

Cybercrime

In this section you will:

- focus on cybercrime and explore its many dimensions
- learn about ethical hacking, using case studies.

A line of enquiry

To understand more about cybercrime and how it is an ongoing and increasing threat to us all, read the statements from the UK's National Crime Agency (NCA) and look at the pie chart. Then answer the questions in Task 3.

Breaches leaked personal data on a massive scale, leaving victims vulnerable to fraud, while lives were put at risk and services damaged by the WannaCry ransomware campaign that affected the NHS and many other organizations worldwide.

Tactics are currently shifting as businesses are targeted over individuals, and, although phishing attacks on individuals are increasing, fewer are falling victim as people have become more alert.

Because the distinction between nation states and criminal groups is increasingly blurred, cybercrime attribution is sometimes difficult.

Although young criminals are often driven by peer kudos rather than financial reward, organized UK cybercrime groups are motivated by profit.

Cyber criminals seek to exploit human or security vulnerabilities in order to steal passwords, data, or money directly.

The scale and complexity of cyber attacks are wide-ranging. "Off the shelf" tools mean that less technically proficient criminals are now able to commit cybercrime, and do so as awareness of the potential profits becomes more widespread.

The evolving technical capabilities of malware mean evolving harm as well as facilitating new crimes, such as the cryptomining malware which attacks digital currencies like bitcoin.

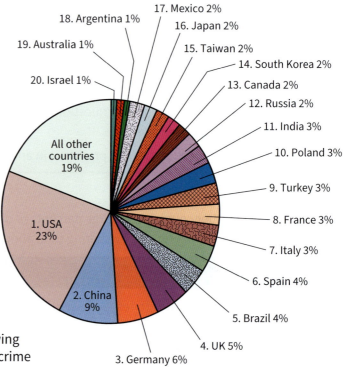

17. Mexico 2%
18. Argentina 1%
16. Japan 2%
19. Australia 1%
15. Taiwan 2%
20. Israel 1%
14. South Korea 2%
13. Canada 2%
12. Russia 2%
11. India 3%
10. Poland 3%
9. Turkey 3%
8. France 3%
7. Italy 3%
6. Spain 4%
5. Brazil 4%
4. UK 5%
3. Germany 6%
2. China 9%
1. USA 23%
All other countries 19%

▶ **Fig. 12.2** Pie chart showing the percentage of cybercrime globally

Task 3

Police officers often have to make clear statements to the public. Using graphs to focus on specific data is also a means of communicating information swiftly, as well as visually.

1. Summarize each of the statements into a clear and direct message. For example, the first statement could be rephrased as "Data breaches in large organizations can result in vulnerable victims and even risk people's lives."
2. Reread your own statements and create one headline to summarize them all.
3. Does any of the data in the pie chart surprise you? Why or why not?
4. Is a pie chart an effective way to present such data? How is it visually appealing?
5. Give a brief talk (about a minute) about the spread of cybercrime globally, using the statements and pie chart. You don't need to comment on all of the data.

Ethical hacking

Hacking can be defined as gaining unauthorized access to a computer or network with the aim of obtaining data illegally. It is a criminal offence. So what is ethical (white hat) as opposed to criminal (black hat) hacking? Read the accounts about two ethical hackers, which show two very different backgrounds.

Kevin Mitnick

Kevin Mitnick has become one of the most famous ethical hackers to have ever lived, and perhaps his skills and insight come from the fact that his hat has not always been white.

In 1995, the law caught up with Mitnick in what became a high-profile arrest; he had been pursued and tracked down due to a two-and-a-half-year spree of criminal cyber activity. His black hat escapades included breaching the security of the Digital Equipment Corporation where, once inside, he copied the software he found.

For this crime he received jail time in 1988 that was followed by a period of supervised release. Before he had completed his punishment, Mitnick was hacking again, gaining entry to Pacific Bell voice mail computers. It is thought that he breached a number of other networks and used tactics including the interception of passwords.

Mitnick ended up receiving a 46-month sentence, with an addtional 22 for violating his period of supervised release in 1989, an event that marked the conclusion of his time on the dark side.

Tsutomu Shimomura

Standing out among ethical hackers, not only is Tsutomu Shimomura a brilliant cybersecurity expert and physicist, his place in our list provides a cyclical effect because he was heavily involved in tracking down Kevin Mitnick, another prominent member of our list.

Shimomura's genius may have been expected by some as he is the son of the 2008 Nobel Prize Winner in Chemistry, Osamu Shimomura. His abilities in physics led him to be taught by the great physicist Richard Feynman.

In 1989, at the University of California, he became a computational physics research scientist, a path that led him to work for the National Security Agency. By testifying in Congress, he raised awareness of the lack of security and privacy in cellular phones.

His part in bringing Kevin Mitnick to justice has been his most high-profile action in terms of using his security skills for ethical purposes. The event led to a feature film called *Track Down*, inspired by the book *Takedown* written by Shimomura and journalist John Markoff.

Standing your ground

In this section you will:

- debate the advantages and disadvantages of the "Stand your ground" law

- engage with a film review and consider questions around the crime of theft.

A line of enquiry

In 2012, in Florida, USA, George Zimmerman shot 17-year-old Trayvon Martin during a fight. Zimmerman was arrested and charged with murder but was later acquitted on the grounds of self-defence. The case raised many issues, including civil rights. It led to a debate about immunity from prosecution that is still ongoing.

Many states in the USA have "Stand your ground" laws.

Read about the advantages and disadvantages of these laws, then complete Task 4.

Advantages

- It allows anyone to protect themselves from the commission of a crime.
- It eliminates the problems that come with a duty to retreat.
- It removes ambiguity from the castle doctrine standards.
- It can provide immunity from criminal prosecution.
- It requires a reasonable belief that harm will occur if actions are not taken.
- It can lead to a drop in crime.
- It follows more than 100 years of legal tradition in the USA.

Disadvantages

- It can lead to an increase in homicides.
- These laws give individuals unfettered power and discretion.
- It can raise the rate of violent crime in the community.
- There could be a racial bias to "Stand your ground" laws.
- It may inspire others to take violent actions.
- Violent crime decline was occurring before the implementation of "Stand your ground" laws.
- It causes people to act on their implicit biases.

Sustainability

In relation to law, sustainability perhaps means that laws should be long lasting and should not need to be changed, amended, or updated. This is the case with some laws, for example, in English law, decisions made in cases several hundred years ago are observed and respected today. In relation to criminals, might sustainability be accepting that there will always be crime and societies therefore need to respect and support criminals after they have been caught? An easier thing to resolve might be crime and laws that are unsustainable.

Task 4

In pairs, you are going to decide on a motion for the whole class to debate.

1. First, explain to your partner what your own position is on standing your ground. What do you think about having or using a gun in those circumstances?

2. Consider alternative perspectives. How might each of these people feel about the issue? Then discuss examples of other different perspectives:
   - a person confined to a wheelchair
   - a member of the armed forces
   - a woman living alone in a large city
   - a pensioner, aged about 75
   - a member of a country's parliament
   - a boxer.

3. In pairs, reread the advantages and disadvantages. Discuss your understanding of the highlighted words and phrases.

4. Do you think the advantages or the disadvantages make the strongest argument? Explain why to your partner.

5. Now agree a good motion for a class debate.

Would you rob a bank?

The film *Bandits*, made in 2022, is based on the real bank robberies of the "Flying Bandit", Gilbert Galvan Jr. Galvan still holds the record for the most consecutive robberies in Canadian history.

Task 5

In pairs, answer the following questions about the issues raised by the film.

1. The film shows Galvan buying a homeless man's ID card for $22. Why would Galvan do this? Were any crimes committed?

2. Act out the scene where Galvin's wife, Andrea, finds out that her husband has been robbing banks. Focus on her social conscience flipping.

3. Do you have any empathy for Galvin and his wife? Why or why not? Is it impressive that he robbed 59 banks?

4. Do the following statements change your response to Question 4?
   - Nobody was ever hurt in the bank robberies.
   - Galvin used an unloaded gun to scare bank staff.
   - He used the money to build a family life.
   - Galvin's wife divorced him many years later.
   - Galvin served his time, spending 14 years in prison.
   - While robbing banks, he flew premium class on airlines.

5. Would you rob a bank under any circumstances?

Viewpoint

In some cases, the "Stand your ground" laws provide the defendant with immunity from prosecution. This means that they cannot be held to account for their actions. Such immunity occurs in other situations too: for heads of state; for diplomats; for people who offer plea bargains to avoid prosecution by trading information. But is immunity ever acceptable?

Empathy

An interesting area of law and criminality is victimless crime. It suggests that some crimes cause no harm to anyone other than the person committing the crime. Examples include some traffic offences and trespassing where no damage is done. Is it reasonable to empathize with criminals when there are no apparent victims?

Moving towards assessment – Individual Report

Making sure you find useful evidence and sources

In your **Individual Report** of 1,500 to 2,000 words, you should evaluate the evidence you present and the sources you use. Try to develop the points you make by focusing on the impact of your research and the arguments the research puts forward.

Skills focus – evaluating evidence and sources

A student is investigating evidence for an Individual Report on the advantages and disadvantages of parole boards.

The three sources below relate to the same case, which is due before a parole board.

The prisoner	A specialist	A victim
I'm innocent! I always said so. When I was arrested eight years ago, I told the police that it couldn't be me as I was somewhere else when the crime was committed. It's not my fault that my alibi became very ill and decided to move to Iceland. Nobody can track her down. Why didn't anyone believe me? Why don't you invest the time and money and send someone to Iceland. It's only a small country. You'll find her.	I have spent several years in the presence of this man who is now up for parole. In my expert opinion he is deluded. Almost everything he says is falsified or a feature of his extremely vivid imagination. He tells me stories which are clearly not real as if they really happened. I have 35 years' experience and a doctorate degree in Criminology. It is my professional opinion that this man is an ongoing danger to society.	Yes, I was a victim of the crime as it was my shop that was robbed. This man had asked me for some supplies that he would use on his next fishing trip. He said he was a local man working as a guide for tourists fishing off the coast. I had no reason to disbelieve him, and I still don't. However, I hadn't seen him before in the shop and I have lived locally all my life. So that seemed a bit odd.

1. Which source would you describe as reliable, if any?

2. What is evidence? What is hearsay?

3. If you were on the parole board, would you recommend parole? Why or why not?

4. If you were researching the issue of parole, what types of sources would you look for?

Proposed research questions

Look at the four research questions that have been suggested for Individual Reports on the topic of *Law and criminality*.

Evaluate each one. How suitable are they as research questions? How could they be modified to ensure that they meet the expectations of a full report?

1. Should hate crime be banned as it is never justified?

2. Does having no laws equal having no crimes?

3. To what extent is crime a social construct? Is anyone a born criminal?

4. Should criminals convicted of violent crime be allowed out on parole?

Sample student evaluations of sources

Three students have decided to write their Individual Reports on the issue of corporate crime. Look at the sections from their reports in which they attempt to evaluate their evidence and sources. Then answer the following questions.

1. What is wrong with Brimma's approach?

2. What is wrong with Fuller's approach? How could Fuller have improved his evaluation?

3. What do you think of Asha's criticism of one of her own key sources?

4. How many sources should you set out to investigate? How many of these should you include in your evaluation?

Brimma

Most criminologists divide white-collar crime into two major types: corporate crime and occupational crime (crime committed for one's own benefit during the course of a legitimate occupation). Most corporate criminals do not view their activities as criminal, since their violations are usually part of their occupational environment. Corporate offenders remain committed to conventional society and do not identify with criminality. Their inappropriate behaviour is often informally approved by occupational or corporate subcultures.

The origins of the concept of corporate crime can be traced to the larger concept of white-collar crime, which was first introduced in the social sciences by US criminologist Edwin Sutherland in a 1939 presidential address to the American Sociological Association.

Taken from: https://www.britannica.com/topic/corporate-crime

Fuller
Evaluation of my source material

Earlier in this essay, I described and analysed four sources which each provided different evidence on the subject of crime committed in the corporate setting. I did this in great detail. It now remains to evaluate the sources I used. All of the sources were obtained from reliable and reputable places — two from well-known .org internet sites and two from regulated social media platforms. I steered clear of blogs and tweets, which are not reliable.

Asha

While Hatfield et al. (2019) was a useful source, and I agree with much of what was concluded about the nature of blue chip corporate crime, there are some issues with it. For example, further investigation reveals that Hatfield herself is an ex-convict and served eight years in prison in Singapore for not disclosing her company's commercial relations with rogue states. This brings into question the assertions she makes. In addition, the report excludes South East Asia in its statistics on corporate crime, which is where the company is registered. It seems likely that Hatfield has a vested interest and could be biased.

Assessment tip

Remember to evaluate the evidence from your sources. Even if you list and summarize your sources earlier in the report, if you fail to evaluate your evidence, you could lose 15 per cent of the available marks. An attempt to evaluate, even if only from one or two angles, will earn you some marks. For example, Fuller set out to evaluate his evidence by using a subheading – a reasonable strategy.

Common misunderstanding

Describing sources is not the same as evaluating them. You do need to explain and analyse your source material, but you need to evaluate its reliability too. For example, you may describe in great detail how a corporate crime revealed a politically motivated spy operation, but how reliable is your source?

What is rural crime?

When we think of crime, we often think of the crimes carried out in towns and cities. The megacities of the world are often referred to as magnets for criminals. It may well be that cities are less safe than rural areas. However, rural areas have been targeted much more in recent years by crime organizations. Why might this be so?

▲ Fig. 12.3

▲ Fig. 12.4

Skills focus – learning from research

Many people think of rural crime as being connected to agriculture. However, it is much broader than this.

Look at the cartoons, then answer the questions.

1. What do you think of the two cartoons in relation to rural crime? What perspectives do they show?

2. To what extent is rural crime in your region connected to agriculture?

3. Discuss how you would define rural crime. Give examples to support your rationale.

4. Why do you think rural crime is on the increase?

5. If your group decides to focus on rural crime for your Team Project, what research would you allocate to each person? Where and how would each of you obtain research data?

6. How motivated would you be as an individual in such a project?

Sample student reflections

Three students decided to raise awareness of the rapid increase in rural crime in their region. They wanted to learn more about the reasons behind the trend and assigned different research roles to each team member. Their action was to film a ten-minute video on a local farm which has invested in a high level of security.

Read each student's reflection, then answer the questions.

1. It looks as if Agnes has been on a steep learning curve. How relevant is her new learning?

2. Does Agnes discuss her role in the team effectively?

3. Darius provides a strong response in this part of the reflective report. Can you give three reasons why this is so?

4. Mikkel provides a strong response as well as a weak one. Where does Mikkel get it right, and why? And where does he fail to reflect properly?

Agnes

I learned a lot. Before the project, I didn't know much at all about rural areas or rural crime. I have only ever lived in a town, so visiting the farm was an eye-opener for me. I have never given any thought to how farming works, so seeing a herd of dairy cows being milked was amazing. Before we made the video, the farmer showed us lots of things. She even let us drive a tractor. I learned how a tractor is automated now, using artificial intelligence to make the tasks 100 per cent efficient. What did I think of my own performance? I slotted into the role well. Farm life is not an easy life and I feel that I was very open to seeing new things and getting very dirty on a farm.

Darius

My role at the research stage was to research for the action, so I visited the farm more than the others and at different times of the day to find out when the farm was most and least active. This was important because Mikkel found statistics that showed that rural crime is committed mostly at night or when not much work is being done. I went on a night security check with the farmer and we found evidence of an attempt at crime – part of a fence had been removed. Luckily, there were no animals in that field but, as the farmer said, it was full of sheep until a few days before. It was scary to think that people had been there earlier trying to steal sheep.

Although people think farmers are strong and can take care of themselves, I learned that farmers are nervous about organized crime. It impacts them financially, but also emotionally. I also learned a lot about my own skills as I'm usually someone who stays home and spends my time on a computer.

Mikkel

I was fine. I did most of the research from home and sent it across to Agnes and Darius. The most interesting research I found was in the *2021 Review of European Rural Crime* on a website called Farmers of Europe. I was amazed by how much money farms have to invest to install high-tech security systems at a time when their profits are being squeezed due to increasing operational costs, especially electricity. I didn't share this with the team, however, as they were motivated by the farm visits. I didn't enjoy being on a farm, I'm afraid. My computer skills are excellent and in this project there was not really anything I could have done to improve them or my performance.

Assessment tip

Learning from research should be approached from the perspective of being in a collaborative team. That means learning from your teammates' research as well as your own. For example, how did research by others help to develop your skills? You might identify some research that you are curious about but then assign it to another team member. What would you learn from that?

Common misunderstanding

Reflecting on your own role in contributing to the effectiveness of the team and learning from teammates is different from reflecting on the challenges of working in a team. For example, Mikkel feels that his teammates were not interested in his research on farm security. However, he failed to reflect on this from two important viewpoints: how not using this research might have affected the success of the action, and what this showed about the help Mikkel needed.

Moving towards assessment – Written Exam

Scan here to obtain the source material you need to carry out this examination practice work.

Question 4 in your **Written Exam** is a question based on all the sources in the insert. Candidates answer by writing an extended response. Candidates are required to assess actions in response to the global issue and explain their judgements with reasons and evidence.

Q4. A government wants to introduce a new policy for reducing crime.

The following actions are being considered:

- Offer the owners of guns a chance to hand them in without penalty.
- Increase the number of police officers on the streets by 25 per cent.
- Run a media campaign to tell people there is no such thing as victimless crime.

Which **one** of these actions would you recommend to your government, and why?

In your answer, you should:

- state your recommendation
- give reasons and evidence to support your choice
- use the material in the sources and/or any of your own ideas
- consider different arguments and perspectives.

Read the two sample student answers, then answer the questions that follow.

Ahmed's response

> Clearly states the chosen action.

I would say to the government to employ more police officers. This is because it will provide 250 police officers in a town, for example, rather than 200 and that has to be a good thing. It might be an expensive policy, but evidence shows that direct regular contact increases trust levels and local people see that money is being spent on them.

> Comes from Source 2.

In my experience, as I live in a difficult town, if we saw more police on the streets we would be friendly to them, and the community will seem more open and sharing. This will mean more foreign tourists will come and more businesspeople, and that will make our town richer.

> Attempts a line of reasoning from own experience and based on Source 2.

Our town is not in any of the countries on the worst gun crime list in Source 1, so we can have more police in the community not wearing firearms. I wouldn't recommend this in the USA, as every member of the community will have at least one gun.

> Uses Source 1 but is the reasoning correct?

> How could this be reworded to make it less assertive?

I don't like the idea of making prison life easier, so I'm not agreeing with the person in Source 4. My uncle had to go to prison for stealing. He was out again after a few months and it seemed like he learned nothing. He was back in prison within three weeks for stealing again. If he'd been there longer and had more lessons about how bad crime is, I think he'd change his attitude.

> A final judgement needs to be more general about the overall issue, not a specific case.

Jai's response

My advice to the government is to run the media campaign. There is strong evidence that social media is the fastest and most effective way to reach a large number of people. The government will need to engage experts in how to create effective social media content. It's highly unlikely that they will have in-house people who can do this. This involves extra costs, of course, but if they are serious the costs will be worth it, as they will probably not need to spend money on increasing the number of active police officers by 25 per cent.

> Gives a strong, direct opening and judgement, followed with relevant evidence from own knowledge.

> Good line of reasoning, engaging with another proposed action at the same time.

Such a media campaign will make people aware of the consequences of having been lenient on crime in the past. This must have been the case as the government are considering actions such as more officers and offering a gun amnesty.

> Useful inference. Does it build an argument to support the opening judgement?

However, the key aspect is exactly what the professor of criminology says: that the victims of crime are not only the people directly affected. For example, in a case of robbery, it is not only the shop owner who suffers, but all of their family. And let's not forget the reputation of the shop, which will possibly put other customers off buying goods there.

> Uses Source 3 well as evidence.

> Follows the evidence by developing a line of reasoning.

My perspective on this is that of the victim. I do understand that offenders should be given a chance to redeem themselves and have time to reflect. A good idea is to make the offender have a meeting with the people that they caused to suffer from the crime and to apologize, showing remorse.

> Shows consideration of different perspectives.

Engaging with Question 4

1. Is Ahmed right to raise the viewpoints of tourists and businesspeople?

2. Does Ahmed interpret the position of the USA correctly on the graph that is part of Source 1? Explain your view.

3. How might Ahmed use the case of his uncle in a more balanced way to support his argument?

4. If you are not going to use a source, you should cover a similar point using your own knowledge or experience. How well does Jai do this?

5. What does Jai's use of the word "amnesty" illustrate?

Media and communication

In this section you will:

- consider the scope of media and communication, and how it raises ethical questions

- look at how adverts can be used in political elections, and when adverts might be not allowed.

A line of enquiry

In 2021, the United Nations estimated that 85 per cent of the global population had mobile network coverage. It is reasonable to predict, therefore, that by 2050 this will have risen to 100 per cent. Imagine being able to connect to anyone in the world easily, inexpensively, and at any time you wish. How does this affect the power of media and how far-reaching it is?

If you wanted a career in communications media, what would you have to research and learn about? What about communications law? Public relations? Marketing strategies? Brand management? Working on television dramas? Music media? Podcasting? Event tourism? All of these are part of the global communications industry.

These areas raise ethics to be discussed. Think about how ethical the media and communications industry is and, in some cases, is not.

▲ **Fig. 13.1** *Broadcast media*

▲ **Fig. 13.2** *Print media*

Quote

Think about the viewpoints these three writers share about newspapers.

"If you don't read the newspaper, you're uninformed. If you read the newspaper, you're misinformed." *(Mark Twain)*

"I became a journalist because I did not want to rely on newspapers for information." *(Christopher Hitchens)*

"It is usually known that newspapers do not say the truth, but it is also known that they cannot tell whoppers." *(George Orwell)*

Using media for advertising

Most countries have their own set of standards for advertising. Have a look at how Brazil approaches one aspect – using the media to advertise during political elections.

Advertising in Brazil

Advertising in Brazil was born in the big cities, where many different services were concentrated as well as large numbers of people. It initially started in newspapers, then extended to radio, magazines, television, and then to the internet.

The advertising industry cannot be separated from the media industry. There are restrictions about what is legal, what was legal, and what it was never legal to advertise in Brazil.

Electioneering

In Brazil, there are laws about what is allowed and forbidden in an election campaign, including advertising. Despite this, there have been campaigns that were illegal in some way.

Main prohibitions

- It is forbidden to distribute items such as T-shirts, key chains, hats, gifts, cestas básicas (basic items given to employees to supplement their wages), or anything that could be regarded as a gift to buy votes.

- It is forbidden to advertise on billboards or promote by *showmícios*, rallies where famous people give free performances or show support for a political candidate, directly influencing the electorate.

- Election candidates cannot spend more than the average spent on advertising over the previous three years.

Sustainability

Sustainability in the media is whether it is able to operate effectively in political, legal, and economic conditions. In a sustainable environment, journalists work without interference or fear of threats, and media organizations enjoy safe and secure business conditions allowing them to pay decent salaries, discourage media corruption, and promote integrity. Under what conditions might aspects of the media become unsustainable?

Task 1

In pairs, answer the following questions.

1. Why do you think Brazil feels the need to have laws about the use of advertising in politics?

2. Do you think other countries need similar laws? If so, which countries and why?

3. The writer states that the advertising industry cannot be separated from the media industry. Do you agree with this viewpoint? Why or why not?

4. Why do you think it might never have been legal to advertise for elections in Brazil?

5. Why are items such as T-shirts and hats with advertising banned during an election campaign?

6. What do you think about famous people supporting politicians in political campaigns?

7. Do you think the last prohibition in the list is sensible? Why?

Investigative journalism

In this section you will:

- consider UNESCO's approach to investigative journalism
- identify news stories you would like to investigate
- explore the work of two prominent, globally respected journalists.

A line of enquiry

Read this extract from the United Nations Educational, Scientific and Cultural Organization (UNESCO) to learn more about investigative journalism.

Investigative journalism means the unveiling of matters that are concealed either deliberately by someone in a position of power, or accidentally, behind a chaotic mass of facts and circumstances – and the analysis and exposure of all relevant facts to the public. In this way investigative journalism crucially contributes to freedom of expression and media development, which are at the heart of UNESCO's mandate.

The role media can play as a watchdog is indispensable for democracy, and it is for this reason that UNESCO fully supports initiatives to strengthen the capacity building of investigative journalism throughout the world.

Causes and consequences

Citizen Nades said that he occasionally self-censored. This would not have been an easy decision for him to make, as his approach seemed to be to investigate "no matter what". Think about some occasions when it might not be such a good idea for the "truth to out". Think about the causes of self-censoring and the consequences of uncovering truths.

Task 2

In pairs, answer the following questions.

1. Discuss the definition of investigative journalism offered by UNESCO. Do you agree? Would you like to change anything about it?

2. Do you think all countries of the world would agree with the UNESCO position on investigative journalism? Which different perspectives might be put forward?

3. What does UNESCO mean by media playing a role as a watchdog for democracy?

4. If you were investigative journalists in your country, which story would you like to uncover? Why?

Perspectives

In 1644 in England, John Milton wrote a speech to argue for the unlicensed printing of material. He was objecting to censorship and arguing for free speech nearly 400 years ago. Censorship remains a global issue, more so in some countries than others. Perspectives on censorship vary, from the suggestion it should not even exist to defending it as central to human rights.

Citizen Nades and Christopher Hitchens

Now look at the work of two very well-known investigative journalists.

Citizen Nades worked in Malaysia until 2016. On his retirement he was interviewed by Robin Hicks, who asked him these questions.

Which of your stories in your career as a journalist have upset the government the most?

Because the nature of the issues addressed in my column point to weaknesses, abuse, or misuse of public funds or power, they naturally upset a lot of government servants. But I think the government is happy that I am keeping the civil servants on their toes. I have in the past received "well done" calls from ministers who feel I am doing the right thing.

What does it take to write a story that rattles the cages of the corrupt? (How do you know when you have enough to run the story? How do you protect your sources?)

When facts and figures are presented, obviously they will get rattled. Instead of addressing the issue, they go on trying to find out how I obtained the information or who leaked the information. I have always maintained that they should not shoot the messenger.

Have you ever knowingly self-censored?

Yes. There have been instances where my discovery and putting it in the public domain would jeopardize security and even, in one case, someone's life was at stake.

Christopher Hitchens (Hitch) worked in Washington, USA and died in 2011. This is his obituary in *The Guardian* newspaper in England.

His targets were the abusers of power, particularly Henry Kissinger (whom he tried to bring to trial for his role in bombing Cambodia and overthrowing the Allende regime in Chile) and Bill Clinton. He was unrelenting in his support for the Palestinian cause. He was a polemicist [someone who enjoys debate] rather than an analyst or political thinker – his headteacher at the Leys school in Cambridge forecast a future as a pamphleteer – and, like all the best polemicists, brought to his work outstanding skills of reporting and observation.

To these he added wide reading, not always worn lightly, an extraordinary memory – he seemed, his friend Ian McEwan observed, to enjoy "instant neurological recall" of anything he had ever read or heard – and a vigorous, if sometimes pompous writing style, heavily laden with adjectives, elegantly looping sub-clauses and archaic phrases such as "allow me to inform you".

Task 3

In pairs, think about the approaches taken by the two journalists.

1. Describe to each other the characteristics of both Citizen Nades and Hitch. What motivated them? What did they stand up for? What did they dislike? How similar and how different are they?

2. Do you think that you would like either of them if you met them? Who might you like most?

3. Imagine you are about to interview them both. Write a list of questions you would like to ask them and of the directions you want the interview to take.

Mass media

In this section you will:

- look at mass media from a wide range of perspectives
- explore specialized television and specific audiences.

A line of enquiry

Mass media is far reaching: it touches almost every part of the globe and almost every one of us. Mass media has traditionally used radio, television, newspapers, and magazines, and now, in the 21st century, the internet to reach its audience. Whether we like it or not, most of us are an intended audience for those who control the mass media. That is not to say that mass media is a negative force in our lives. You are going to look at various perspectives.

▲ **Fig. 13.3** *Mass media addiction*

▲ **Fig. 13.4** *One way to the truth*

Task 4

In pairs, answer the following questions.

1. Look at the two photographs. What message is each sending about the power of mass media?

2. Do you think they are valid messages? Why or why not? Or perhaps it's not that straightforward?

3. Now consider a different perspective. The musician David Bowie said, "I think that we have created a new kind of person in a way. We have created a child who will be so exposed to the media that he will be lost to his parents by the time he is 12." What did Bowie mean? Do you think this is true now, many years after Bowie said it?

4. Look at the cartoon. How does it show a positive message about the media?

▲ **Fig. 13.5**

5. Look at the graph. Is this a trend you would expect to see for the period 2004–21? Do you think this regional trend is a global trend? Would you expect to see a similar trend in your country?

6. Write a list of the advantages and disadvantages of mass media. Focus on new media, giving examples and advantages and / or disadvantages. An example of new media could be tweets. An advantage is sharing a platform and a disadvantage is that it can lead to hatred.

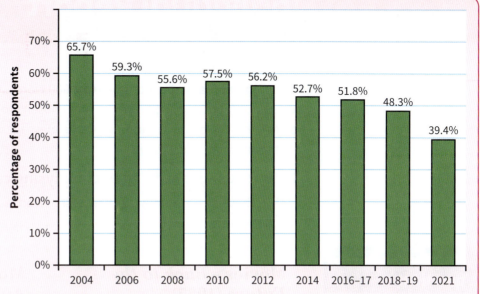

▲ **Fig. 13.6** *Graph showing trust in the mass media in Latin America and the Caribbean, 2004–21*

Audiences

Mass media is especially effective when it targets a particular audience to achieve a specific aim. In Italy, television audiences are higher than those in many other countries. For example, Italian television has a large number of programmes dedicated to food and cooking.

Task 5

In small groups, answer these questions.

1. Why do you think Italy has such a large television audience? Can you think of another country that might have a larger than average television audience?

2. What about your own country? Do many people watch traditional television, or are people moving over to social media instead?

3. What other types of specialist shows for specific audiences might there be? Think of examples which are specific to certain countries, regions, or local areas.

Reflect

Have there been times in your life when you felt that you were losing control of your time as a result of your interaction with mass media? Many people think that one of the most precious things in life is time – to relax, think, or do nothing if you prefer. Does mass media take advantage of the free time that people have and need? Think of some moments when you wanted to just "switch off".

Empathy

The way in which mass media targets specific audiences can result in people making complaints about the effects of its power. Sometimes this is a personal issue, with harm done directly to an individual. Sometimes an organization will object when many people have been affected. For people who are frequent users of mass media, are there grounds for empathy? Or could we argue that they deserved what they got?

Moving towards assessment – Individual Report

Causes and consequences

In your **Individual Report** of 1,500 to 2,000 words, you should explain and analyse some causes and consequences of your chosen global issue. You are going to look at how the media communicates its messages, focusing on the causes and consequences of censorship.

Skills focus – identifying and analysing causes and consequences

Look at these three examples of censorship from a range of media types. Then complete the task that follows.

Proposed research questions

Look at the four research questions that have been suggested for Individual Reports on the topic of *Media and communication*.

Evaluate each one. How suitable are they as research questions? How could they be modified to ensure that they meet the expectations of a full report?

1. Twitter is the gatekeeper of free speech.

2. We will not be truly globally connected until we have at least 20 international space stations covering at least 50 languages.

3. Media moguls are more powerful than monarchs and presidents.

4. The solution is that every government should have its own media channels.

Movies – *Back to the Future* (1985)

The time travel within *Back to the Future* results from Emmett "Doc" Brown's experiments, which always fascinated teenage Marty McFly. After stealing plutonium for his modified DeLorean, several men appear to take revenge and kill Doc. Marty narrowly escapes in the DeLorean after Doc is shot, not realizing the car is actually a time machine.

This movie was banned by the Chinese government.

Music: 'Spasticus Autisticus' by Ian Dury and the Blockheads (1981)

Dury wrote 'Spasticus Autisticus' to protest against what he saw as the patronising International Year of Disabled Persons, and then it was blocked by the BBC, which deemed Dury's descriptions of physical disability offensive. Redemption finally came at the 2012 Paralympic opening ceremony, where it was sung by a group of performers with disabilities.

Books: *Of Mice and Men*

The Steinbeck novella about two migrant ranch workers came out in 1937 and has been challenged by school boards ever since for offensive language, racial slurs and, according to a coalition of clergy in Mobile, Alabama, "morbid and depressing themes". Somewhat hilariously, the book was also taken to task due to Steinbeck's noted "anti-business attitude", and was thus nixed as a summer youth program reading assignment in Chattanooga, Tennessee, in 1989.

1. What is your reaction to these examples of censorship? What do you think their causes and consequences might have been? Do you agree or disagree that they should have been censored?

2. Can you think of other examples of media censorship? What are the causes and consequences of your examples?

Sample student extracts

Three students decided to write their Individual Reports on the issue of censorship. Their research question was: "Should there be a global agreement about what should and should not be censored in the media?"

Below are extracts from their reports where they identify and analyse the causes and consequences of censorship. Read the extracts, then evaluate each one using these questions.

1. Do you think Star makes a valid point using an appropriate example? Why or why not?

2. Angela decided to present and evaluate research on a case of national security in Poland, but not to discuss its causes and consequences. What do you think about this?

3. Do you agree with Kiana? What point is she making? She fails to mention any consequences. What might they be?

4. Which of the three students do you think produced the strongest report? Explain your reasoning.

Star

Not everything about censorship causes a controversy. Sometimes it can be a positive thing and therefore has a good cause, for example, censoring the identity of victims in court to protect them against organized crime. The consequence of not doing this could be fatal. Take the example of my research into Jonas Lillywhite in Kenya, whose identity was mistakenly revealed by a Nairobi judge during a case in which a drug baron had been brought to court.

Angela

It is not against the law for authors, publishers, or other creators to censor their own work. The causes of self-censoring are worthy of analysis as they can vary from case to case. In my research, I focused on two different perspectives: uses of censorship to protect national security and uses of censorship to prevent hate speech spreading. I closely examined the former in my research using a case in Poland, so that is self-explanatory, but in the latter, I would like to draw attention to the increase in hate speech censored by Twitter.

Kiana

The cause of censorship is obvious — intolerance. It doesn't matter who is being intolerant — a person, a nation, a government, the owner of a media company, or even you or me — it is never right to be intolerant. When I researched this global issue, I came across examples in Japanese culture of what I would call intolerance, for example, not being allowed to print facts that are different from information given to reporters by the Japanese police force.

Assessment tip

Try to compare different causes of your main global issue. Some causes are more important than others, so target those. You should also look at a national perspective to contrast the global viewpoint – maybe look at how the effects or impacts vary. For example, if your issue is how to deal with hate speech, the causes are likely to come from a wide range of cultural backgrounds.

Common misunderstanding

You need to do more than just describe causes and consequences. For example, you might think the lack of freedom of speech in a country is due to a military regime that holds the balance of power. Don't just describe the power and influence of the military and focus on historical and traditional values. Instead, analyse why the military is still very influential in the modern era and how it uses the media to its advantage.

Moving towards assessment – Team Project

A brief history of communication

Alexander Bell experimented with the first telephone line in 1875 and Alexandra Palace in north London issued the world's first higher definition television broadcast in 1936. The decade we are living in has faster access to media and to a greater range of types of media than ever before. Is there an argument for using slower forms of communication? Do we need to be informed of issues around the world as they happen? How do you see this trend of instant communication developing by 2075 – the bicentenary of the telephone line?

Skills focus – writing content for a local radio programme

Imagine this scenario: a new independent radio station has opened and wants to connect with teenagers in your area. The producer wants to establish a 'Teen Weekly' segment of 30 minutes and is looking for people to provide content. The station has put out a poster to attract interest, asking for "stories of local interest that must also have global reach".

1. Decide on a local story you want to cover. Make sure it raises an issue that has global appeal but that you can provide evidence for locally.
2. The station requires teams of four members. Assign roles to each team member. They should each bring a different perspective to the issue.
3. Are there any other things to bear in mind, given the story you have chosen to cover and the angles you are taking? Remember, your aim is for each person to contribute to the activity on an equal basis and to avoid situations where the team is not working together in balance.
4. Are you able to predict any flashpoints? Any times when the pressure will be on?

Sample student comments

A team of three students made their first-ever radio show, as part of the 'Teen Weekly' series. Read their notes commenting on their contributions to the project, culminating in the radio broadcast about the lack of opportunities for teenagers to voice their opinions outside of their school. Then answer the following questions.

1. Who do you think was the most flexible team member? Explain why.
2. If you were Paloma, how might you do things differently next time you work on a similar project?
3. Is Estella right to say that equality was taken too far? Can you think of other examples in teamwork where this might be the case?

Proposed projects

Look at the following four ideas that have been suggested for a Team Project on the topic of *Media and communication*.

Evaluate each one. How suitable are they as projects? How could they be modified to become more appropriate and viable?

1. To examine the history of the BBC and its global role in creating television media.
2. To work as a team of investigative journalists seeking out the truth about a local issue.
3. To show by visual and musical examples how censorship has been carried out in our country.
4. Demonstrating that it's difficult in our region to become a journalist due to local factors.

4. Was a fair and reasonable solution found as to who should feature in the main part of the broadcast?

5. How much of Luisa's notes are valid from the perspective of individual contributions?

6. What do you infer from Luisa noticing that another team member was struggling?

Paloma

At the concept meeting I made it clear to the team that we should allocate 15 hours' work each to plan the project, but not on Tuesday or Thursday as I have a part-time job and that must take priority. It's not that I need the money, but I do relish the independence. There were some complaints in the team but I brushed them aside. Every team needs a strong leader.

I was very disappointed to have been given a minor role for the broadcast. I only did the two-minute introduction.

Estella

It was difficult today working with Paloma. She insisted that we each commit to 15 hours of our time and it wasn't just me who made the point that this was taking the idea of equality too far. I am happy to give more of my time and you never know who needs more support, do you? I was probably too passive, however, letting Paloma take the lead.

It didn't matter after all as we each met our own targets, and in the studio the evidence was there as we ran a 30-minute show almost to perfection! It was right that Luisa took the main chunk, as we all agreed (except Paloma) that she has natural talent on the microphone.

Luisa

We achieved our main aim, which was to use the radio show to illustrate an irony, which was that on the whole, teenagers' voices are not heard in our community. We worked well as a team to bring this to a wider audience. Estella and I will develop this further by writing another show that hinges around the unheard voices of teenagers in another town in our bordering country of Indonesia — a nice trip, and this could become a theme for a series!

When we were in the studio, I noticed that Paloma was struggling. She looked frustrated. I'd also noticed this in the planning stages. She did keep going, so we valued her contribution.

Assessment tip

It is important to reflect on the impact of your individual contribution to the Team Project and not just describe what you did. A strong contribution adds value to the project and motivates other team members. For example, in Paloma's team, a useful impact would have been to ensure equality in the team and a fairer sense of allocating tasks and time, not just to describe how Paloma ran the show.

Common misunderstanding

In order to justify weaknesses in your own role and contribution, it is not enough just to identify roles or provide a list of what went wrong with certain roles. Such comments may be valid when reflecting on team collaboration, but for individual collaboration you can only make these comments about yourself. Estella does this well as she reflects on her strengths and weaknesses in how she contributed her own time and energy.

Moving towards assessment – Written Exam

Scan here to obtain the source material you need to carry out this examination practice work.

Question 1 in your **Written Exam** is a structured question based on several sources. There will be three or four parts to the question. Candidates are required to read the sources and analyse the information, arguments, and perspectives presented about the global issue.

Q1. Study Sources 1 and 2.

  a. What is the general trend predicted for social media usage in South America from 2022 onwards?

  b. Using Source 2, identify three factors which raise concerns relating to social media usage.

  c. What do you think is the most positive perspective of social media? Explain your choice.

  d. Which of the challenges provided by social media do you think is the most significant? Explain why.

Read the two sample student answers, then answer the questions that follow.

Leila's response

1 a) It's an upward trend.

  b) 1 The trend of use seems to be getting worse.
  2 People using it too much at work.
  3 Disability is not given equal status.

  c) I think that social media provides an alternative to watching television and streaming channels all the time. It's one thing to be stuck in your room as a passive viewer, but social media is interactive, so this means you ==feel like you are connected to people==.

> Connects to a factor in Source 2.

> Starts well with a clear opinion.

  d) ==I think it's the challenge of keeping your identity a secret==. I follow a lot of people on Twitter and their profiles are there for all to see. I also follow a lot of influencers, but I guess they want to be known by as many people as possible. I think it's not fair when influencers are attacked, for example, by trolls, ==as they are only trying to do good things==. Children under 12, in my opinion, should be kept safe but the question is how to do it?

> While this might be an argument, it tries to support her opinion.

  The issue is really about vanity. It's the people on social media who have big egos and are the ones that cause all the problems. The challenge, therefore, is to have a separate space for these people who all know each other but to have private spaces for the rest of us.

Lennon's response

1 a) The use of social media is levelling off.

b) 1 Everyday use suggests too much dependency.
2 Too much social media can reduce life quality.
3 Students achieve less in terms of grading.

c) Of the issues raised in Source 2, <mark>I think the most positive perspective</mark> is that social media is being used by police forces to reduce crime. While I am aware that criminals use social media to commit a lot of online crime, cybercrime, it's good to see that the police can use the power and speed of some social media platforms to raise awareness <mark>and send the message</mark> to criminals that they are trying to find them.

d) I would say it's the one faced by employers. Many times I have been in shops, restaurants, offices, and even schools where the staff seem always to have their phones in their hands. It must be difficult for the employer to know if this is work use or personal use. <mark>That must be quite a challenge and it raises the connected issue of trust</mark>. You'd think that because it's so difficult to keep anonymous, employers do know which of their employees are abusing the trust.

<mark>On the other hand, it's clear that in the past decade the reliance on social media has gone up a lot</mark>, and this may well be because of how useful it is for companies to promote their interests. I can see that for many, social media is invaluable for them to make better profits.

As people spend most of their time at work, and if they are active social media users, <mark>what would happen if they were banned</mark> from using their phones while working? I think this could result in some of the other issues, such as losing touch, loneliness, not getting enough sleep and quality of life going down. All of these lead to less efficient working, surely.

So the reason this one is the most significant is that it involves different perspectives, and from the graph seems to be different in different places in the world. It also brings in causes and consequences.

Recognizes that it is indeed a perspective – a viewpoint taken by the police.

Picks up on positives hinted at in the sources.

Lays a foundation for details to support his opinion.

Looks at the issue from another useful angle. A good clear signpost.

Nice use of rhetorical question and follow up connections to source material.

Engaging with Question 1

1. Do you think Leila's answer to Question **1a** is correct? How can trends in graphs and charts be described?

2. Look at both students' answers to Question **1b**. Have they identified appropriate factors?

3. Question **1c** focuses on the use of the two sources. To what extent has each of the students referred to the sources?

4. Question **1d** is really getting at understanding an issue and providing a supported opinion about it. The specific issue here is the challenges that social media can bring about. Which student do you think deals with this best? Why?

14 Migration and urbanization

In this section you will:

- explore the impact of urbanization
- analyse the attractions and problems of living in big cities
- compare present and future settlement trends around the world.

A line of enquiry

Congratulations! Since 15 November 2022 you are officially one of 8 billion people living on planet Earth. According to the United Nations (UN), most of us now live in cities. In 1950, only two cities – New York and Tokyo – could be classed as megacities, which are cities of more than 10 million inhabitants. Now there are many.

Many young people move to cities because of better work opportunities. Finding a well-paid job or setting up a business is often more profitable in a city than in smaller towns or rural areas.

What is your experience of city life? Do you think living in a city is something to aspire to or aim for? A famous writer once said that nothing happens in the countryside – everything happens in the city. Do you agree?

▲ **Fig. 14.1** *A megacity in Asia*

Megacities

Begin by thinking about the economic, social, and environmental impact of megacities.

Task 1

In pairs, decide if the following views are positive or negative. Is the type of impact they describe economic, social, or environmental? For example, the first statement is clearly a positive view of city life and it describes a social impact.

a. I've made a lot of new friends here. There are so many opportunities to socialize. We often go to restaurants or the cinema.

b. The area I live in looks dirty. The bins are collected once every week, but there is a lot of rubbish in the street.

c. I had to move for my new job. But I now have a higher salary so I can buy a bigger apartment.

d. I feel lonely. My apartment is in a big block of flats and I don't know my neighbours. I worry that if I needed help, I wouldn't know who to ask.

e. My neighbourhood is well connected. There is a bus stop in front of my house and the subway is just a ten-minute walk away.

f. My son is going to secondary school next year. There are so many good schools near where we live.

g. My dad's car got broken into last month and some shops have problems with shoplifting.

h. My area has improved with new shops, cafes, and restaurants. Houses have been renovated at great expense, but now you can't afford to buy a house.

i. When I look out of my window, I can see into my neighbours' flat opposite. I live alongside a busy road with traffic all day and night.

j. My business is thriving. I hardly had any customers when the shop was on the outskirts of the city, but now there is a lot of passing trade.

Future cities

In the future, more and more people will move to cities, expecting to find jobs and opportunities to improve their lives. The graph below compares the number of cities on each continent in 2018 with the expected number in 2030. Think about the changes that will occur.

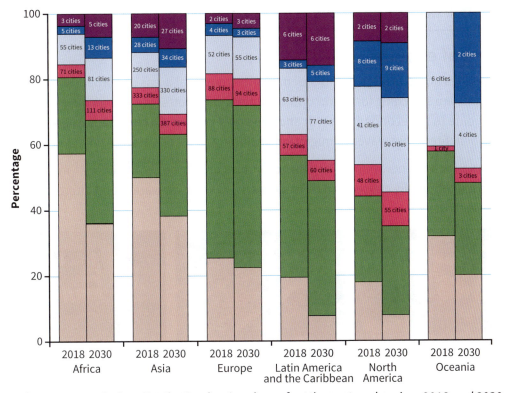

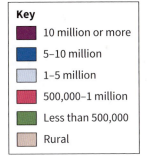

Key

- 10 million or more
- 5–10 million
- 1–5 million
- 500,000–1 million
- Less than 500,000
- Rural

▲ **Fig. 14.2** *Population distribution by size class of settlement and region, 2018 and 2030*

Sustainability

Rapid, sprawling, and unplanned urbanization is unsustainable. Developing countries face major challenges with waste disposal, resources, and infrastructure management. Should each city be allowed to set its own targets for reducing pollution and aiming for net zero?

Task 2

In pairs, look at the graph and answer the following questions.

1. Where in the world will we see the biggest changes by 2030? Look at the percentage trends and also the number of cities in each classification. Give details.
2. What does the graph predict about rural areas in 2030? What consequences could this have for agriculture and farming?
3. Where will we see the biggest increase in the number of cities that have 1–5 million inhabitants? Explain why this might be the case.
4. In which region are the number of megacities not increasing? What could be the reasons for this?
5. Which parts of the world change the least and which the most? Give reasons for your answer.

Argument

Inequality, social segregation, and urban social exclusion are all connected to urbanization. For example, London is an unequal city. It is known for its banking sector and economic performance, but many Londoners struggle to find good-quality jobs and affordable housing. In this megacity there is a wide gap between rich and poor.

Endless opportunities or a never-ending nightmare?

In this section you will:

- consider the different factors that make people want to move to cities
- evaluate the socio-economic impacts of migration.

A line of enquiry

Many cities accept a large number of migrants from rural areas or abroad. Most migrants are searching for better opportunities and a better life. Urban migration can contribute to the economic growth and cultural diversity of a city. Many major cities have benefited from waves of migration, including New York, Hong Kong, and Sydney.

Migration is not a new thing. There are examples of it throughout history – including mass migration, the causes and consequences of which are varied and interesting to research.

▲ Fig. 14.3

▲ Fig. 14.4

▲ Fig. 14.5

▲ Fig. 14.6

▲ Fig. 14.7

Task 3

Look at the photographs showing different aspects of city life.

In pairs, work through the following.

1. Identify whether each picture shows a push or a pull factor, explaining why and how people are drawn to cities.
2. Give some examples of other push and pull factors relating to migration.
3. Is migration a choice? Give reasons to support your answer.
4. Which push or pull factors are the most important for young people under the age of 25?
5. If you had the choice, would you rather live in a big city or elsewhere? Give reasons for your answer.
6. Categorize the push and pull factors you have identified, such as environmental, technological, health, economic, social, or cultural. Is there a pattern? Explain your answer.

Migrant workers in China

According to Chinese government statistics, the current number of migrant workers in China is estimated at 130 million, approximately 9 per cent of the population.

Every Chinese New Year, millions of Chinese migrant workers embark on a temporary migration back to their home town to reunite with their loved ones. The Chinese-Canadian director Lixin Fan tells this emotional journey in her 2009 documentary film *Last Train Home*.

Read through the following film review, then answer the questions that follow.

▲ **Fig. 14.8**

Last Train Home

The film tells the story of the Zhangs, who left their home in the countryside 16 years ago, just after the birth of their daughter, to work in the factories of Guangdong province, making cheap goods for Western countries. They only return home once a year for a few days during New Year. This is often the only occasion when they can spend time with their children and parents.

The story is about the Zhangs' attempt to leave the city, having to fight the inhuman crush of workers who crowd into Guangdong's dirty railway station to secure tickets. The trip covers more than 2,000 kilometres and is an exhausting and stressful journey by train, bus, and ferry. When they finally arrive home, they are able to spend only a few days with their son Yang (10) and daughter Qin (17), who have grown up under the care of their grandparents and hardly know their parents. During the last ten years, Qin has become resentful at never seeing her parents, even though the economic necessity of the arrangement is self-evident. The parents' only conversation is to tell the children to study hard, but they show no interest in what they study. In a rebellious frame of mind, Qin decides to leave school and go to work in a factory just like her parents, thinking that it is the path to freedom. In exploring the dark side of the Chinese economic miracle, *Last Train Home* has plenty of tunnels along their journey but little light at the end.

Task 4

In small groups, answer the following questions.

1. What perspective on migrant workers does the film review take?
2. Why do you think the parents, and later their daughter, Qin, work as migrant workers in factories?
3. What are the socio-economic effects of this decision?
4. What is the impact on the family – children, parents, and grandparents?
5. Create a dialogue between Qin and her parents expressing why she has left school and what she hopes to find in the big city. Include a concluding section, with suggestions on what will happen to Qin and what kind of life she will live.

Empathy

Migrant workers often work long hours and can become isolated and socially excluded, sending much of their earnings to their families back home. Migrant workers bring with them skills, ethnic culture, cuisine, music, and entrepreneurship. They are also a crucial factor for economic growth. Think about any migrant workers that have relocated to a city you know well and how much value has been added.

People on the move

A line of enquiry

Climate change and wars are major reasons for migration, with the poorest often hit the hardest. Around the world, millions of people try to escape droughts, floods, rising sea levels, conflict, or violence. The maps show that, in 2021, conflict forced more people to leave their homes than natural disasters did. In many cases, the line between those who choose to migrate and those who are forced to migrate (displaced) is not clear cut.

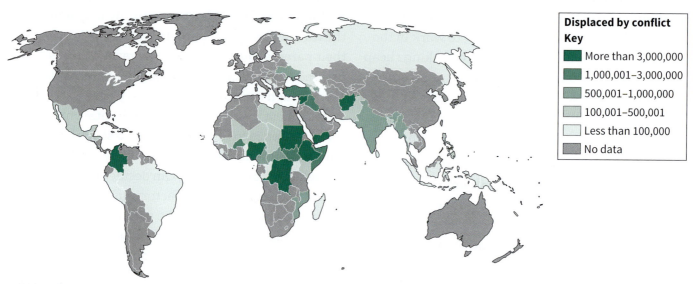

▲ **Fig. 14.9** *Conflict and violence in 59 countries resulted in 53.2 million internally displaced people in 2021*

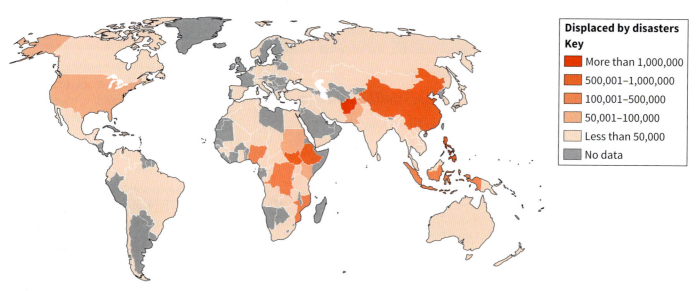

▲ **Fig. 14.10** *Natural disasters in 84 countries resulted in 5.9 million internally displaced people in 2021*

Read about four teenagers from different areas of the world. They all wrote a blog with the title "People on the move".

Nur Salam, 16

My family lost everything in the floods. Our house was destroyed, all our belongings and animals were swept away. We could barely escape ourselves. It was traumatic. My dad decided to move us to the capital city. He has a job in a restaurant and we have started to rebuild our lives. I was sad to leave my friends behind, but I can finish my education now and maybe even go to university.

Abdul, 15

We have had two major droughts in the last five years. My dad is a farmer. He usually sells his vegetables and livestock in the nearby city but, with the drought getting worse each year, no one can live here anymore. There is no water for us or the crops. Everyone else has already moved to the city. My dad doesn't want to leave. He is worried about finding another job at his age. I will have to give up school and move to the city on my own. I am very worried about the future.

Fabienne, 17

A hurricane took the roof off our house. Trees fell on cars, shop windows got smashed and the rain caused a mudslide that covered many houses. Our family has thought many times of moving to another country, but we love our island and we haven't got enough money to move. My dad says that if I study hard, I could get a scholarship and study abroad one day, but that's just a distant dream.

Mykola, 16

My mum and I were forced to flee our country. It was very scary. My dad and grandad stayed to fight for our country. I don't know if I will ever see them again. I try and focus on school, but I often lie awake at night and cry. I can't believe political decisions can destroy my life. We didn't want this war. We had no choice but to move to another country. People here are very friendly, but I just want to go back home. I don't feel settled here.

Task 5

In pairs, answer these questions.

1. What impact did moving to the capital city have on Nur Salam?

2. How could the situation have been improved for Abdul?

3. Why was Fabienne not able to move? Is migrating always the best solution? Refer to the idea of a "brain drain" in your answer.

4. How would you help Mykola if he was in your class?

5. Which of the four teenagers do you think has adapted best to their new life? Explain your answer.

6. Now create a role play to explain why someone had to move to your city and how they were helped. Include different viewpoints towards migrants.

Causes and consequences

Migrants who flee violence or natural disasters are often traumatized and suffer from mental health issues, not helped by having to leave behind loved ones and belongings. As a result, migrants may suffer from post-traumatic stress disorder (PTSD), depression, and anxiety. Art therapy has been used to help with trauma. For example, NGOs in Lebanon have organized art therapy for children from Syria to help them deal with their traumatic experiences of war.

Ever-changing world

Low-lying islands such as Kiribati and the Maldives are under threat from rising sea levels. None of Kiribati in the Pacific Ocean is more than 2 metres above sea level. There are plans to raise the islands, but this will cost billions. During COP27 in 2022, President Maamau of Kiribati called on the wealthy nations, who he thinks are responsible for rising sea levels, to pay for this plan.

Structure, clarity, and cohesion

In your **Individual Report** of 1,500 to 2,000 words, you should aim to write a well-structured report that is clear and easy to follow, providing analysis of the global issue with relevant supporting information.

Skills focus – structuring a report

Put the following ideas in order of importance, from first (1) to last (9).

- Sense check the report to check that my arguments are clear and coherent.
- Use the internet to search for ideas about migration and urbanization.
- Allow time for reflection to see if my perspective has changed.
- Note down the title or website of articles and books that I will use.
- Decide on the title of my report.
- Include a global, national, and personal perspective on the topic.
- Explain the causes and consequences of migration and urbanization.
- Explain which sources are reliable and which are not.
- Include sustainable and inclusive solutions to urban growth and explain why they solve the issues that big cities face.

Sample student first drafts

Three students have completed the first draft of their Individual Reports on climate migration. Feedback from their peers was given focusing on structure, the use of connectives, and how the essay could be improved. Answer these questions, supporting your answers with reasons.

1. Which student's first draft was easiest to follow?

2. Which student should develop their sentences and focus on checking grammar and punctuation?

3. Which student wrote a report that was difficult to read and not well structured?

4. Which student needs to learn how to link paragraphs together better in order to write a more cohesive report?

5. Which student included effective topic sentences in their paragraphs?

Proposed research questions

Look at the four research questions that have been suggested for Individual Reports on the topic of *Migration and urbanization*.

Evaluate each one. How suitable are they as research questions? How could they be modified to ensure that they meet the expectations of a full report?

1. The benefits and challenges of megacities.

2. How can migrants be integrated into communities?

3. To what extent are future visions of urban spaces sustainable?

4. Should climate migration be managed globally rather than on a national level?

Feedback given to Pippa

Your essay was clearly written with many references. You obviously did a lot of research. I like that you supported your perspectives well throughout the essay, not just in one paragraph. I also liked your introduction and the facts and statistics about climate migration. Your reflection at the end was very honest and thoughtful. Try to include more paragraphs though, to make it easier for people to read. For example, the paragraph below could be split into two.

"I had heard of climate change and rising sea levels, but I never really thought about people being forced to flee their homes because of this. I assumed they would be able to go back to their houses afterwards. Now, after doing research, I understand that climate migration affects you on all levels, your finances, your mental health, your education and your social wellbeing. More research needs to be done about the effects of climate migration on school children. It would be interesting to see how much schooling they lose and how their traumatic experience affects their learning."

Feedback given to Leanne

You write as if you are speaking. I think you need to adapt a more academic style of writing. Your paragraphs are not clear as you haven't included clear topic sentences, which makes your report incoherent. There are also mistakes with grammar. You have used the past tense when you should have used the present. Check your punctuation and include some more passive phrases such as "research has shown" or "it is predicted that …". This will make your report sound more academic. Here is an example of a part to improve.

"Millions of people were escaping natural disaster, which can come in forms of floods, droughts, tsunamis, earthquakes and so on. This is totally unacceptable and we must do something about it. The politicians only talked, they never did nothing about climate change. Soon whole islands are going under and there is nothing we can do about it. Sure, people were afraid that migrants were stealing their jobs and houses, but I think we need to show some solidarity here."

Feedback given to Ollie

I couldn't really follow your report. You jumped from one point to the next without linking the paragraphs, which did not logically connect. Your essay does not really flow. It has too many headings and there is repetition. There are lots of mistakes, so you need to read the report again and use a spell check. For example, you wrote:

"Causes and effects of climate migration

Causes for climate migration. The causes for climate migration are floodding, earthquakes, tsunammis and wars. Millions of people are now displace because of this.

Efects of climate migration. The Effects of climate migration are stress, PTSD, anxiety and depression, but there are also people who end up homeless or unemployment because they

Cause, effects and solutions

Possible solutions could be to give climate migrants free visas and social housing. The causes and effects are that they are in need of help."

Assessment tip

Plan an effective structure and avoid writing that does not flow well. For example, Ollie tried to include some useful headings, but there is repetition and not enough content. It would have been better to write an extended paragraph for each heading. Don't forget to use the spell check on your computer.

Common misunderstanding

Migration and urbanization is a big topic. Some students try to fit everything they know into their report and then run out of time to evaluate the strengths and weaknesses of their perspectives. Pippa's approach is better. She comments on the limitations of the report. This way, she can zoom in on fewer issues but explain and analyse them in more detail.

Moving towards assessment – Team Project

The future of megacities

What vision do you have for cities of the future? Do you see driverless cars racing around energy-efficient, high-rise buildings with vertical gardens? Or endless traffic jams in noisy, polluted cities with few green spaces?

Tokyo gives a glimpse of what sustainable cities of tomorrow could look like. At the foot of Mount Fiji, 60 kilometres outside of Tokyo, Woven City is a 175-acre experimental smart city – a testing ground for robots, smart homes, and driverless cars. Buildings are made of wood, transportation is carbon neutral and automated, and homes measure your daily vitamin intake and blood pressure.

Skills focus – approaches and strategies for research

1. What changes are likely to happen in the megacities of the future? How would you go about researching something that might happen in the future?

2. Explain some methods countries are developing to make towns and cities more sustainable. For example, how are some countries accommodating a high number of refugees? Where would you look for appropriate research and evidence?

3. Reflect on the idea of driverless cars and other automated transport. Do you think this is a good idea or problematic? How would you research this to show different perspectives and opposing viewpoints?

Sample student extracts

A team of three students decided to work on the issue of transportation in their city. Read these extracts from their Reflective Papers. Think about how well each student fulfilled the criterion of clearly communicating their research findings.

1. Which student communicates with the most clarity?

2. Which students have included clear perspectives?

3. Which student has summarized their research findings most effectively?

4. Which student has the most structured extract? Explain why you think so.

5. Which student do you think is producing the highest quality work? Explain why you think so.

Proposed projects

Look at the following four ideas that have been suggested for a Team Project on the topic of *Migration and urbanization*.

Evaluate each one. How suitable are they as projects? How could they be modified to become more appropriate and viable?

1. Refugees and asylum seekers are welcome in our town.

2. The city is getting too crowded. We need to create more safe places for children and teenagers to play in.

3. Is our city's transportation network fit for purpose?

4. Vision 2050 – our hope for a sustainable future city as a model for others to follow.

Cullum

I have an interest in engineering and really enjoyed the part of designing a future city. If future cities are to be sustainable and energy efficient, then architects, designers, urban planners, and city governments have to work together to make it happen. I took the political perspective and looked into how local governments could promote the use of automated buses, driverless cars, and cycling lanes. I found some exciting and innovative examples, one in Tokyo where a future city called Woven City is already trialled by Toyota and the other one in Amsterdam where the Nieuwe Meerstad is a new ecological city development. I really enjoyed researching these ideas and they helped us all to be more positive and inspired. To learn about what happens already in other countries really moved our project forward.

Anthony

Our city is very polluted because of the many cars. Everybody drives a car and something needs to be done to stop this pollution. It makes people ill, with asthma and so on.

My research took me to places like South Korea and Germany, and big international companies such as Samsung, Audi, and VW. They had some ideas on their website that I could use for suggesting driverless cars in our city. Everybody imagines driverless cars and drones and so on but it was important to show my teammates how it can work in practice.

Technology is one thing, but people also need the will to stop whatever is convenient and switch to, let's say, electric cars, if the whole sustainability should work. And what about housing all the climate migrants? They may arrive by train or bus but where do they get housed? Just making the transport system carbon neutral won't make our city sustainable.

Ying

I live in the city and my parents drive me to school every day. Sometimes the highway is so congested, we sit for one hour in traffic. I have even arrived late to school on occasion. So I wanted to look at the health perspective when we discussed transport in our city. Many studies show how polluted our city is and I found some statistics about the link between pollution and illnesses such as asthma and cancer. Working in a team of people who all have a positive vision for our city really changed my attitude to what can be done. It made me more responsible and "green". I now use public transport to travel to school and it benefits my whole family. I have to change trains twice, but we are all less stressed and I even persuaded my mum to walk to the local supermarket rather than drive all the time. We are now much fitter and healthier.

Assessment tip

Ying's Reflective Paper was 1,200 words long. She saved some of her best ideas for the conclusion, but her teacher could not credit the conclusion because it was over the word limit. So Ying had to revise what she thought was a good piece. The Reflective Paper should not be longer than 1,000 words, so check the word count before you submit it.

Common misunderstanding

Some students summarized what they found out through their research and others wrote from a certain perspective about their research. You don't have to do both. For example, both Cullum and Anthony have started to explain how their research influenced the Team Project. This is sufficient, but don't forget to include references of your sources.

Scan here to obtain the source material you need to carry out this examination practice work.

Question 3 in your **Written Exam** is a question based on a source that presents different arguments about the global issue. Candidates answer by writing an extended response. Candidates are required to analyse and evaluate the arguments, and make a reasoned judgement about the quality of the arguments.

Q3. Study Source 4.

Which argument do you find more convincing, Yukiko's or Stefan's?

Your answer should:

- consider both arguments
- evaluate their reasoning, evidence, and use of language
- support your judgement with their words and ideas.

Read the two sample student answers, then answer the questions that follow.

Emma's response

I think Yukiko's argument is more convincing. Big cities attract young people because they want to go out with friends and have fun at cinemas, restaurants, and discos. I also understand Yukiko's argument about getting better services such as education and healthcare in a city. We moved to the city when I was five. My mum thought there are better schools and hospitals and I think she was right. Yukiko could have used some more keywords such as push and pull factors but instead gave a personal example and that is always really persuasive, I think. In addition, the experience that she had at her gran's house, when the internet didn't work and she could not chat with her friends, has happened to me. I'm addicted to my phone and I was stressed out when the internet didn't work. I understand what Stefan says about the pandemic. Some people thought that moving to the country is best because you have less chance of getting the virus. That is counter-urbanization, but I'm not easily scared. In conclusion, Yukuko's answer convinces me the most. Stefan seems a bit boring.

Demonstrates understanding of a perspective, supported by material from the source.

States why she thinks Yukiko's answer was convincing, but this is the only argument she writes about, limiting opportunity for evaluation.

This is emotive. Try to express criticism in a more constructive way.

Karl's response

There are many reasons why people move to cities and also why they prefer to stay in rural areas. Moving is not easy and so it is not surprising that both Yukiko and Stefan like to stay where they currently are. There are push and pull factors for living in cities but there are also reasons why the countryside can be a place to enjoy

A good start. Starts to evaluate the two arguments.

▶

life. In the following, I will analyse which arguments are the strongest and conclude that <mark>Stefan's answer is the most convincing.</mark>

Firstly, people who move to the city are attracted by entertainment. As Yukiko mentions, for many young people, going out in the evening and meeting your friends in bars or having a meal in a restaurant are important social factors that make city life more attractive.

Moreover, business owners find cities the best place for trade because of banks and better transportation, and generally they are more connected with other countries. Therefore, it is more convenient for you to live in a big city. This is the economic perspective.

Finally, older people rely on healthcare and other services such as public transportation. <mark>As Yukiko's mother rightly points out, hospitals offer a much better service in cities</mark> than in the countryside where you may have to wait longer for an ambulance, which can be a matter of life and death.

<mark>On the other hand,</mark> big cities are polluted and can cause health risks and environmental problems. There is often a high crime rate and it can be very expensive to live in one of the megacities such as Tokyo because space is limited. In addition, the arguments raised by Stefan that big cities can be lonely places, where the poor desperately try to make a living and the rich drive up the prices for housing and enjoy entertaining themselves <mark>makes sense</mark>. It seems that more and more megacities have developed areas with slums and inhumane sanitary conditions. Stefan mentions cities in Brazil and India, but the same inequality can also be observed in New York or London.

Despite the fact that Stefan advertises farm life as idyllic, living in the countryside also has disadvantages such as having to rely on your own transport. <mark>What Stefan hasn't mentioned is that climate change has forced many farmers in other countries to move to the city because droughts or floods</mark> have destroyed their crops.

However, in conclusion, I still believe that Stefan's arguments are far more convincing than Yukiko's personal examples.

> States a choice, which needs to be supported.

> Keep adding perspectives if they add to the analysis.

> Clear discursive marker indicates a counter-argument.

> Implies positive analysis.

> Stay focused and evaluate what has been said, not what has been missed.

Engaging with Question 3

1. Explain whether Emma has fairly considered both arguments.

2. What different perspectives does Karl bring to his response?

3. Can you find examples in either response where relevant source material has been clearly referred to?

4. Identify any bias in either answer. How does that bias show?

5. Do you think Karl's final judgement is balanced? Explain your choice.

In this section you will:

- discuss the role of government and political power in creating happy populations

- consider arguments for and against different political actions.

Perspectives

Political actions have the goal of affecting political structures (such as who is ruling a government) or policies (such as who pays taxes or what a country invests in). There are many forms of political action, including campaigning, lobbying, petitioning, writing, voting, sharing information on social media, and protesting. Different countries have different rules about what political actions are legal and who can participate in them.

A line of enquiry

Do you think young people should be involved in politics? Political theorist John Wall argues that children should be able to vote in elections. They will be affected by government policy for much longer than older people, so they should have a say. How do you think your society would change if everyone over ten years old was allowed to vote on all government policies? Would the government's priorities change?

Philosopher John Stuart Mill argued that more educated citizens should have more votes in politics. What do you think? Should political participation involve everyone or should it be limited to those with more education or experience?

Thomas Hobbes argued that humans need a government to set rules and protect them. Without a government, Hobbes wrote, life would be "nasty, brutish, and short" as each person would seek their own interests, even if it hurt others.

Politics and happiness

Whether governments should use political power to seek human happiness is still debated. Since 2002, the World Happiness Report has measured the happiness of countries in the world.

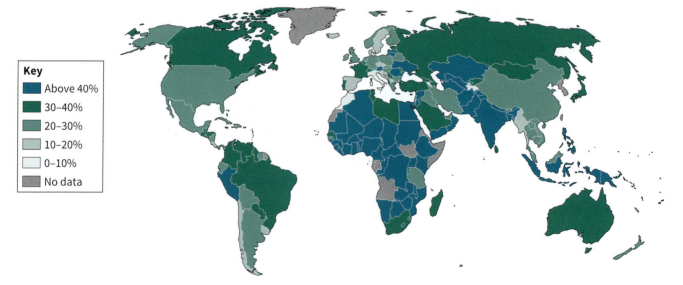

Key
- Above 40%
- 30–40%
- 20–30%
- 10–20%
- 0–10%
- No data

▲ **Fig. 15.1** *The countries with the highest percentage of happiness in their populations around the world, 2022*

Task 1

In small groups, answer these questions.

1. Look at the map. How does your country rank in terms of happiness?

2. Do you think governments should use their power to make their populations happier?

3. What do you think a government can do to make its population happier? Think of as many ideas as you can that are linked to different areas such as politics, environment, culture, economics, and society.

4. Perform a role play. Two members of your group should act like politicians running for office. They need to convince the rest of you to vote for them by presenting proposals to make either your country or the world happier. The rest of the group must ask questions and vote for a winner.

Jubilee 2000 – action for poverty

Can ordinary people change the world? Jubilee 2000 set out to prove that they can.

Jubilee 2000 was a political campaign organized to ask wealthier countries to wipe out the debt owed to them by poorer countries. The campaign argued that indebted countries would be better off spending their money on education, health, and infrastructure, rather than paying high interest on loans.

▲ **Fig. 15.2**

The campaign had several components. Famous people such as Bono, Muhammad Ali, and Willie Colón used their popularity to publicize it. Also, people around the world signed petitions, wrote letters to their governments, and went to government meetings. Jubilee 2000 entered *The Guinness Book of World Records* for the largest petition, with over 24 million signatures. In Birmingham, UK, during a G8 meeting, 70,000 people created a human chain, holding hands for over nine kilometres to show their support for people in countries suffering from debt and poverty.

Jubilee 2000 led to more than 100 billion dollars, owed by 35 of the world's poorest countries, being cancelled.

Task 2

In pairs, answer the following questions.

1. What was the goal of the Jubilee 2000 campaign?

2. What perspectives did Jubilee 2000 consider?

3. What political actions were part of the campaign?

4. What arguments for and against the campaign can you think of?

Who has power?

A line of enquiry

Have you ever considered the question, "Who has power?" Sometimes the answer is obvious. A president or prime minister, for example, has power. They can shape the rules by which people in their country live. However, what gives these heads of state such power?

Global power

In international relations, who has power on the global stage and how does one power balance another? Some political theorists argue that, without balance, chaos and disorder will take over. During the Cold War, the world was balanced between the USSR and the USA. Since the fall of the USSR, new global powers have emerged.

Task 3

Answer these questions.

1. As a class, take a vote on which countries you think are the three main global powers at the moment.

2. Make a list of what you think gives a country political power.

3. In small groups, look at Figure 15.3 and the data opposite. Do they provide evidence for your views on who the current global powers are?

4. Looking at the graph and tables, do you think military or cultural power is more important? Why?

5. How does your country rank in terms of global power? What particular areas do you think affect your country's standing as a global power?

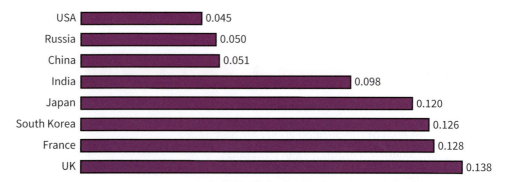

▲ **Fig. 15.3** *Graph showing the world's most powerful militaries; countries ranked highest on the Global Firepower Power Index (0.000 = most powerful)*

Powerfulness ranking	Country	GDP (US$)
1	USA	56,084
2	Russia	25,965
3	China	14,340
4	United Kingdom	41,499
5	Germany	46,974
6	France	41,476
7	Japan	38,142
8	Israel	34,054
9	Saudi Arabia	53,802
10	United Arab Emirates	67,217
11	South Korea	36,612
12	Canada	45,602
13	Turkey	20,420
14	Iran	17,346
15	Switzerland	58,647
16	India	6,187
17	Australia	47,644
18	Italy	35,781
19	Sweden	48,199
20	Pakistan	4,906
21	The Netherlands	49,624

Countries with the greatest cultural influence, according to US News & World Report	
1	Italy
2	France
3	USA
4	Japan
5	Spain
6	United Kingdom
7	South Korea
8	Switzerland
9	Germany
10	Australia

Empathy

When you are the one in power, it can be difficult to imagine what being powerless feels like. Have you ever considered what it would be like to live in a place where your views on what should be done, even your views on whether you should be alive, were not considered? A great way to develop empathy is to read accounts of the lives of those oppressed by power, such as *The Diary of a Young Girl* by Anne Frank.

Ever-changing world

Who has power changes as countries and societies evolve. For example, Brazil was once in the power of Portugal, ruled by a military dictatorship. In 2022, Brazil was a democracy led by a president. In many countries, women were only granted the right to vote in the late 20th century. Indigenous peoples and minorities are still fighting for the right to have their voices heard.

The power of words

In this section you will:

- explore different views on what power is
- evaluate whether social media should be limited, given its political power
- consider how to use social media for a political cause.

A line of enquiry

There is great power in words. They can be used to highlight injustices committed by those in power, as the former enslaved person Sojourner Truth did when she demanded, "Ain't I a woman?" Words can be used to inspire political change, as Martin Luther King Jr did when he said, "I have a dream that my four little children will one day live in a nation where they will not be judged by the colour of their skin but by the content of their character." Words are key in fights for political power.

> "There will be no end to the troubles of states, or of humanity itself, till philosophers become kings in this world, or till those we now call kings and rulers really and truly become philosophers, and political power and philosophy thus come into the same hands." *(Plato)*

> "You must make women count as much as men; you must have an equal standard of morals; and the only way to enforce that is through giving women political power so that you can get that equal moral standard registered in the laws of the country. It is the only way." *(Emmeline Pankhurst)*

> "Political power grows out of the barrel of a gun." *(Mao Zedong)*

> "The most common way people give up their power is by thinking they don't have any." *(Alice Walker)*

> "The greater the power, the more dangerous the abuse." *(Edmund Burke)*

Task 4

Read the quotations, which give different views on power. In pairs, answer the questions.

1. When do you think Pankhurst made her statement? Is it relevant now?
2. Look at Plato's quotation. What do you think a philosopher would be like as a political leader?
3. Do you think Mao Zedong was correct in his view on guns and power? Rewrite the quotation, changing the "barrel of a gun" to a phrase you think is more appropriate.
4. Explain Walker's quotation in your own words.

5. Discuss which quotations you agree with, if any, and why. Make sure you clearly state your arguments. For example, you might disagree with a quotation because it focuses too much on only one aspect of society. Or you might agree with a quotation because you think its focus is key to justice.

6. Write your own quotation on power.

7. Present your quotation to the class as if you were running for political office. Be clear, be loud, and say nothing more than your quotation!

Social media and political power

Information shared on social media can affect people's political views. In particular, those with millions of followers, including celebrities, political leaders, and millionaires, can have great influence when they share their views.

▲ **Fig. 15.4**

How can social media influence political power? In 2013, a group of young people in the USA started a movement by using the hashtag #BlackLivesMatter on Facebook. This hashtag inspired people all over the world to ask for just treatment for people of African ancestry and other minorities. Political action at a local level, such as a personal post on Facebook, can affect global political demands.

▲ **Fig. 15.5**

Task 5

In pairs, answer these questions.

1. Discuss this proposition: "Social media should have no rules in order to allow full freedom of expression."

2. Do you think there should be rules to limit the influence of wealthy individuals and celebrities on social media? Explain your reasoning.

3. Think of two arguments for and two arguments against the view that social media platforms should be responsible for fact-checking posts to prevent incorrect and fake information from being shared. For example:

Social media platforms *should* check for fake news	Social media platforms *should not* check for fake news
Young people using social media are naïve and need to be protected.	Each person is responsible for checking information they see to make sure it is true.

4. If you were going to use social media to create social change, what would you seek to change? Think about a hashtag that might draw attention to your movement, such as #celebrateminoritylanguages.

Viewpoints

Social media can impact politics in a number of ways. It can help to create and spread new ideas, influencing social and cultural changes. It can create new wealth, which can support new political movements. It can serve as a way for political candidates with little money to get their message across to millions of people. Social media can also have a psychological impact by making people feel certain ways about candidates or issues.

Moving towards assessment – Individual Report

Explaining causes and consequences

In your **Individual Report** of 1,500 to 2,000 words you should highlight and analyse the causes and consequences of the issues you are spotlighting.

Skills focus – identifying and analysing causes and consequences

You are going to look at the impact of an international treaty on a country, focusing on the treaty's causes and consequences. Here are three examples of international treaties that have had far-reaching consequences for governments around the world.

The Geneva Conventions, 1949

These are a set of internationally recognized agreements that apply during armed conflicts. They specifically protect those who are either civilians or were soldiers but are no longer taking part in hostilities because they are wounded or have been captured following their surrender.

UN Convention Against Illicit Traffic in Narcotic Drugs and Psychotropic Substances, 1988

This treaty is focused on helping governments fight drug-related organized crime. It requires nations to trace and seize the assets of drug-related criminals. Much of the focus is on requiring governments to pass laws that will force banks to release financial records.

The Paris Agreement, 2016

This agreement was written to help countries adapt to the effects of climate change by making finance available to all. Under the agreement, each country is required to regulate, plan ahead, and document its efforts to achieve its own pollution controls and emissions reductions.

1. How well do you think your own country is performing in relation to these treaties?
2. Are there any other kinds of treaties that you feel are needed – globally and in your own country?

Proposed research questions

Look at the four research questions that have been suggested for Individual Reports on the topic of *Political power and action*.

Evaluate each one. How suitable are they as research questions? How could they be modified to ensure that they meet the expectations of a full report?

1. Is democracy the right tool to address climate change?
2. Describe the political power that social media has globally.
3. Why political leaders should be held to higher ethical standards only on certain global issues.
4. Why political power should be shared among everyone around the world.

Sample student extracts

Three students wrote their research on the theme of *Political power and action*. Read the extracts from their reports where they explain the causes and consequences of the issues they are researching. Then answer the questions.

1. Do you think Mirabel makes a valid point using an appropriate example? Why or why not?

2. George discusses what political leaders need to do but it is quite general. How do you think he might improve his statement?

3. Niyati seems to suggest that protests are nearly always inevitable. Do you agree with her?

4. Which student do you think produced the strongest report? Explain your rationale.

Niyati

Research question: "Should governments ban protests?"

Protests are an important way for people to make their voices heard in a political process. In countries where protests have been banned, people eventually disobeyed the rules and protested anyway. Johnson says, "Protests have led to political changes by bringing up issues governments wanted to ignore" (2020). Stevens states, "Political power is always, ultimately, in the hands of the people" (2019). We need to think about why people protest and their causes. The Carnegie Endowment for International Peace Protest Tracker notes three main causes for protests around the world: corruption (most often), economic complaints, and desire for political change (2022).

Mirabel

Research question: "Can youth change politics by actively getting involved?"

Research shows that young people are becoming more politically involved around the world (Stevens, 2022). Young people's involvement in politics can be traced to their interest in current issues. A social media survey of young people in 37 countries found that they are intensely interested in environmental causes (90 per cent) and social justice (92 per cent) (Knox, 2019). The sense of urgency for change was mentioned in the survey as the main reason for joining protests (Knox). Some also mention being inspired by the actions of teenagers in other countries. Young people's involvement in politics has had dramatic consequences in history.

George

Research question: "How can political leaders help to solve the climate crisis?"

Political leaders are responsible for addressing our climate crisis but to do so they need to understand what causes it and its consequences. Climate crisis is caused by rising global temperatures and melting glaciers. Plants and animals cannot exist in these changing conditions. The effects of climate crisis are severe and this is why governments need to act.

Assessment tip

If your report does not have a clear global issue as its focus, it will be difficult for you to research and present causes and consequences. Each of the three student responses clearly identifies their global issue, allowing them to think about what causes this issue and what are its effects. Starting with a clear global issue is key to being able to research causes and consequences.

Common misunderstanding

Global issues are likely to have multiple causes or reasons, and they are likely to impact the world in many different ways. When you research your issue, consider which are the most important causes and which are the most significant effects of the issue. Using more than one cause can help you demonstrate a deeper understanding and build a better argument in your report. Do not just focus on one cause and its consequence.

Food deserts

A food desert is an area where local inhabitants, often on low incomes, have limited access to affordable and nutritious food. This is because the low level of economic prosperity makes the location unattractive to large supermarket chains and independent suppliers of fresh foods such as meat, fruit, and vegetables. Very often, only convenience foods are readily available, and they tend to be low quality and high in sugar and fats.

How might you explain the concept of food deserts to someone who is unaware of them?

Do you think you have food deserts in your local area? If so, how would you characterize their locations?

Skills focus – completing an action

There are issues that surround food deserts, such as poor diet, which can lead to ill health and physical and mental degradation. However, possible solutions to the problem of food deserts will counteract many of these consequences.

1. What are the social and political implications of food deserts on a population?
2. Can you think of a positive community response to the removal of a food desert?
3. If you were asked to raise awareness in your local community, and perhaps even globally, of the problem of food deserts, how would you draw attention to it? What action would you carry out to get a good, clear message across?

Sample student reflections

A team of three students gave a presentation at their local community centre to local residents and government officials. They did it to raise awareness of food deserts both in their local area and globally. Read what they thought about the impact of their presentation. Then answer the questions.

1. Compare the role of each student in this presentation. Which role do you like best? Why?
2. Why was Dominic's role not entirely successful in the end? How could the group have improved this?
3. Is there evidence from Simon that the action had any effect? Explain your response.
4. What could have been done to make Josy's role more successful?
5. What do you think of the team's action? What action do you think would work best to raise this issue in your local area?

Proposed projects

Look at the following four ideas that have been suggested for a Team Project on the topic of *Political power and action*.

Evaluate each one. How suitable are they as projects? How could they be modified to become more appropriate and viable?

1. Organize a meeting that allows younger people to meet with and discuss important issues with local government officials.
2. Create a video about the importance of voting.
3. Create an international online forum with like-minded students to compare views on global issues.
4. Use social media to get the viewpoints of young people.

Simon

Our group thought it would be a responsible thing to raise awareness in our local area about food deserts, as we considered that we have many of the telltale characteristics of being in a food desert area. We wanted to do this by giving a public presentation that detailed some of the reasons, issues, and possible solutions of the problem. We felt that if this knowledge was shared we might be able to inspire action from the community and local government officials. In the presentation, we illustrated the consequences of food deserts and got a good deal of interest and positive feedback from local residents because they took all the information sheets we had to support our presentation.

Josy

We thought that if we could highlight and discuss some community-based solutions to our local food desert, we might be able to begin the process of our local community shops potentially producing their own fresh food. In my part of the presentation, I talked about how food co-operative groups worked and that some areas have bus stops at farmers' markets, but it was difficult to explain these concepts clearly and effectively without actually having an example to illustrate the point. The audience seemed unsure about how we might get things started and who would take charge. In reality, it was hard to maintain enthusiasm in the audience. We perhaps should have tried a different approach regarding the idea of a community food group.

Dominic

I talked about funding and fundraising, and the feedback was somewhat mixed. The local people, who would be the ones to use the food co-operatives, were quite enthusiastic about the whole idea and were even able to offer fundraising suggestions. However, the local councillors, who would be the ones responsible in part for funding, were less keen. They said they did not want to give money to grow local produce unless it was professionally organized. They also said that the suggestion of improved bus routes to make travelling to supermarkets easier was impractical and unaffordable. I think this part of the presentation was less well prepared than the other parts, as we didn't really get the message across clearly about the long-term economic impact of improving health benefits, and it could have gone better.

Assessment tip

Part of your assessment will look at how well you completed your action. To do well, you need to have selected an achievable action. So choose something you can realistically complete successfully within the timeframe of the course and with the resources, skills, and people available. A well-focused and confidently delivered presentation on the advantages and disadvantages of education spending is going to be better than a rambling lecture about governments wasting money.

Common misunderstanding

When reflecting on a Team Project, it is important to highlight the impact of your chosen action. For assessing evidence of your action, show that what you actually did resulted in a positive difference to your chosen issue (if you did it well). For example, if after Dominic's presentation the councillors said they would definitely help, then he has an opportunity to reflect upon why.

Scan here to obtain the source material you need to carry out this examination practice work.

Question 3 in your **Written Exam** is a question based on a source that presents different arguments about the global issue. Candidates answer by writing an extended response. Candidates are required to analyse and evaluate the arguments, and make a reasoned judgement about the quality of the arguments.

Q3. Study Source 4.

Which argument is more convincing, Lilia's or Joshua's?

Your answer should:

- consider both arguments
- evaluate their reasoning, evidence, and use of language
- support your judgement with their words and ideas.

Read the sample student answer, then answer the questions that follow.

Dev's response

Two opinions are presented in the source discussion as to whether the United Nations Security Council (UNSC) should expand its membership. Lilia argues that the UNSC needs to expand its permanent members, while Joshua argues for it to stay as it is. After considering each side's reasoning, supporting evidence, and the objectivity of their writing, I think Lilia's argument is more convincing.

Lilia's argument calls upon history to give a historical understanding of why the UNSC was set up as it was. She then builds on this historical argument to note that, as the world has changed since 1945, it makes sense for the UNSC to change as well, as it is meant to represent the power divisions of the world. This is a logical argument. Lilia then presents some arguments for the ways in which the UNSC could change, noting where political power now lies in countries with nuclear power, and in countries with large populations. If the UNSC is about power, this is a logical argument. However, Lilia's argument could have been strengthened by listing some of the countries with nuclear power or large populations she is thinking about. Finally, Lilia brings up an argument of balance, where she also

Shows understanding of what the task requires and that there will be a comparison.

A general statement that needs supporting with evaluation.

Shows how Lilia develops her justification for change and presents a logical process.

Critical evaluation of the source highlights where it is weak.

A clear discursive marker shows that a second argument is about to be considered. However, there is never any clear comparison between the two arguments.

highlights her own perspective: the idea that the largest part of the world is not represented at all in the UNSC. Throughout her argument, Lilia is logical and organized.

A clear judgement on the logical flow of the argument.

On the other hand, Joshua's argument is far more generalized and some of the judgements made seem to be based upon his personal assumptions rather than any stated facts. Joshua questions whether the ability of the council to perform its primary function would be compromised if the UNSC is changed just for the sake of being more inclusive. Effectively stating that there will always be someone that is unhappy with the situation is not a good argument for not doing something different. However, he does then go on to try and justify why avoiding this might be the case, but again his reasoning is just based on personal assumptions rather than supporting evidence. Joshua fails to explain how the existing nations "are a representative balance" or how they work effectively. As such, his argument that the UNSC "functions as required" is unsupported and "It is not perfect but it is effective" cannot be measured, as people with different perspectives of the consequences of the actions of the UNSC might not consider this to be the case.

Critical evaluation of the validity of the source material.

Brings together a core theme of Joshua's argument and highlights the weakness it contains.

A good final evaluation of Joshua's argument, highlighting potential weakness.

A final comparison of the two arguments would have been effective at this point.

Engaging with Question 3

1. What do you think about the quality of Dev's evaluation of both viewpoints in the source?

2. Would you add any other points to Dev's response about Lilia's argument?

3. What other evidence could Dev provide to support his view that Joshua's argument is weak?

4. Do you think Dev engaged with both sources critically enough, covering all aspects of the question? Explain your answer.

▲ **Fig. 16.1**

A line of enquiry

"*Give a man a fish and you feed him for a day. Teach a man to fish and you feed him for a lifetime.*"

Think about what this ancient Chinese proverb suggests and how it might relate to poverty. When you hear the term "poverty", what comes to your mind? Having no money? Homelessness?

To help you, think about these statements.

> Poverty is not being able to afford the new trainers you want.

> Poverty is a problem mainly found in inner-city areas.

> If you have a laptop and a mobile phone, you can't be living in poverty.

> Globally, 385 million children live in poverty.

> Real poverty is only found in less economically developed countries (LEDCs).

> Working hard always gets people out of poverty.

> Not having a job means you live in poverty.

Causes of poverty:
- having little or no money
- being unemployed
- having a disability
- living in a region where droughts are common
- a corrupt government
- not having a full education
- living in a war zone
- disputes arising in a family or in close relationships.

Consequences of poverty:
- not having the chance to escape from family poverty
- becoming disabled or having poor health, including mental health issues
- being forced to fight in a war
- not having access to social media or the internet
- not being able to gain employment due to an incomplete education
- being tempted into crime as "the only way out"
- the breakdown of relationships
- losing your home and having to migrate.

The cost of living crisis

In 2022, many countries experienced a cost of living crisis. Everyday items such as food, energy, fuel, and insurance increased significantly in price. Not only LECDs were affected by the rising prices. People in Europe and North America also felt a strong impact. In the United Kingdom – the sixth richest economy in the world in 2022 – there were parents who could not afford to cook a warm meal for their children or to pay for school lunches. As a consequence, some charities set up food banks where people could go to receive a box of essential food items to support them through difficult times.

▲ **Fig. 16.2**

Task 1

You are going to volunteer to help out in a food bank, showing how useful they can be and engaging with some of the challenges involved.

As the cost of living crisis worsens, you are receiving fewer donations and you realize that you will have to raise money and buy certain items in for your food bank to continue operating. Your manager has asked you to suggest a fundraising plan and a budget for the next three months. You need to decide how much food to stock in order to continue handing out nutritious food boxes to the 1,200 households in need of food in your community. However, each household has families of different types and sizes.

In small groups, produce a detailed plan for your food boxes, a financial costing sheet, and a leaflet or poster to advertise your food bank to people and companies who may be able to donate. Divide your tasks and answer the questions below.

1. Decide what food items need to go into each box. How will you account for the variation in family types and sizes?

2. Include a budget sheet. Each food item in your box needs to be costed and then multiplied for the number of households you are budgeting for. How much does each box cost? How many boxes do you need to feed people in your local community? How much does a delivery service add to the total cost?

3. Design a leaflet or poster to attract additional donors. You should use techniques of persuasion, appealing to people's emotions. Present the poster to the other groups. How effective is your poster?

Sustainability

Food banks work towards achieving the second United Nations Sustainable Development Goal (Zero Hunger) by reducing food waste and redistributing food to places of food insecurity and poverty. In this way, food banks also contribute to the circular economy as they reuse and recycle food.

The widening gap between rich and poor

In this section you will:

- explore the way that poverty is divisive in society
- use a movie to show how poverty and crime are linked.

A line of enquiry

According to the World Bank, the number of people living in poverty globally has increased since the Covid-19 pandemic. For more than two decades, extreme poverty was declining and, at the end of 2020, China declared proudly that it had achieved its goal of eliminating extreme poverty. However, since then, the gap between the wealthiest and poorest of the population is widening again. Globally, the richest 10 per cent of the world own 76 per cent of the wealth, while the poorest half of the world's population owns a mere 2 per cent of the total assets. A useful distinction to make is the difference between absolute poverty and relative poverty. The World Bank states that if you live on less than $1.90 a day, you live in absolute, or extreme poverty. Relative poverty, by contrast, means you are poor in relation to other people's income in your country.

Task 2

1. In pairs, discuss the following quotations. Explain what they mean. Which one do you like best, and why?

"As long as poverty, injustice, and gross inequality exist in the world, none of us can truly exist." (Nelson Mandela)

"Poverty is the parent of revolution and crime." (Aristotle)

"You can't get rid of poverty by giving people money." (J. O'Rourke)

"Poverty is like a punishment for a crime you didn't commit." (Eli Khamarov)

2. The extract from a blog below, highlights how poverty affects many parts of society – how poverty can create a gender gap, a generational gap, an ethnicity gap, and a health gap.

   With the same partner, use this list to fill in the missing words, taking note of the implication in the heading.

   lower / unemployed / unaffected / increased / less / more / poorer / more / afford / more / likely / relative / extreme / rich

   ### Poverty is unfair

   Children born into _____ poverty are _____ likely to stay in poverty and have _____ access to education. They are _____ likely to suffer abuse and become damaged by it. As a result, they are likely to have _____ aspirations than more affluent peers.

   Between the late 1980s and mid 2000s, UK house prices _____ dramatically. This made people who already owned houses _____ because they could sell their house for a profit. It meant that many young people whose parents weren't wealthy and who didn't have savings were unlikely to be able to _____ a house of their own.

Black and ethnic minority people are _____ likely to experience _____ poverty than white people in the UK.

Women are more _____ to be unemployed or on lower pay.

People with disabilities who are unable to work are more likely to be _____ than non-disabled people.

Extreme weather, Covid-19, conflicts, and the cost of living crisis have resulted in the poor becoming _____ while wealthy people remain mostly _____ by it.

Poverty as a theme in movies

Many artists and film makers have highlighted and criticized the gap between those who are well-off – the upper classes, the rich and powerful – and those who rely on help from others for their survival – the poor and disadvantaged.

One such criticism was made by director Bong Joon Ho in his film *Parasite* (2019). The film won four Oscars and focuses on the resentments that divide the "haves" and "have-nots". The director introduces us to two Korean families who, although the same in size and nationality, differ vastly in their way of life. The Kim family live in a basement flat that is bug-infested and frequently flooded with sewage. Unemployed, but aspiring to a more comfortable life, they get entangled with the Park family. They are wealthy, privileged but nice people who live in a mansion on top of a hill from where they can look down on the city.

Task 3

The disadvantaged family in the film *Parasite* end up committing a series of crimes. Studies by the World Bank confirm that places with high income inequality, such as big cities, have higher crime rates.

In pairs, choose a large city or town as a background for a film script. Imagine you are directing the film and you want to draw attention to the widening gap between rich and poor in your country. Create a scene for your film.

1. Give your movie a suitable title.

2. What sort of film will you make? Will it be an animation, a documentary, or a feature film?

3. Who will you cast as your main actors?

4. Which city or town is your film based in?

5. What social issues will you highlight in your scene?

6. Include some dialogue between contrasting characters. Show the feelings and opinions they have towards each other. How did they meet?

7. Finish your scene by drawing attention to the unfair nature of such an unequal society.

Empathy

Poverty is not a choice. It can have a detrimental effect on health and wellbeing. What if you cannot join your friends to go to the cinema to see a film because you don't have enough money? How would you feel?

Poverty results in feeling powerless, excluded, and alone. The next time you see someone who is not able to join in, ask yourself what the possible reasons might be.

The advantages and disadvantages of giving financial aid to LEDCs

> **In this section you will:**
> - examine the dilemma of offering financial aid to countries in need
> - explore several aspects of donations to charities, whether giving money or donating in other ways.

A line of enquiry

There are many factors that influence a country's development, and some affect whether or not a country needs international aid. These factors can be historical, social, political, or economic. Some countries are in debt to other countries because of their acceptance of financial aid.

For those countries handing out financial aid there is often a dilemma. For example, it is necessary to support countries that need money to pay for emergencies such as natural disasters. However, if some of the financial aid is in the form of loans, the receiving country may only ever be able to pay the interest back and not all of the money loaned. This creates a debt trap.

Donating to charity

Read through the charity advert calling for urgent donations for Afghan children. Then complete the task that follows.

Donate now to protect children from starvation in Afghanistan!

Afghanistan is one of the toughest places on Earth to be born. After the Taliban came to power, poverty levels jumped from 54 per cent to 70 per cent, with more than half of the population living in extreme poverty. Political instability, Covid-19, frequent droughts, earthquakes, high unemployment, and an opioid addiction crisis are just some of the contributing factors that have led to over 13 million Afghan children being in need of urgent international help. Acute malnutrition affects 1.1 million children who need immediate humanitarian assistance to survive.

Rashid, 8, from Kabul, is one of thousands of orphans. He lives with his uncle and his extended family in a makeshift tent on the outskirts of Kabul. His uncle used to work in a small restaurant, but since the pandemic he has lost his job. Now Rashid and his male cousins are forced to look for work. Sometimes Rashid carries water. On other days, he polishes shoes or collects cardboard. In Afghan culture, especially under the Taliban, few women are able to seek employment outside the house. Now Rashid cannot attend school anymore and there are days when he is so hungry that he cannot sleep at night.

Please donate! Only £20 a month provides life-saving food and water for a family for a whole month.

Task 4

There are different ways of responding to a charity appeal. Some people will give money and others are unwilling to donate.

1. Why might some people not want to donate money to other countries?

2. Is giving money to charity the best way to reduce hunger and starvation in a country? What other options are there?

3. "Poverty exists because of greed. If everybody donated money to charity there would be no poverty." Do you agree or disagree? Explain why.

4. In small groups, divide the following roles between you:
   - an international charity worker (a cultural viewpoint)
   - a government minister (a political viewpoint)
   - a homeless person from your local community (a local viewpoint)
   - a wealthy religious businessperson (an ethical viewpoint).

   Then work alone and write a short paragraph that illustrates your person's perspective on giving financial aid.

5. Return to your group and discuss how much financial aid your country should give. The following factors may help you:
   - the top five countries that the money should go to and why
   - what the money should be spent on (e.g. infrastructure, food, weapons, hospitals, and medical care)
   - a list of rules and conditions for countries who receive the money. Refer to examples such as infrastructure, and when and how the money should be repaid
   - whether or not you should spend more or less on foreign aid in the next 20 years.

Viewpoints

Controversial topics are very useful for understanding and developing different viewpoints. The more controversial the topic, the stronger the opinions and disagreements. It takes openness and tolerance to listen to someone's opinion and understand why they have it, especially if you disagree with their point of view.

Argument

You may have heard the terms "shared prosperity" and "common prosperity", but what is the difference? Shared prosperity is one of the recommended goals set by the World Bank arguing that to achieve it means to increase the welfare and income of the bottom 40 per cent of society, wherever they are. In contrast, common prosperity is often suggested by Chinese leaders to address income inequalities and limit excess wealth in Chinese society.

Moving towards assessment – Individual Report

Identifying causes and consequences

In your **Individual Report** of 1,500 to 2,000 words, you should explain some causes and consequences of your chosen issue and then analyse them from a range of perspectives.

Skills focus – causes and consequences

Look at the following series of actions that highlight causes and consequences.

Complete the following statements using either *as a result of* or *resulting in* in the gaps.

1. Homelessness among young people has increased _____ relationship breakdown.

2. _____ the pandemic, shop closures and lockdowns have caused economic hardship and mental health issues for millions of people around the world.

3. Many teenage girls in Afghanistan no longer go to secondary school _____ the religious and cultural perspectives of the Taliban government.

4. Lebanon's economy has contracted _____ the collapse of the Lebanese pound, the national currency.

5. In many countries, hate crime is on the rise _____ income inequalities.

6. A 6.7 magnitude earthquake has destroyed most homes in the area _____ thousands of people becoming homeless.

7. _____ international emergency funding, millions of children received food and safe drinking water.

Proposed research questions

Look at the four research questions that have been suggested for Individual Reports on the topic of *Poverty and inequality*.

Evaluate each one. How suitable are they as research questions? How could they be modified to ensure that they meet the expectations of a full report?

1. What causes poverty and how can we address the negative effects of it?
2. Can foreign international aid eliminate global poverty?
3. Should the international community write off the debts of LEDCs?
4. Describe how poverty contributes to an increase of crime in Europe.

Sample student extracts

To achieve a high level in your Individual Report, you need to work at perspective level. This means you must support your viewpoints. In the extracts from reports below, three students have compared the causes and consequences of poverty.

1. Does each student cover both causes and consequences?
2. Which perspectives does each student begin to explore?
3. Which student has identified causes and consequences but failed to explain them?
4. Which student has written the most effective extract? Explain why you think so.

Aliyah

The root of poverty is having no money. If you cannot find work, because you have no suitable knowledge or skills, you won't earn any money and then you cannot pay the rent for your accommodation or buy food. This can make you hungry and homeless. One of the reasons for being homeless is living on the streets, because some people have to sleep under bridges or in shopping malls. This shows that having no money leads to being without a home or decent food and so you are stuck in the cycle of poverty.

Donnie

In Scotland, almost one in five children are brought up in poverty. It is therefore important to recognize the impact poverty has on the mental health and education of children. Children who grow up in poverty experience a significant level of stress as a result of their family being unable to pay bills or afford to cook regular meals. Research has shown that poverty is often linked to unemployment, illness, or debt. If a parent loses their job due to long-term illness, they may at first accumulate debts on their credit cards, but soon they won't be able to afford day-to-day items such as food and clothing. Tensions then run high. This in turn has an impact on the child's education and mental state, as they might not be able to concentrate in school with an empty stomach or they could be bullied at school because they do not have the newest mobile phone or clothes. Thus, poverty negatively impacts on the education and mental health of a child.

Jacey

Homelessness is one of the worst consequences of poverty. Many people who end up on the streets have addictions such as alcohol or drugs. In my city there are many homeless people. They often beg and have a dog as it is dangerous and lonely to sleep outside, especially in winter. They also get ill more often. In my opinion, it is good to support a poor person by giving them food or some money, but I wonder if it really helps them in the long term to get off the streets. I think some people may waste the money on alcohol and drugs. Many charities are helping homeless people.

Moving towards assessment – Team Project

Raising awareness of some causes and consequences of poverty

Advertising on social media is a useful platform to reach millions of people worldwide. Social media is used by charities, worldwide aid organizations, and governments to raise awareness for goals such as ending child poverty or fundraising for an emergency. Those who can influence others to make decisions use trendy hashtags, blogs, and fundraising campaigns to make a big change in people's lives.

Have you seen any advertisements recently that promote charities? Think of examples with global reach that offer support to people in need wherever they are. Can you think of any examples which target local or regional needs, such as homelessness?

Skills focus – considering the suitability of actions that attempt to raise awareness

Evaluate the efectiveness of each of these five ideas that a group discussed for their project.

1. To create an app that lets people find their nearest local food bank and pick items for delivery.

2. To install a community refrigerator in schools that are located in areas of high deprivation.

3. To give a presentation in a school assembly to inform your peers about a newly emerging spread of poverty in a part of town that was previously doing well economically.

4. To create a petition and influence followers on social media to sign up and agree that greater equality is needed in your local town.

5. To invent a new product which filters dirty and undrinkable water and turns it into clean drinking water.

Proposed projects

Look at the following four ideas that have been suggested for a Team Project on the topic of *Poverty and inequality*.

Evaluate each one. How suitable are they as projects? How could they be modified to become more appropriate and viable?

1. To what extent do poverty and inequality cause an increase in crime globally?
2. Our team will explore the controversy of helping LEDCs by giving foreign aid.
3. To show how the cost of living crisis is affecting people in our local community by raising awareness of availability and prices of food and drink.
4. Are food banks and social housing good enough to prevent people from becoming homeless in our community?

Sample student planning

A team of three students has agreed to work on the topic of homelessness in their local area. Each student has their own ideas for improving the problem of homelessness. In their first meeting, they each present their ideas of an effective action. Read through each student's approach and answer the following questions.

1. Which perspective does each student explore?
2. Which approach is likely to make the biggest impact? Explain why.
3. Evaluate the validity and viability of each proposed action. Which one might work the best?

Assessment tip

Analysing and evaluating potential approaches, showing the strengths and weaknesses of each of them, will help your team to decide which of your ideas would have the most valuable impact on your community. Explain in detail how your team's planning will be evidenced, and therefore be effective in highlighting a local issue.

Kirsten

Homelessness is just wrong and it needs to stop. I have teamed up with a local church and we decided to start a soup kitchen here in our local community. Every Friday, we go out into the town centre and give out free soup, sandwiches, and hot drinks. This kind of work has not been done in our town and it is therefore a pioneering solution. It really makes a difference to the people who are on the streets and because it is done regularly and long term.

Natalia

Many homeless people have mental health issues due to the stress of being on the streets. My approach is to have a mobile clinic parked in each district. It would be staffed by a team of health workers and social workers who have free medicine available. Homeless people can just come in — it's a walk-in clinic — and get free treatment. Any minor injuries can also be dealt with. It's really important and can save lives, especially in the winter months. Homeless people would know about it through word of mouth or through adverts in homeless shelters.

Akeem

Let's make stricter laws for landlords too that they can't ask for too much rent and can't kick people out in the first place. Many people can't afford to rent anymore as rents are so expensive. With stricter laws and regulations, the government can tackle the homeless crisis and get people off the streets, and we will see immediate results in our local areas.

Common misunderstanding

Natalia has included a detailed plan about her mobile clinic, and you can tell she feels really passionate about it. However, Natalia has not included any methods to measure the success of her idea. She could have added a sentence such as, "We could show this programme works by asking our customers to complete a short survey at the end of their treatment about why they came, and how they felt after the treatment."

Scan here to obtain the source material you need to carry out this examination practice work.

Question 4 in your Written Exam is a question based on all sources in the insert. Candidates answer by writing an extended response. Candidates are required to assess actions in response to the global issue and explain their judgements with reasons and evidence.

Q4. A country wants to eradicate child poverty. These actions are being suggested.

- Provide one free cooked meal a day for all children in school.
- Deliver free training on how to grow your own food and supply free vegetable seedlings and agricultural tools.
- Provide low-income households with vouchers for food, rent, and energy bills.

Which one of these actions would you recommend to the government and why? You should:

- state your recommendation
- give reasons and evidence to support your choice
- use the material in the sources and / or your own ideas
- consider different arguments and perspectives.

Read the sample answer and answer the questions that follow.

Aliya's response

Many countries around the world have recently entered a cost of living crisis. Natural disasters, wars, and pandemic lockdowns have led to global food shortages and growing food prices. Families on low incomes struggle to even provide one cooked meal a day for their children and often have to decide between paying bills or buying food. In the UK, 1.4 million children had food insecurities in 2021 and in Afghanistan poverty levels have risen from 54 per cent to 70 per cent, resulting in 13 million children in urgent need of help.

> Uses facts from the sources.

During these hard times, I would recommend that governments provide free vouchers to the poorest in society. Vouchers have the advantage that they can be used in local stores and food markets, and people can choose what they want to buy with them. For instance, they could use the vouchers where they are most needed, be that for food, rent, or energy bills. Additionally, receiving regular vouchers provides stability for families who are responsible for providing food for their children and a warm and stable home to grow up in. This will give a sense of normality in these unprecedented times. Low-income households will feel supported and cared for by the government, which in return will result in happy and grateful citizens who support the politicians in charge. Still, the most important reasons why a voucher system is the best solution to end child poverty is that it offers a measurable and sustainable way to reduce poverty.

It will be measurable, so that the government can budget for them and can measure their effect, and sustainable because it produces a more equal society with a shared prosperity.

> The argument for food vouchers is supported by a rationale.

Critics may argue that the cost of providing vouchers is too high and that it will get the country into debt because the money has to come from additional taxes. My response to this is that the government should tax the rich a bit more, thus supporting the most vulnerable in society. If the wealthiest in society were taxed more, we would create a more equal society and shared prosperity.

> A counter-argument is considered.

However, from an educational viewpoint, providing free school dinners could be argued as a better way to reduce child hunger. It would be an incentive for parents to send their children to school and it could be argued that a voucher system is open to abuse and some parents may buy non-essential items such as snacks, fizzy drinks, or other unhealthy food and drink with them. Some may even claim that vouchers hinder rather than help as they patch up the pain rather than deal with the cause of why people are poor in the first place.

> The counter-argument is only partially supported as free school lunches need to be explained and analysed more clearly.

Despite these objections, I believe that vouchers provide the best way out of poverty as they not only feed the child but help the whole family live a more sustainable life. Helping people to grow their own food is a long-term option and it won't bring the quick results needed in an emergency. Likewise, providing free school lunches only helps children who are in school, and we know that there are a growing number of children who do not attend school as they have to help their family out and earn a living.

> Personal viewpoint links back to the question and refers to the sustainability theme.

Engaging with Question 4

1. Evaluate whether Aliya has fulfilled all the requirements of the question.

2. Identify how many arguments in favour of food vouchers Aliya has presented.

3. Evaluate whether Aliya has used a wide range or a good enough range of evidence and reasons to support her answer.

4. Explain the viewpoints and perspectives that Aliya considers in her response.

In this section you will:

- learn about a social identity theory and social categorization
- experiment with the use of stereotypes.

A line of enquiry

Social identity is our sense of belonging within the social world, which to a great extent is conditioned by the groups we have to be in and the groups we choose to be part of. For example, family is a group that most people are born into; a school class is a group that is usually compulsory under a country's law. Groups we choose to belong to include circles of friends and also groups like sports teams.

Being in a group usually brings a feeling of inclusion and also a sense of pride. In contrast, people who find themselves excluded from a group often experience a sense of loss, feeling like an outsider.

Think about the groups that you choose to belong to. What is it that attracted you to them? Think also about the groups that you feel you have to belong to. Is it possible for people to feel lonely in a group? What about people who don't like groups and who prefer to do things alone? Can groups be a negative thing?

Them and us

Social categorization can result in a "them" and "us" syndrome. About 60 years ago, the sociologist Henri Tajfel proposed that placing items into groups is a human trait and that we tend to do this in many situations in our daily lives. For example, we provide young children with sorting games, where we give them different coloured objects and ask them to group them. When we collect our books, games, or music, we tend to put them in a genre or some other grouping. Tajfel suggested this was cognitively normal – in other words, to do with how our brains process things.

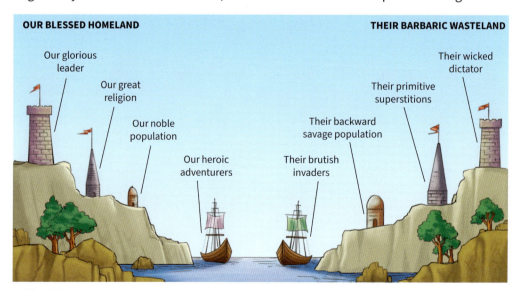

▲ **Fig. 17.1**

Task 1

In pairs, answer these questions.

1. How much do you categorize things? How often do you find yourselves placing things together in some sort of grouping order?

2. Do you think we are conditioned to organize things? Are our brains preset to do this? Or do we perhaps seek to organize things for other reasons?

3. Look at the cartoon in Figure 17.1.

    a. How much or how little do you agree with it?

    b. Do you think it shows what happens now or just what happened in history, when people were ignorant and scared of other groups?

    c. What do you think is its key message?

4. An argument in social identity theory is that members of one group will try to find negative aspects of another group. Why might they do this? Can you think of any relatively harmless examples, when two or more groups have a positive outcome?

5. Think of situations where the division of society into "them" and "us" can create more serious problems. You can include historical situations. Copy the table and extend it.

Groups in conflict	Problem	Resolved
Male and females	Females not allowed to vote in elections	In the USA, in 1918, for example
Upper class and lower/working class		

Stereotyping

Stereotyping is making assumptions about a person or group of people based on things such as gender, race, religion, and physical traits. People who stereotype make generalizations about other people, especially based on the groups in society they are part of. The problem with stereotyping is that it's mostly based on false assumptions.

Look at the words and phrases in the word clouds, then attempt Task 2.

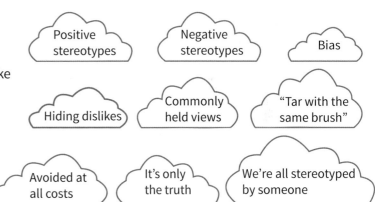

Task 2

In pairs, answer these questions.

1. Fill in the gaps with words or phrases. Feel free to choose the words you like but, of course, try not to offend anybody.

    All white people are ___.

    All politicians are ___.

    Women are only concerned with ___.

    Men who spend ages on a computer ___.

    Women are not good at ___.

    Men are better at ___.

    All teenagers are ___.

    People who come from ___ are usually ___.

    In the USA ___.

    Women always___ and woman take ___.

    Only men ___ and only men like ___.

2. Join with another pair and compare your completed sentences. How similar or different are the results? Did you do the task in the same way?

Traditions

In this section you will:

- explore some unusual traditions from around the world and what they tell us about social grouping
- engage with the experience of global nomads and a modern nomadic lifestyle.

A line of enquiry

Many people look to the past and local or national traditions to find a sense of belonging. Some traditions are common to several countries, some are unusual and unique, and some appear to be strange to an outsider. It could be argued that the wide variety of traditions makes for a diverse and wonderful world. Others might suggest that traditions don't allow humanity to synchronize and meet its common aims.

Greece, Cyprus, and Bolivia share an unusual New Year tradition of baking cakes with a coin inside. It is said that when the cake is sliced, whoever receives the coin will have a year of good fortune.

▲ Fig. 17.2

La Tomatina is a festival held in August in Valencia, Spain. Thousands of people take part in a friendly encounter where tons of overripe tomatoes are thrown at each other in the streets.

▲ Fig. 17.3

Each spring, competitors take part in "cheese rolling" at Cooper's Hill in Gloucestershire, UK. Competitors chase a 4 kg round of cheese down a hill. The prize awarded to the winner is a Double Gloucester cheese.

▲ Fig. 17.4

Task 3

In pairs, answer these questions.

1. What do you think about baking a cake, or any food, and putting a coin in it?

2. Can you see any connections between the three countries and why they have these traditions?

3. Would you enjoy taking part in a mass tomato-throwing event in the streets? Why or why not? Would a cleaner, safer way to do this be better?

4. What do you think the origins of such an event are? Suggest some ideas to explain to an outsider.

5. Why do you think cheese is rolled? Would the event work just as well with round loaves of bread, for example?

6. The event in Gloucester is 200 years old and was created by a group of like-minded locals. It now attracts professional, international competitors. What does that tell you?

7. Can you think of any traditions which are global, rather than quirky events that bring local people together?

8. You have been invited to discuss traditions on a talk show. One of you must argue that traditions only serve the interests of local people who share history and interests, and exclude outsiders. The other must argue that without traditions the world would be far less interesting and less inclusive.

Global nomads

You have looked at aspects of strong cultures, where each member would have a strong sense of belonging to their social group, whether it is for a day or for a lifetime. What about people who don't want or need to belong in the same way? People who drift away from their roots and seek an international life?

Read this introduction to global nomads and answer the questions that follow.

A global ==nomad==, or glomad, is a person who is living a mobile and international lifestyle. Global nomads aim to live ==location-independently==, seeking ==detachment== from particular geographical locations and the idea of ==territorial belonging==. There is no one way of being a global nomad; it is a broad term and can include:

- **digital nomads** – people who earn a living working online in various locations of their choosing (around the same country or internationally)
- **remote entrepreneurs** – people who have a location-independent business that they can run remotely from one or more countries (freelancers, self-employed, or company founders, etc.)
- **remote workers / employees** – employees who do not need to commute or travel to a central place of work such as an office building, warehouse, or store
- **perpetual travellers / permanent tourists** – people who base different aspects of their lives in different countries and do not spend too long in any one place.

Task 4

In pairs, answer these questions.

1. Look at the four highlighted words and phrases. What do they tell you about the mindset of global nomads? Do you think these words and phrases show a positive or negative viewpoint?

2. Would you like to be a global nomad? If so, which of the categories appeals to you, and which don't? Do you know any global nomads?

3. More countries are offering global nomad visas for people to live in one country but work or run a business in another. What do you think about the idea of global nomad visas? Think about different perspectives.

4. Is being globally nomadic a new world order? Is this how we will all be living in 50 years' time? Is this a good thing? Do you think it will lead to breaking down cultural barriers and a more peaceful world?

Sustainability

While global nomads may think it's an attractive lifestyle to be always on the move, what are the implications of this from a sustainability perspective? If more people follow the global nomadic way of living, the increases in air, train, and boat travel will add to their carbon footprints. That poses the dilemma of globalizing work, for example, but compromising the environment.

Evidence

What is the current evidence regarding the increase or decrease of strong cultures which stamp their identity on people's beliefs? What about evidence of the increase of more diverse, global cultures – people having similar beliefs but living across a wide range of countries? Think about the global superpowers and compare evidence of diversification. Think about a theoretical argument that if 4 billion people share the same belief, the rest of the world should follow.

Famous real-life spies

In this section you will:

- learn about some of the most famous spies in history
- compare real-life spies to spies who feature in movies.

A line of enquiry

You can consider the theme of inclusion and exclusion from the perspective of espionage (spying). You might think that spying doesn't happen in the modern world. You might assume that it was a historical activity, in recent history particularly connected to the period during and just after World War II, which ended in 1945. You might think that now spying is the stuff of fiction, as in spy movies.

Read about some real-life spies from history.

Melita Norwood	British 1912–2005	Melita was a lifelong communist who spied on Britain for the Soviet Union. She wanted a balance of nuclear weapons and felt that the USA and Europe had dominance in the 1950s.
Sir Francis Walsingham	British 1532–90	Sir Francis was a secretary to Queen Elizabeth I of England. She faced many threats to her life so Francis built up an extensive international intelligence network. He was known as "The Spymaster".
Sidney Reilly	Russian-born 1874–1925	Known as the "Ace of Spies", Sidney is said to have spied for at least four different states. He studied chemistry in Vienna, before going to Brazil. There he started working for British Intelligence services.
James Armistead Lafayette	African American 1748–1830	James was a slave who worked as a double agent during the American Revolution. He worked as a spy and infiltrated British Intelligence. His reports helped to defeat the British at the Battle of Yorktown.
Frederick Joubert Duquesne	South African 1877–1956	Frederick was a conman who used many disguises. He worked as a spy (nicknamed "Black Panther") during the Second Boer War and as a German spy during World War II. He was captured many times but always escaped.
Harold "Kim" Philby	British 1912–88	"Kim" attended Cambridge University from 1929 to 1933 when he was possibly recruited as a spy by the Soviet Union. He was a British Intelligence officer and also a Soviet spy for 30 years until he defected to Soviet Russia.

Task 5

In pairs, answer these questions.

1. How many of the spies did you already know about? Can you think of some real-life spies who are not on this list?

2. Do you have any empathy for Melita Norwood's viewpoint?

3. In one way, Sir Francis Walsingham was a very modern spy. Why do you think that was?

4. Sidney Reilly's loyalty was questionable. Why? What does that tell you about spies?

5. What skills did Frederick Duquesne have? What other skills do you think spies excel in?

6. Kim Philby is known as one of the most successful spies in history. He held very high positions in the British government until he defected. What does "to defect" mean? Why might a university be a good place to recruit spies?

7. James Armistead was also a double agent. Do you think he felt included or excluded when he was in the British Army? Can you think of other aspects of life where people pretend to be included but really feel excluded?

8. Why do you think many of the spies in the list are connected to the UK?

9. Why do you think there is only one woman in this list? Can you think of any other famous female spies in history?

10. Do you think espionage is as common in the world now as it was in history? Why or why not? Where do you think spies are working?

Fictional spies

Look at these photographs of fictional spies.

▲ **Fig. 17.5** *James Bond*

▲ **Fig. 17.6** *Ethan Hunt in* Mission Impossible

▲ **Fig. 17.7** *Nick Fury in* The Avengers

▲ **Fig. 17.8** *Harry Hart in* Kingsman: The Golden Circle

Research

The movies in the photographs all have male main characters. However, there were some very famous real-life female spies, such as Melita Norwood, Josephine Baker, and Martha Cnockaert, a spy who wrote spy novels. The dominance of male spies in movies has been challenged with movies such as *Salt*, *La Femme Nikita*, *Red Sparrow*, and *Black Widow*, which have prominent female lead characters.

Task 6

In small groups, answer these questions.

1. Are these famous movie characters really spies? Based on what you know about real-life spies, do these and other movie spies have anything in common with the real thing?

2. Why are spy movies so popular? Movies like the James Bond and *Mission Impossible* series have global audiences of millions and make billions of dollars in profit. What is it about these movies that make us feel included?

3. Can you think of any movies or television series that make you feel excluded? Think about why you would feel this way.

4. In your group, play a "truth or lie" game. The topic is "Times when you told the truth but nobody believed you".
   - Decide on a story that is true.
   - Think of two other stories that are not true, just as spies do.
   - Now join another group and tell them the three stories, trying to make them think that they are all true. Each story should last about a minute.
   - The other group will ask you questions for five minutes. Their aim is to reveal which one of you is telling the truth.

Ever-changing world

Spying has taken on a different meaning in the modern, digital world. Modern technology has redefined what spying is. It is now easier to use Wi-Fi networks and the internet to gain illegal access to someone's life. Think about the historical reasons for spying, and contrast that with why people closely observe others in more modern times. Has spying changed from a curious, intriguing pursuit to a very different thing?

Citation and referencing

In your **Individual Report** of 1,500 to 2,000 words, you should reference and record your source materials in a clear, logical, and systematic way.

Skills focus – using referencing systems and writing paragraphs from notes

There are several referencing systems you can use. Of the two most popular systems, one is commonly used in humanities subjects.

Proposed research questions

Look at the four research questions that have been suggested for Individual Reports on the topic of *Social identity and inclusion*.

Evaluate each one. How suitable are they as research questions? How could they be modified to ensure that they meet the expectations of a full report?

1. As we plan to travel to Mars, people on Earth are getting more scared of each other.

2. Crime is the reason for extreme nationalism and this is the reason for people losing their sense of identity.

3. Social identity is not a global phenomenon and it is fake news to think that it is.

4. Is it fair to say that the internet is the leading force in a new social identity?

Harvard referencing is the most commonly used style at UK universities. It uses author and date in-text citations corresponding to an alphabetical bibliography or reference list at the end of the writing. For example:

- In-text citation: This argument can be found in his book about how identity is formed in young professional footballers (Roberts, 2022).

  Reference list: Roberts, D (2022): *Life in the Leeds Utd Fast Lane.* 2nd edn. OUP.

MHRA referencing

This system is used in the humanities. It uses footnotes in the text with source information, in addition to an alphabetized bibliography at the end. For example:

- In-text citation: This argument can be found in his book about how identity is formed in young professional footballers.[1]
- Footnote: [1]Dean Roberts: *Life in the Leeds Utd Fast Lane*, 2nd edn (OUP, 2022).
- Bibliography: Roberts, D: *Life in the Leeds Utd Fast Lane*, 2nd edn (OUP, 2022).

Quoting is when you copy some text directly from a source and enclose it in quotation marks to indicate that it is not your own writing. For example:

- Roberts states that "a 16-year-old footballer's identity at Leeds United starts with a blank sheet" (2022, p. 37).

Paraphrasing is when you rephrase the original source in your own words. You don't use quotation marks, but you still need to include a citation. For example:

- In his opening chapter, Roberts argues for the idea first introduced by John Locke in his *Tabula Rosa* and applies this to establishing a clean-sheet mindset in a young player on the training grounds of Leeds United (2022, p. 37).

In-text citations are intended as quick references to your sources. These can be checked and verified by a reader.

Note: if the source has more than three authors, include the first author followed by "et al.", which means "and others".

1. Read these notes from the drafts of an essay. Write up the notes into formal paragraphs. First use the Harvard system, then the MHRA system.

   - Proposed (Stewart and Nabos and Steele and Chin) in 2011 that social exclusion always precedes social inclusion.
   - They say, "Our study of Panama in the 1970s demonstrated that politicians chose first an exclusion policy." So it was impossible for some people to feel included and they felt like outsiders, they said.
   - (2015) Peters challenged that. He said, "It's not true." His most useful statement: "social inclusion is complex and cannot be predicted". He went on to argue that exclusion was often a consequence of inclusion.
   - Paraphrasing, I'd say Stewart and friends would reply that it's a small sample and in only one country.

2. How well does your paragraph read? Ask someone else to read it.

Sample student referencing

Two students decided to write their reports on the issue of national identity. The title is: "There is more nationalism, tribalism, and extremism in the world than there has ever been." In the extracts, the students wrote about specific elements of this and how they used citation and references. Evaluate each extract using these questions.

1. Where has Pennie gone wrong in her citation and referencing?
2. If you were researching inclusiveness policies on social media channels, how would you go about it? Where would you look? What about Tweepforce and #twitterignite? How would you cite and reference them?
3. Erika researches fandom nationalism. What do you think about how she does this?
4. What do you think of Erika's citation?

Pennie

My research on inclusion led me to social media. I consulted all the popular global channels to analyse their inclusiveness policies. For example, You Tube[1] has a policy that you cannot exclude people unless they are shown to be adding inappropriate content. Twitter (2022) doesn't have the same policy and operates on a case-by-case basis. Instagram has a special policy at instaseepolicy.com so please look there. Facebook has a policy that we are all aware of so it doesn't need a bibliography reference. Finally, I researched Weibo and they use a downloadable PDF. That's in my reference list under "Weibo — social media".

Erika

I find that fans' comments on *Squid Game* are inextricably related to fandom nationalism in the post-Covid era. As Liu (2019, p. 126) defined, "fandom nationalism" means netizens love their nation in the way fans love their idols in the Chinese media ecology. That is, in the context of cyber-nationalism, similar to idol culture, the nation becomes the object of unconditional worship and defence. Chinese netizens become fans of the nation, seeking to purge all negative comments against it on social media, and feuding with all potential competitors or threats to the nation.

Assessment tip

When quoting from your sources and also when paraphrasing, clearly show where the text has come from. If you do not add clear references, you could be accused of plagiarism, as it will appear that you are trying to make the words and ideas look like your own. Pennie doesn't plagiarize, but you can see that in another part of her report she might do.

Common misunderstanding

Even where you carry out primary research, for example, to explore different perspectives, it's important to reference this research. For example, if Erika interviewed a fan of *Squid Game* and then wrote about this, she would need a reference either in her main text or in her bibliography. If she used statistics and did not want to include these in her report (to save words), she should add a note to her bibliography.

Different perspectives on inclusion

Is it possible to feel included globally but excluded locally? Or perhaps included nationally but excluded globally? Is there a relationship between local, national, and global inclusion? Can you think of an example of being included or excluded in all three contexts?

Skills focus – carrying out and communicating research

A team decided to run a project on how inclusive their local sports centre is. Here are the aspects they looked at, who they interviewed (primary research), and how each team member wrote this up to use in their reflective reports.

<table>
<tr><th>Professional practice:
a paralympic swimmer</th><th>Financial costs:
manager of the centre</th><th>Membership:
a regular client</th></tr>
<tr><td>She told me that the pool was 25 years old and had not been upgraded. Once she fell over and had a shoulder injury for five weeks. An alternative pool is 80 km away. Her funding is limited.</td><td>She said membership cost was relatively high to attract serious- level members. There is no other nearby centre to compete with. Investment is mainly going into the new café, opening in a year.</td><td>She runs a business so needs her own space for workouts from 5pm to 7pm every day. She likes this centre because it has people like her — strong, fit, and active. She enjoys the social side, but events don't have vegan menus.</td></tr>
</table>

1. How might the swimmer feel excluded?
2. After interviewing the swimmer, what further research should the student do?
3. What does the manager mean by "serious-level"? Can you make this note clearer?
4. Is investment in the new café an inclusive action? Why or why not?
5. Do you think the regular client feels her needs are met? In meeting some of her needs, how are other people's needs ignored?
6. A fourth team member wrote notes on their research on a different aspect of inclusivity at the sports club. Suggest what aspect they might have chosen, who they interviewed, and what notes they made.
7. Would you join this sports club? Why or why not?

Sample student reflections

A team of three students decided to look at different ways that their local town approached inclusiveness. Here are extracts from their Reflective Reports that comment on the research they did.

Proposed projects

Look at the following four ideas that have been suggested for a Team Project on the topic of *Social identity and inclusion*.

Evaluate each one. How suitable are they as projects? How could they be modified to become more appropriate and viable?

1. To interview four people from four different countries to find out how social identity differs in each.

2. To invite two local people who have experienced exclusion and have had bad experiences to tell.

3. To put on a local sports event in which males and females are equally represented.

4. To attend an art display in the local centre which is focused on inclusiveness in the local area.

Read the extracts, then answer these questions.

1. In one aspect, Leela's observation is useful, but in another, it's disappointing. Explain why that might be the case.
2. How much credit would you give to Leela for reflecting on her research?
3. Evaluate the strengths of Charlie's reflections. Is there a weakness?
4. Consider how Daria could have improved this part of her Reflective Paper.
5. Do you think this was a successful Team Project? Why or why not?
6. Given the research that was done, what would have been a good Evidence of Action?

Leela

If we look at the three perspectives we covered, it's clear that we missed out a key aspect. This was the local politics perspective. Given that the town has a new mayor and a new political party, we should have gone to their office and asked to speak to someone about whether the inclusiveness policies had changed. Charlie's research was the closest to this aspect as he looked at the national government's approach to inclusiveness. But he didn't get any local input. I did change my approach, however, so I deserve some credit for that.

Charlie

In looking at the national perspective, I was able to carry out primary research by interviewing the Minister for Change Management. Dr Aziz provided detailed and insightful evidence that the government is looking to support local communities to modernize their policies on inclusion. Money has been allocated and the development channels are in place. My interview was recorded and the full transcript is provided as a source. One key moment was when Dr Aziz said, "This country has a poor record on this issue and many people have contacted us about how much they feel excluded at the national level and also the local level. It's up to me to correct this."

The secondary research I investigated was a report that I found in the national library, entitled "The major barriers to social inclusion" (Kogan, 2017). In this paper, it is clear that many towns have suffered from many years of underinvestment from those in power who, it could be argued, prefer to promote exclusivity.

My research influenced the project in a positive way as it led to a team member refocusing her research from shopping facilities to leisure facilities and how they are funded.

Daria

My role in the group was to research how open our town is to outsiders like tourists – not only tourists from other countries but also from other parts of our own country. I interviewed ten tourists over two days, all from different places. The vibe I got was that our town was very welcoming. It's a shame I didn't record these. On reflection, I should probably have also got data from the tourist centre. But to summarize, my research was positive and we are inclusive.

Assessment tip

In a team, you will have divided responsibilities to look at research from different aspects and viewpoints. For example, Daria makes it clear that her personal research duty was to look at the aspect of tourism, and she does reflect on this in her report. It's also important for Daria to consider the primary and secondary research uncovered by her team and, ideally, to comment on how her research added to the whole.

Common misunderstanding

Depending on the nature of your project, your group may decide that someone should carry out research of a national or global perspective. This is fine as it could add value to the project and have an impact on the action you choose. Charlie looked at the national perspective and his findings resulted in the team making a change. His findings could also have been used to enhance the key message about the issue as a local issue.

Moving towards assessment – Written Exam

Scan here to obtain the source material you need to carry out this examination practice work.

> Question 4 in your **Written Exam** is a question based on all sources in the insert. Candidates answer by writing an extended response. Candidates are required to assess actions in response to the global issue and explain their judgements with reasons and evidence.

Q4. A government wants to find ways to promote and improve social identity.

The following actions are being considered:

- making its economy strong so that social mobility moves upward
- every young man and woman aged 18 will serve in the military for a year
- invest in sports facilities.

Which **one** of these actions would you recommend to your government, and why?

In your answer, you should:

- state your recommendation
- give reasons and evidence to support your choice
- use the material in the sources and / or any of your own ideas
- consider different arguments and perspectives.

Read the sample student answer, then answer the questions that follow.

How relevant is this to the issue?

Is this assertive enough?

Is this appropriate?

Starts to engage with perspectives.

Gnonto's response

According to Source 1, which comes from the World Economic Forum, social mobility is strong in cold countries. But it's difficult to see the link here. Why would a cold country improve the standard of living over time for the next generation? It might be that all the countries are in Europe though. The European economy is usually strong and they have a good record of human rights and equality also.

In Source 2, I agree with all the factors in the list. Before a government can improve people's chances of being secure with their identity, they do need to research all of the factors. I can think of examples of all five that have happened to me and people I know. Where I live, the key factors are location and gender. I'm sad to say that my society is behind the world in equal opportunities, especially for women living in rural areas.

Source 3 is an interesting argument. I know that some countries have military service. I think Finland is one of them, and they feature in Source 1 as being highly upwardly mobile. I suppose if you are in the army, for example, you have to be strong and you have to feel 100 per cent part of your unit. But isn't this about the identity of the whole army or navy – I mean it's not exactly a personal perspective, is it?

Source 4 is more up my street as I play a lot of sport. Therefore, I recommend that the government invests in making sport more widely available to more people, and the idea of building more sports facilities must be a great idea. How could anyone object to that?

The reason I am giving this advice is because in my own country I have seen us grow from a lowly nation, with hardly any Olympic athletes and a cricket team that, until three years ago, nobody had heard of. That was until our women's team made the World Cricket finals. All of a sudden we are competing against the best, such as Australia and India. ==We didn't win, but the media focus we got improved the access of sport to women hugely.== I agree with the lady in Source 4, that sport is a great way to get to gender equality. And, like her, I feel it needs to done by government making women's sport a priority and by having new policies. It won't happen naturally.

> Shows clear line of reasoning which can be followed easily.

The man is not wrong. He's right that sport strengthens body and mind. It's what he doesn't say that matters. ==Sport can also lead to people feeling like outsiders,== as sport is often based on strong social groups or teams. I would think there is evidence to say that this applies equally to male and female players in sports teams. Also, sport can lead to failure, which causes anxiety, loneliness, and being shy to try new things. And what about getting injured? This must be the same for men and women.

> Implies these are factors that should also be considered.

==Perspectives of a government spending money on sport are:==

* ==people who don't like sport will say that it's a waste of money==

* ==scientists will argue that it's more important to do space travel or solve diseases like cancer==

* ==an economist might argue that the success of a country makes money — just like our cricket team did three years ago.==

> Lists personal, ethical, and economical perspectives.

So, yes, I think all three actions are valid, ==but sport is the one that is balanced best.==

> Gives a conclusion but does it have clarity?

Engaging with Question 4

1. After reading Question 4, analyse Gnonto's approach to structuring his response to the question.

2. Identify where Gnonto begins to engage with Question **4**.

3. Gnonto uses rhetorical questions. Do you think they work? Explain your answer.

4. Evaluate to what extent Gnonto's response is based on evidence.

5. Consider whether Gnonto shows a good understanding of what social identity is.

6. Does Gnonto cover alternative perspectives effectively?

In this section you will:

- explore the wide range of emotions that sport brings about
- analyse what sport means to a university student
- consider the impact of professional sport from personal perspectives.

A line of enquiry

The word "sport" can trigger a range of emotions in people. For some, it brings joy, excitement, and anticipation. For others, it brings displeasure, nervousness, and fear. However, the word "recreation" doesn't trigger a similar range of emotional responses. What does sport mean to you? What about recreation? In what ways are the two similar and / or different?

Sport and recreation form a part of every country's culture, but with different emphases and to different extents. Can you think of some countries where sport seems to be a major part of the culture and other countries where sport seems to be a minor part of the culture?

In this section, you will look at two aspects of sport – sport for students and sport as a career.

A student's viewpoint

Read the account below by Adam, a university student in Glasgow, Scotland. He was studying during the Covid-19 pandemic when contact between people was severely limited. Then answer the questions that follow.

Although competitive sport causes worry and stress, sport in and of itself is still a way for students around Scotland and the UK to relax. Now, as we enter a period where many students will spend hours on their laptops attending Zoom tutorials and online lectures, sport will become more of a break than ever. A chance to get out of your room, see friends in person, and be active will be more than welcome to many Glasgow students.

For me, sport is all these things and more. I train with my best friends, I can escape from university stress through sport, all while staying relatively in shape. So, as we enter an academic year like no other, with the possibility of no nights out and many societies relying on Zoom socials, sport at university can offer a break from the laptop screen and a chance to (briefly) stand within two metres of someone you don't live with!

Whether a fresher or a final year PhD student, a nationally ranked swimmer or amateur footballer, with over 50 sports in Glasgow at levels ranging from international competitions to recreational sessions and everything in between, sport really can be whatever you want it to be.

(By Adam Paton, Glasgow Guardian *blog page)*

Task 1

Adam is posting to a blog which has the title "What does sport mean to you?"

1. As he begins his blog, Adam talks about how sport can help students.

   a. Give two ways he thinks sport can help.

   b. What do you think he means by "a chance to get out of your room"? Where else in the blog is there evidence to support what he means?

   c. Are the positives he mentions specific to students in the city of Glasgow?

2. What do you think Adam means when he says that sport is all these things "and more"? What does he mean by "more"?

3. Adam concludes that sport can be whatever we want it to be. Look at his final paragraph. How many different perspectives are covered?

4. Choose a country that you believe is very different to Scotland. How might the perspectives differ? What are the causes of the different viewpoints?

5. Now it's your turn to write a blog post, by responding to Adam's post directly. Write about 100 words.

Reflect

Several personal perspectives have been explored on these pages, along with how sport can provoke emotions. However, think about the global stage for sport. Is it possible that major events, such as the Olympic Games and the football World Cup, bring the people of the world together? Is that what Shakespeare meant when he said that "all the world's a stage"? Or when you reflect on global sport, do you have mixed feelings?

Sport as a career

In his blog, Adam mentions that competitive sport causes worry and stress. Why then do we have professional sport? In all countries in the world, there are people who have made sport a career. Some of them began their sports careers at a very young age. For example, gymnasts often reach their peak at 18 years of age. In other sports, some continue their careers beyond 50 years of age, such as professional golfers.

▲ **Fig. 18.1** *The star attraction*

Task 2

Look at Figure 18.1. Some of the photographers have very sophisticated wide-angle lens cameras.

1. What event do you think these photographers are capturing?

2. Why are there so many of them there?

3. What does this tell you about professional sport?

4. What stresses might a professional sportsperson experience? Give two examples.

5. Salman, aged 19, is just about to begin his professional cricket career in front of those photographers. Look at each of these perspectives.

What might each person be thinking:

   a. Salman's parents

   b. his brother or sister

   c. his trainer since he was 13 years old

   d. his teammates on the field of play

   e. the captain of his cricket team

   f. his sponsor – Salman is advertising the company on his shirt?

Sport, money, and politics

In this section you will:

- consider how sport sometimes finds itself in the political arena
- examine how sports can be affected by external forces
- give a talk considering specific sports and how fair and passionate they are.

A line of enquiry

Look at the cartoon. It is followed by an extract, which was written in January 2022.

◀ Fig. 18.2

"IT'S NOT DOUBLES. THAT'S HIS AGENT BACK THERE."

Amnesty International introduced the term "sportswashing" in 2018 to describe the practice of those who use sports to polish reputations. Specifically, it is used to divert attention away from political and cultural matters. Traditional examples of sportswashing include the 1936 Olympic Games in Berlin under the Nazi regime, which Hitler hosted in an attempt to showcase the so-called superiority of German and Aryan peoples.

The sheer amount of sport that is played now has led to a massive increase in global coverage, especially on television networks, streaming services, and all over the internet. Take football, for example – a truly global game. Almost a quarter of the global population, just under 2 billion people, watched the 2022 World Cup final between France and Argentina.

By its very nature, sport is divisive – one team or player wins, the other loses – and the world watches. In international competitions, teams or individual players represent their home countries, so it is easy for politics to creep into these competitions. Which team / country do you support? Which team / country is better? Can international focus on an important sports event enhance the host country's reputation? Or does it focus attention on other issues, such as human rights, to be faced and questioned?

Put sport and politics together and you will get a wide range of views, all coming from very different perspectives, with people shouting and securing their interests. It all depends which side you are on.

Task 3

In pairs, answer the following questions.

1. Why do you think the writer uses the word "polish" in the opening paragraph?

2. Can you think of any other sporting events in history that attracted attention for reasons other than the sport being played?

3. Why do you think only a quarter of the global population watches the football World Cup? What do you think the other three-quarters are doing?

4. Do you agree that sport divides people? Can you think of any sports where this is not the case?

5. Put the highlighted sentence in your own words. Focus on "shouting and securing". What is implied by this?

6. What about the argument that major sporting events can focus on social, cultural, and political issues?

7. What does the cartoon suggest about the role of agents in sport?

8. Imagine you are the agent of an up-and-coming sports player. Your partner is the sports player. Role play your very first meeting. What's on offer? What does the sports star want, or even demand?

The many sides of being a successful sports star

Sports stars are increasingly being asked to talk about their politics. Many choose not to do this and concentrate solely on their sport and their performance. They argue that they are paid to play sport and not to talk politics. However, some sports stars are very wealthy, have a lot of influence, and are tempted to get involved in politics.

Task 4

Pretend you are a successful sportsperson. You are going to give a short TED-style talk, and you have been given the following prompts to include in your talk. Some of your talk can be political.

- Why did you choose your sport?
- How fair do you think your sport is for all the people who compete in it?
- What role does passion play? Could your sport be called violent?
- How much money are you paid and how do you justify this?
- Is "big money" involved in your sport? In your opinion, how does this affect the sport?
- Should sport and politics ever be mixed?
- Do you think your sport has ever been "sportswashed"?

Gender equality and inclusion in sport

In this section you will:

- examine the argument that gender equality is being achieved in sport
- look at the progress that women have made in being represented in the Olympic Games.

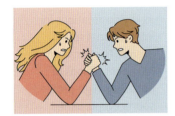

▲ **Fig. 18.3** *We should make this an Olympic sport!*

Reflect

Reflect on your own experience relating to sport – either taking part or watching. Reflect also on how others around you have reacted to sport. It could be argued that sport brings out the full range of emotions, and that it generates positives, or high points, and as many negatives, or low points. Sport is often associated with strong mental and physical health – but there are two sides to the argument.

A line of enquiry

In 2022, Thomas Bach, the president of the International Olympic Committee (IOC) was quoted as saying:

> *"Yes, we have made progress. Yes, we can be proud of this. No, we are not complacent, there is still a lot to do."*

Participation
Access and opportunities for athletes on the field of play and for staff of sports organizations
Leadership
Positions with decision-making powers and/or influence
Safe sport
A sporting environment that is respectful, equitable, and free from all forms of harassment and abuse
Portrayal
The language (words and expressions), images, and voices used, the quality and quantity of coverage, and the prominence given when depicting individuals or groups in communications and the media
Resource allocation
The distribution of funding, facilities, and non-financial support
The IOC as leader of the OLYMPIC movement
The IOC as owner of the OLYMPIC GAMES
The IOC as an Organization
+++
Impact
+
Control
Influence

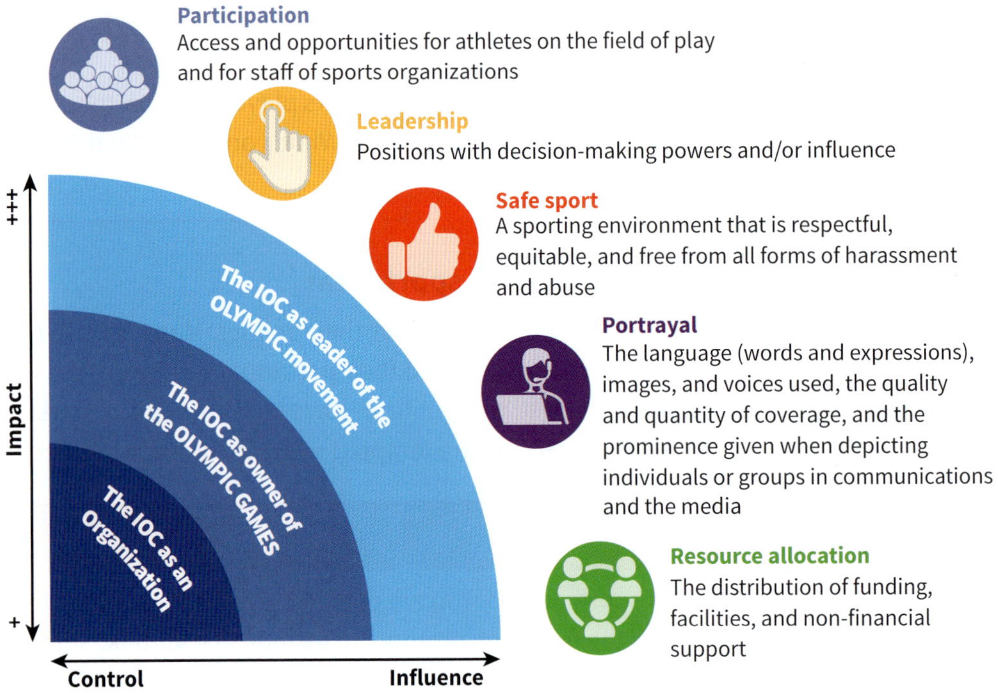

▲ **Fig. 18.4** *The values promoted by the IOC*

The IOC set out a vision for 2021–24 called "Accelerating progress". The Committee set a target that the Paris Olympic Games of 2024 would be the most gender-balanced and inclusive Olympic Games ever.

Task 5

1. What message is Figure 18.3 trying to send?
2. Do you think the cartoon aligns to what Thomas Bach meant when he said that "there is still a lot to do"? Explain why or why not.
3. Give some examples of sports which you think are gender-balanced and some sports you think are not.
4. Look at Figure 18.4. In your own words, what is the relationship between impact, control, and influence?
5. For the five areas focused on in Figure 18.4, imagine that there might not be gender balance. Copy and complete each sentence to put forward an argument.

a. I don't see why all the senior coaches in our women's football team are _____.

b. Wouldn't it be a great idea if the President of the IOC _____?

c. They talk about safe sport, but a simple example like _____ shows that it's not as safe for women.

d. I get really frustrated when the media portrays women's sport as _____.

e. I recently looked at some statistics on how much my country spends on sport, and _____.

Gender equality through time

A counter-argument showing a different perspective can be seen in Figure 18.5.
Study the diagram, then in pairs answer the questions that follow.

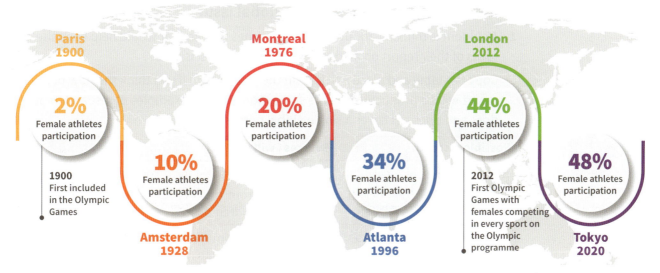

Paris 1900
2% Female athletes participation
1900 First included in the Olympic Games

Amsterdam 1928
10% Female athletes participation

Montreal 1976
20% Female athletes participation

Atlanta 1996
34% Female athletes participation

London 2012
44% Female athletes participation
2012 First Olympic Games with females competing in every sport on the Olympic programme

Tokyo 2020
48% Female athletes participation

▲ **Fig. 18.5** *Gender equality through time at the Olympic Games*

Task 6

1. What trend does Figure 18.5 show?

2. What do you expect the percentage statistic to be by the time of the Paris 2024 Games?

3. On the diagram, it looks as if good progress was made from 2012 in London to 2020 in Tokyo. Do you agree, given that Thomas Bach said, "There is a lot still to do"? What more should be done to improve things for Paris 2024?

4. Look at the two photographs. How do they make you feel?

▲ **Fig. 18.6** *Egyptian beach volleyball player celebrating*

▲ **Fig. 18.7** *Women's rugby forwards in a scrum*

5. Do you think the media presents sport in a gender-balanced way?

Perspectives

Sport is without doubt a global issue. It functions at all levels from local to the world stage, such as the Olympic Games. Think about your local area and how sport friendly it is. Think about your country and how much your local area reflects sport in your country. Also think about international sport. Isn't it the ultimate aim of all sport to succeed on the international stage?

Focusing on a global issue

In your **Individual Report** of 1,500 to 2,000 words, you should aim to focus on a single global issue, providing an analysis of the issue with relevant supporting information. You should be clear about who holds the global perspective, for example, a global organization such as the World Health Organization (WHO). If the perspective is held by a group of people, you should bring together the supporting evidence to show clearly what their global perspective is.

Skills focus – analysing a single global issue

1. A student is thinking about some approaches to take that would help keep the focus of their report on an easily identifiable global issue.

    Copy the table and place a tick (√) in the last column if you think the flow of the report will be productive. Create some more rows as examples of research that does and does not cover a single global perspective.

Possible research	Sources I will use	Tick?
a. The number of local areas for children to play games in is decreasing.	1. My own country – local council report. 2. A report from the WHO on how much exercise children aged 7–11 get.	
b. It is easier to become a professional sportsman than sportswoman.	1. Case study from our local female tennis hero – a European champion. 2. Case study from our local male baseball player.	
c. Television and streaming rights have resulted in wider access to sports for all.	1. Interview with a content planner for the local sports channel. 2. Interview with Stan Lee in Laos, who doesn't have a TV or a computer.	

Proposed research questions

Look at the four research questions that have been suggested for Individual Reports on the topic of *Sport and recreation*.

Evaluate each one. How suitable are they as research questions? How could they be modified to ensure that they meet the expectations of a full report?

1. Is it true that local and national sports are being underfunded and underdeveloped by most countries?

2. To what extent do the issues of money, corruption, drug use, and nationalism affect sport at the global level and also in different countries?

3. In Switzerland, Roger Federer has shown that a professional sports player can raise the reputation of the nation.

4. The use of performance-enhancing drugs cannot be properly understood without a detailed analysis of the chemical substances being used.

Sample student extracts

Three students have decided to write their Individual Reports on the issue of money in competitive sport.

Look at the extracts from their reports, in which they provide the basis for the main essay. Then answer the questions.

1. Identify what Antonia's global issue is.

2. Evaluate whether Antonia utilized the data from *Forbes* magazine appropriately. Why or why not?

3. In Guido's report, the issue seems to be clear. Explain his issue in your own words.

4. Identify what obstacles Guido is likely to face later on in his report.

5. Carlos raises a promising single issue to research. However, at times, his choice of words is unusual. Which words would you replace to make his issue even clearer?

Antonia

The amount of money that the governments of China and Russia allocate to the development of professional sport is astounding compared to how much countries such as Vietnam and Estonia spend. Data drawn from the article from *Forbes* magazine illustrates this and suggests a clear contrast between wealthier countries and less developed ones. The global issue raised is that sport is corrupt from the top down.

Guido

The Israeli government has reviewed its annual funding for the development of sport and recreation in the community and has decided to decrease it by 8 per cent. In the article by Cohen (2022) in the *Israeli Times*, a government spokesperson is quoted as saying that "the global economic crisis of 2022 and 2023 as a result mainly of the pandemic and the Ukraine conflict has forced us to either increase taxes or make cuts to public services". What this means is that sport and recreation at the local level has been sacrificed for the national interest. The global trend is the same: all countries are reducing their spending on such facilities.

Carlos

The issue I want to raise in this essay is the global trend of money killing sport. It can be seen in all of the major world competitions, such as the Beijing Olympics and the Qatar World Cup for football, and also in sports such as alpine skiing, professional cycling, and Formula One car racing. On the other hand, representatives of those sports exclaim that it's a natural economic trend — more investment is a no-brainer to get better quality sport for players and viewers. If we look at how the men and women's New Zealand rugby teams dominate internationally, we can see the glory of high investment.

Assessment tip

Be absolutely clear about what your global issue is from the outset and, ideally, contrast this by using a national or local context. For example, if a student's issue is the gender balance in professional sports, they can quote the International Olympic Committee with its assertion that, by the time of the Paris 2024 Olympic Games, there will be more female athletes taking part than male.

Common misunderstanding

A report should build up its global and national (or local) perspectives using different information sources that feed back into the single main issue being researched. Antonia, for example, covers a good range of countries, but she should be careful not to prioritize global coverage, with information from many countries, over a more in-depth analysis of the global issue and the local or national issue in a prominent country that perhaps goes against the global position.

Moving towards assessment – Team Project

Proposed projects

Look at the following four ideas that have been suggested for a Team Project on the topic of *Sport and recreation*.

Evaluate each one. How suitable are they as projects? How could they be modified to become more appropriate and viable?

1. We want to raise the issue of problem areas in our local community and show how providing free sports facilities will help make people's lives better.

2. There is too much violence in the town. We should try to relocate that violence to the sports fields.

3. We are worried about the environment and how these extra sports facilities will reduce local areas of nature which, after all, are supposed to be protected.

4. Not enough people play chess. We could start a chess club for everyone.

Can greater access to sport and recreation help with local issues?

In many countries around the world, people play games with their friends and families and compete in amateur sports on a regular basis. The games and sports vary in different places and with different climates. It's fair to say that sport has a global dimension. Many people use sport to meet their need for exercise; walking football, for older people, is an example of when sport becomes recreation. It makes very good sense, therefore, for all local communities to prioritize sport and recreational facilities, with easy access for local people.

1. Look at the two photographs. What does each one tell you about the facilities needed for each activity?

2. What do you think is involved in organizing these two recreational activities? How much of that is likely to include teamwork?

3. What factors might cause recreation to change into a sport?

▲ Fig. 18.8

▲ Fig. 18.9

Skills focus – evaluating the success of a project

Assume that the aim of these projects was to increase the accessibility of organized recreation for local people. Consider each evaluation point. Are they taking the correct approach? Why or why not?

1. The success of this activity was that local people realized that they need to take part in more team sports.	3. Within days, we saw people from other countries flying in to take part.
2. Before our event, only older people came to the Chinese yoga class. Now it's full of younger people coming after work.	4. Nobody turned up. Our team doesn't know why. Peter, who leads our team, said there's no point in being negative.

Sample student evaluations

A team of four students decided to raise the issue of limited facilities for sport in their local area by holding a sponsored 24-hour football game. Their aim was to raise awareness and to use any donations for a new sporting facility. Read each of their accounts and answer the following questions.

1. What do you think about the aim that Mirat mentions.
2. Consider how well Mirat evaluates his own contribution.
3. Evaluate how well Vladimir managed his own task. What opportunities to develop the project has he missed?
4. Identify the strengths of Natasha's account.
5. Identify the weaknesses of Victor's account.

Mirat

I'm useless at football. I argued all along that we should have had a sponsored debate about the issue, but I was voted down by three to one. To play football for 24 hours was a ridiculous aim for our team project. I did turn up and played for four hours, but I resisted doing much else. From my perspective, it was a pointless venture as we could have raised awareness in a much less physically demanding way.

Vladimir

I love football. I play it whenever I can. I always have a ball close to me. I support Russia and we have a strong national team. It's a shame, in my view, that my local area is lacking in football facilities. Playing for 24 hours attracted attention from a wide range of people, including a spotlight piece on our local TV channel. I was interviewed and was able to report how well I was playing – I scored 14 goals.

Natasha

The way we went about this activity to make local people realize that we need more places to take part in sport was impressive. I know that Mirat wasn't keen as he hates football, but I took him aside and pointed out the bigger issue and he said he would play for four sessions of one hour. Vladimir has a good heart but he used this occasion to showcase his skills as a striker. I feel that we did well to spring so many local people into action to come and support us, and we raised enough money to start a fund for a new climbing wall in one of the disused town centre buildings.

Victor

I did really well. I could see that if we attracted the local media, we would increase our chances of success. That was my role – to organize the media. Everyone worked well as a team and the game was a roaring success.

Assessment tip

When you are evaluating the action, try to provide at least two different points and develop both. For example, if the action is a sponsored 10 km run in a coastal town to raise awareness about how the local marine sports industry has been affected by central government policies, you don't need to evaluate those policies. Focus on how much awareness was raised, even if the run was cancelled after 6 km due to bad weather.

Common misunderstanding

The reason you are doing a Team Project is to show that your collective work can achieve a positive result. It is better, therefore, to focus on the team's strengths than to describe tasks that team members failed to carry out. For example, consider Mirat's approach. What do you think about how he wrote about his team members' roles and tasks?

Scan here to obtain the source material you need to carry out this examination practice work.

Question 2 in your **Written Exam** is a structured question based on a source that describes some research or evidence about the global issue. There will be two parts to the question. Candidates are required to evaluate the research or evidence, and suggest ways to research or test a claim related to the global issue.

Q2. Study Source 3.

a. Developing body strength should be a priority for people globally.
Explain the strengths and weaknesses of the research outlined in Source 3.

b. "Most people would have better lives if they took part in more sport."
Explain how this claim could be tested. You should consider the research methods and evidence that could be used.

Read the three extracts from the two sample student answers, then answer the questions that follow.

Norrie's response to Question 2a

a. The trainer has a vested interest in more sports being played as he earns his money from it — and he gets to travel around the world as well! His skill is body training and building up core body muscles. He appears to have a strong argument, as we all know how important it is to take regular exercise. However, people can take exercise in a wide range of ways, such as walking, cycling, and swimming, and they don't have to be intensive.

The research quoted varies from reasonable to weak. It is reasonable to state that boxing builds up core body muscles. The 15 per cent factor is not supported with any methodology, though. We have to take his word for it. The view that doctors would prescribe these kinds of fitness classes is arguable. It looks as if it's the trainer's viewpoint rather than proper medical research. Building up brain muscles in the university study sounds promising, and I can make sense of this as you do need to be focused mentally while playing sports.

This may be true but it's not relevant to the question.

Gives a personal view, which is not considered in the source.

Avoid assumptions and stay focused on the research and evidence presented.

Good evaluation in this paragraph.

Engages directly with two aspects of the research presented to balance things out.

Cary's response to Question 2a

Correct, but only describes this and does not evaluate.

a. The writer uses assertion about boxing being the best sport to test his exercise regime. ==This is matched by more assertions== of doctors actually making patients do tougher exercise. A strength is that the writer has travelled globally and also that he has worked with Olympic teams – ==we can take it that he is an expert==. Daily workouts of 45 minutes seems like a strong case to me – then more ==people will lose weight and get fitter==. Working with ordinary people in schools and old people's homes is ==strong research as ordinary people make up most of the world==.

Not a strength of the research, though.

But what research was done?

Maybe so, but the evidence should be contested as an opinion.

Norrie's response to Question 2b

b. To test this claim, I would look at a range of information that would be available globally. For example, there ==must be a lot of data from medical studies in hospitals== in lots of countries. I would focus on case studies showing the effects of being involved in sport on people's mental condition – how much ==their state of mind improves during and after playing==.

Gives a good source of evidence.

Gives useful case studies to establish some research data.

There would be no point in studying professional sportspeople because their lives must already be good as they have chosen to play the sport. If they have failed (played in losing teams or not won in the Olympics), then maybe it would be worth researching to provide a counter-argument.

Useful data could be gathered from sports clubs – a ==questionnaire for new members, perhaps after six months== to see if they feel their lives are any better.

Includes a range of methods and builds up different sources.

I think it's also important to find cases where people's lives have been made worse, such as those with long-term sports injuries and people who hate sport. I could interview people from both areas.

Engaging with Question 2

1. Analyse the three student responses, stating where there is a lack of credibility.
2. Look at Norrie's second paragraph in his answer to Question **2b**. Identify what additional support, if any, this brings to the answer.
3. Give three pieces of advice to Cary to improve his response.
4. Can you contribute any more relevant and useful research methods and types of evidence that Norrie hasn't covered in his response?

In this section you will:

- explore how insects have been used as inspiration for designs for AI robots
- evaluate the advantages and disadvantages of investment in AI projects.

A line of enquiry

"You have to talk about *The Terminator* if you're talking about artificial intelligence. I actually think that that's way off. I don't think that an artificially intelligent system that has superhuman intelligence will be violent. I do think that it will disrupt our culture." *(Gray Scott)*

The debate about whether we should be developing artificial intelligence (AI) systems has been running for decades. It has perhaps become more real in the 2020s, as we have started to see humanoid robots displaying facial expressions that make us feel excited but, at the same time, nervous.

For some people, AI poses threats and challenges. For example, we might feel inferior to an AI humanoid robot. However, think about nature and its complexity. Do you sometimes look at the natural world and think that it is so much more sophisticated than we are?

Others see AI as the only way to solve all of the problems facing the human race. One thing is certain, AI is upon us and may be unstoppable.

Robotic insects

If you look at insects very closely, you will see that they are very clever creatures with lots of features that are extremely functional. Their bodies have three main parts:

- a head with eyes, mouth, and antennae
- a thorax with legs and / or wings
- an abdomen that contains their organs.

Now look at the photographs, which show how the National Aeronautics and Space Administration (NASA), USA, is using AI and the features of insects to explore our solar system.

▲ **Fig. 19.1** *RoboSimian is an ape-like robot that could respond to disaster scenarios too dangerous for humans.*

▲ **Fig. 19.2** *SpiderBot is a micro-robot designed to chart the terrain on other planets and explore smaller bodies, such as comets, asteroids, or the Moon.*

▲ **Fig. 19.3** *SPARROW would be propelled by steam and hop across icy terrains, like those found on Jupiter's moon Europa and Saturn's moon Enceladus.*

▲ **Fig. 19.4** *Geckobot is a gripping system inspired by the tiny hairs on the bottom of geckos' feet, allowing this robot to cling to vertical walls and other surfaces.*

Task 1

In small groups, consider how NASA is using AI and the features of insects, and the broader issues this raises.

1. Why did NASA feel that insects were such a good inspiration for their aims?

2. Choose one of the insect robots. What specific challenges would it face if it was exploring a planet, moon, or asteroid?

3. The development project will have cost millions, perhaps billions of dollars. What is your group's view on funding the building of insect robots?

4. Use the views from Question 3 to complete a advantages and disadvantages table. Copy and complete the table below. Be creative!

Advantages	Disadvantages
They could be used to carry out repairs rather than risking humans.	They could be used as spyware by other nations because they are small and easy to move around without being noticed.

5. Now it's your turn to create a robot. In your group, consider another animal as inspiration for an AI robot – but this time, one that is useful to us on Earth, not in space. Think about these factors:
   - your animal robot's name
   - the animal's features that you will mimic in your design
   - the functions of your animal robot
   - the purpose of your animal robot
   - the environment you are designing it for and the challenges you face in designing it
   - how you will incorporate AI into your robot.

6. Decide on how you will present your new animal-like robotic prototype to your class. You might give a team talk, draw a detailed picture, or have a panel show for a television station.

Causes and consequences

It can be argued that one of the causes of AI is the human need to make progress. To go faster, to go further, to lessen the workload for humans, to transfer our brain power to a machine that can optimize it.
Some negative consequences, however, could be that we waste money that could help people in greater need (e.g. through poverty, floods, drought), and the ultimate consequence might be that we destroy all of humanity.

Sustainability

"Humans are not sustainable; machines are." Think about this. How true is it? In 2021, the James Watt telescope was sent into space. It is a machine with a degree of AI built into it. However, it will not last forever and when it reaches a distance of about 2.4 billion kilometres from Earth, it will cease to function and drift off into the universe. It raises the question of what sustainability is in relation to the universe.

Big Tech

In this section you will:

- look at how the Big Tech industry is benefiting society
- expose concerns that some people have about the growth of Big Tech
- explore how images can send messages by using targeted language and clever visuals.

A line of enquiry

A few large technology companies, known as Big Tech companies, tend to dominate the IT industry. Much of the industry is based in the USA, but in the 2020s, China and other countries are catching up fast and developing alternative technologies. Read the extract below, from an article written in 2021, and answer the questions that follow.

Big Tech companies have incredible influence

Big Tech companies have so much power and resources that their impact spreads far beyond single entities. For example, Facebook owns Instagram and WhatsApp. Its acquisitions include a drone manufacturing company, a video software brand, and a street-level imaging service.

Plans from Google, Apple, and Amazon to develop health services or collect patient data also show the growing influence of these companies. Such growth often blurs the lines between once distinctive industries. For example, people in select areas can pay for parking and transit fares through Google Maps. Apple's engineers want to break into the electric driverless car market.

Starting in 2017, Facebook assisted employers by publishing job openings via the platform. Amazon worked on an internal hiring algorithm that ultimately showed bias against women.

These entrances into multiple markets and industries back up government officials' claims that Big Tech has too much power. However, that's not the universally held opinion. Many government bodies invite these companies to meetings that entities with less influence cannot attend.

As Big Tech companies exert power in more areas, positives become apparent, too. Increased technological investments and commitments to innovation are some examples. For example, Facebook's involvement in campaigns to increase internet access could decrease the digital divide. Still, their intentions aren't always benevolent, as seen with its Indian internet scheme that placed the company's services at the center of the internet, leaving potential users little choice but to hand data to the company.

These businesses also research ethical uses for artificial intelligence, achieving progress while reducing potential dangers.

(Shannon Flynn, 2021)

Task 2

In pairs, consider the issue of the impact of Big Tech on the IT industry.

1. What does the author say are some of the benefits of Big Tech?
2. Which areas does the author show concerns about?

3. Is this a balanced piece of journalism?

4. Look at some of the language the writer has used. Does it indicate a viewpoint or a bias?

5. From your own experience, and your use of some of the applications mentioned in the article, can you think of any additional benefits and concerns?

6. Where might the Big Tech companies go next in their desire to grow and move into other economic marketplaces?

7. At the end of 2022, there was a crash in the market value of the main Big Tech companies. What might have caused this?

Task 3

Images can convey several ideas, often intentionally, but sometimes unintentionally. With a partner, look at Figure 19.5, which raises the issue of Big Tech, and answer the following questions.

1. What is the main message that the image is conveying?

2. What other less obvious messages could it be sending?

3. Add a speech bubble to the image. Here are the criteria for your challenge.

   - You are limited to 25 words.
   - There should be an element of surprise for the viewer.
   - Your words should provoke a response.
   - Ideally, there will be a political or ethical message.

▲ Fig. 19.5

Perspectives

Satirical cartoons often use humour to convey a viewpoint that may well be a global perspective – that the rise of Big Tech companies is an issue for us all, irrespective of which country we live in. However, does this type of humour – satire – cross borders? Would everyone, of every nationality, understand it? Where in the world might it not work at all?

Reflect

Reflect on what type of humour you find funny. For example, do you enjoy seeing people falling over, even if they get hurt? Or do you prefer a more subtle kind of humour, with hidden messages that the audience has to work out? Think about times when you have found something funny but those around you couldn't see the humour. Social media platforms often have clips that amuse some people but not others.

Innovation in the fishing industry

In this section you will:

- learn about an innovative device that is being used to help the fishing industry

- apply to the European Commission for your own idea of an innovative technology project related to the fishing industry.

A line of enquiry

The European Commission has lots of agencies that implement a wide range of European Union (EU) programmes. You are going to investigate a specific project in the fishing industry funded by the European Commission.

Read the extract below about STARFISH 4.0. It is an innovative device that is being tested to improve the safety of fishers and the sustainable management of small-scale fisheries.

The STARFISH 4.0 project addresses the small-scale fisheries (SSF) sector of the blue economy, a sub-sector of the extraction and commercialisation of living marine resources. Small-scale fisheries play an important role in the European Union from a biological, economic and social perspective, amounting to 85 per cent of all fishing vessels. But SSF are not currently monitored as large, industrial fishing vessels are.

To solve this gap, this project helps bring to market an innovative product for SSF. This product includes a solar-powered device with an Internet of Things (IoT) / satellite / GSM communications system and dedicated applications.

One hundred fishers in Greece and 50 fishers in Mauritania will be involved for 18 months to test the product at sea. Various characteristics of the product such as robustness, battery life, ease of use, and data accuracy will be field tested. Their feedback will be collected through several questionnaires, which will be used to further refine and improve the product.

Scientists and authorities will have precious information about SSF fishing activities, which will serve as crucial decision-making tools for sustainably managing resources. The willingness of fishers to use such a system will be enhanced and the business model refined and de-risked; the outputs of this validated and improved system can be directly transferred to other European countries.

Task 4

With a partner, discuss these issues and answer the following questions.

1. Do you think it is possible to work out what the acronym STARFISH means?

2. Where is this project based?

3. In your own words, what is the "blue economy"?

4. Look carefully at paragraph 1. Are other perspectives relevant here?

5. The innovation is a "solar-powered device with an IoT / satellite / GSM communications system and dedicated applications". What do you think this is?

6. What does "field tested" mean? Is it the same as evidence?

7. What are some benefits of this project?

Global spending on the fishing industry

With a partner, analyse and evaluate the graph by completing Task 5.

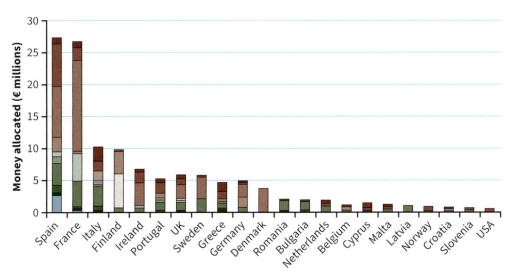

▲ **Fig. 19.6** *Bar graph showing money allocated to different countries, by category, from the European Maritime and Fisheries Fund*

Task 5

Carry out this task in small groups.

1. Look at the colour coding used. What do the browns represent? What does the darkest green represent?

2. Which countries appear to benefit from funding? Why do you think this is so?

3. What is your interpretation of the reason for the allocation of funds to tourism?

4. Coastguard operation funding is relatively high. Why might this be so?

5. What does the funding allocation for dealing with marine litter tell you? Are you surprised to see the countries it has been applied to?

6. Why do Spain and France attract the most funding?

7. Your challenge is to design an innovative project that benefits people working in the fishing industry and submit it to the European Commission to get funding. It does not have to be a device. It can be broader, such as something connected to a career, tourism, the coastguard, or managing marine litter. Take time to discuss your project and check its viability with your teacher.

Evidence

All the evidence in this section points towards humans neglecting the potential of the seas and waters of Earth to support us in the next 100 years or so – and we are trying to make amends with sustainable corrections to our current actions. Seventy per cent of Earth's surface is covered in water. So isn't the management of our water resources a global issue, and evidence that we should value water as it is essential to our existence?

Moving towards assessment – Individual Report

Concluding your Individual Report with a reflection

In your **Individual Report** of 1,500 to 2,000 words, you should aim to reach a conclusion based on what you have learned about the different perspectives you have researched, analysed, and evaluated in the body of your essay.

In a conclusion, the focus should be on a reflection of your own viewpoint on the issue. Has your viewpoint changed? Is it still the same? If you have set yourself a good research essay title, it will be easier to write your conclusion as you can return to your question and answer it directly.

Skills focus – presenting your own viewpoint on an issue

Find a small group of friends or classmates to discuss how much each of you already knows about the important skill of presenting your own views in an essay.

Instructions

1. Cut some A4 sheets of paper and make eight of these notes each. On one side of each note, write "Entry". Write "Exit" on the other side. On the Entry side, write one thing you already know about how to present your views in an essay.

2. Your group then puts all the cards into the centre of the table. Each of you reads all the cards.

3. Now deal out the cards around the group. When you receive a card, turn to the Exit side and add one thing you have learned during the activity.

4. Return the cards to the table, shuffle them again, and hand them out a second time.

5. Has your level of knowledge gone up?

Proposed research questions

Look at the four research questions that have been suggested for Individual Reports on the topic of *Technology, industry, and innovation*.

Evaluate each one. How suitable are they as research questions? How could they be modified to ensure that they meet the expectations of a full report?

1. What is the solar industry?
2. Capturing solar energy by using satellites beyond the Earth's atmosphere is ten times more efficient than solar capture on Earth. If we can capture the Sun's energy in this way, we can go a long way to solving the problem of dwindling energy supplies, which the Earth will face in the late 2020s.
3. "Had President Obama and the Desoto Solar Farm been honest about the dangers it contained, the solar power industry would be distinctly different to what it is today." (*Steven Magee)*. This essay will explore what is meant by that quotation.
4. Is it better to have the carbon problem now but have clean energy later?

Sample student reflective conclusions

Three students have decided to write their Individual Reports on the issue of factory fish farms.

Look at their concluding remarks, then answer these questions.

1. Identify two major problems with Adebola's approach.

2. Evaluate whether Adebola's recommendation of further research is valid. Why or why not?

3. Evaluate Adebola's approach overall.

4. Is it acceptable, as Mahmood says, to not hold a view on the issue being investigated? Explain your answer.

5. Consider how Mahmood's research question had an impact on his concluding remarks.

6. Mahmood appears to have satisfied the requirement of writing at least 1,500 words, propose how his marks could have been improved.

7. Evaluate Suraya's approach.

Adebola

My view, which is opposite to the view presented by the two sources, is that factory fish farming is a good thing. It means that we can get much cheaper seafood. Where I live, on the coast near the Andaman Sea, that benefits our local community and fishing industry, so it's a win-win situation. I can see that the position globally might be different, but my research was into positive effects in the Andaman Sea area. I have reflected on how our community can gain more from its rich source of seafood, and I recommend further research into digital technologies to increase efficiencies.

Mahmood

I learned nothing from this essay. I already knew a lot about both perspectives and why they are different. People involved in the fishing industry are bound to have opposing views — that factory fish farming is bad, or that it benefits people who want to eat a lot of seafood. My research question was to explore the advantages and disadvantages of factory fish farming, and I did that extensively. The two sides will never agree, and I don't have a view on the issue.

Suraya

When I was young, my father took me out on one of his fishing boats. I remember the excitement of the adventure. We set out while it was still dark, and when dawn arrived we had the nets in the sea and the fish were jumping into them. When I reflect on this now, I feel that fishing ought to be a natural pursuit; although fishing crews work hard chasing the fish, there should be some chance that the fish might escape the nets. Factory farming removes all of this and is not fair to the fish. This is why I disagree with that perspective.

Assessment tip

Try to have a clear idea of the different viewpoints in the sources you have researched. For example, if you decide to write about factory fish farming, choose two sources that include different arguments. One might argue that large artificial lakes of shrimp make economic sense, while a different view is that it makes no sense to waste the time and money, and it is better to fish for shrimp in the open seas. These are related viewpoints – different to each other, but not opposing.

Common misunderstanding

The objective of a reflection is not to demonstrate your knowledge of a topic. For example, if you are researching the conditions of people who work in the factory farming industry and you have significant evidence in your sources of very bad practices and the exploitation of workers, don't get carried away with summarizing these at the end of your essay and showing how much you empathize. A reflective conclusion is not a summary.

Moving towards assessment – Team Project

A new hi-tech factory is coming to town!

The growth of the technology industry has resulted in the need for many more manufacturing, storage, and distribution factories across the world. Consumers' need for items produced by digital technology is becoming a global need. Can you think of any country, for example, that doesn't want smartphones, the internet, or better gaming platforms?

To ensure the development and production of hi-tech products, we need more places where the industry can flourish.

Skills focus – submitting evidence of what a team has done

Choosing an effective action will make a Team Project more successful. The five teams listed below were working on the actions for their projects on *Technology, industry, and innovation*. Use the scale to decide on how much you agree or disagree with their ideas.

Strongly disagree	Disagree	Undecided	Agree	Strongly agree
1	2	3	4	5

1. Our satellite will be launched and even though it will only rise one metre, it will demonstrate that we need to send people to Mars.

2. Due to the difficulty of the science, we won't actually demonstrate how the solar tool works, we will just tell people about it.

3. It's easy to show how this new $400,000 quantum-driven temperature control device can change the ambient temperature in a small room by $+/-20°C$ in less than a minute.

4. The four of us will each do an eight-minute segment in a team video, showing different perspectives on the issue of a new hi-tech factory coming to our town.

5. The local community centre will display our interactive screen about the benefits of the planned new specialized digital arts centre for 14 days.

Proposed projects

Look at the following four ideas that have been suggested for a Team Project on the topic of *Technology, industry, and innovation*.

Evaluate each one. How suitable are they as projects? How could they be modified to become more appropriate and viable?

1. Why California doesn't need any more hi-tech industry.

2. Researching the negative impact of hi-tech factories in several countries.

3. The impact of a hi-tech development zone in our rural location, where the agricultural industry is declining rapidly.

4. How the new Google research and development facility on the edge of town will benefit our community.

Sample student planning

A team of five students is planning a Team Project on the news that a major global hi-tech company is going to build a manufacturing plant in their local town. Each team member has presented their ideas about what form the action should take. They have to settle for one action only. Examine their ideas and answer these questions.

1. Identify which viewpoints feature in each team member's suggestion.
2. Based on the suggestions, what do you infer is the aim of their group? Perhaps currently there is more than one aim.
3. Rank the actions from strongest to weakest.
4. Modify each team member's approach to make a more suitable action.
5. Identify another action that you feel would work better.

Adrian

The factory will be right next to the town's nature reserve, which is visited by thousands of people, locally and from across the country. So I think the best action would be a protest held in the nature reserve.

Pete

As the factory will be in the heart of the town, and they are promising a state-of-the-art ergonomic working space, we should consult workers in large industrial plants in the town to see what they think of it. We could do a questionnaire.

Lapita

Let's follow the company on their website and see how they operate. I'm sure we can find some previous examples of how they have exploited local places like ours. We can interview employees who no longer work for them and run a vox pop video that we post online.

Gene

We need to show two sides of this: those who support this venture and those who have concerns about it. I suggest we go with a slideshow and a talk at a conference centre in town to make people more aware of the benefits and consequences.

Jai

We need to show it's a sound investment. I will get the projected accounts and profits from the company and then we can make a spreadsheet to prove that it is a worthwhile addition to our town.

Assessment tip

From the outset, when designing your Team Project try to ensure that the action at the end matches your aim. Another way of looking at this is to make sure that the action is viable, that it can be carried out with relative ease with good planning. For example, don't attempt to demonstrate how a quantum computer works to a group of primary-age students!

Common misunderstanding

Remember that the action is not the most important part of your Team Project. It is necessary to carry out the action, as this will give you scope for the reflection you need to do. For example, if you tried to launch a satellite to Mars and it failed to leave the ground, you can reflect on this in your Individual Report when evaluating the action.

Moving towards assessment – Written Exam

Scan here to obtain the source material you need to carry out this examination practice work.

> Question 1 in your **Written Exam** is a structured question based on several sources. There will be three or four parts to the question. Candidates are required to read the sources and analyse the information, arguments, and perspectives presented about the global issue.

Q1. Study Sources 1 and 2.

a. Referring to Source 1, what is the trend in investment for the USA and China?

b. Using Source 2, identify two arguments against space exploration.

c. Which benefit of space exploration do you think is the most important? Explain why.

d. Explain how space exploration has important personal consequences.

Read the two sample student answers, then answer the questions that follow.

Cassie's response

a. It's a downward trend ==as the two bars in the chart are both less== than the higher ones.

> This is a misunderstanding as the trend is upward.

b. Firstly, exploring space ==gives us too many resources==, and secondly it is really expensive.

> Source 2 states that resources might be an argument for exploration but doesn't mention how many there will be.

c. I think that it will be great for us to ==use the Moon and Mars as a base to welcome life== from the whole of the universe. There are lots of films I have seen where we go out and meet life, such as *ET* and *First Contact*. Life must be out there as the universe is just so big. If we explore space far enough ==we will surely find it==. The cost of exploring is definitely worthwhile. I'd say it's always a good investment for countries like the USA, China, and Japan to do this for us. ==India should spend more== as they are a huge country and they have a lot of IT in Bangalore.

> This doesn't best describe how we might benefit and therefore doesn't answer the question.

> This explanation is not based on source materials.

> Engages with an economic perspective and is a reasonably argued point. However, the question asks for only one benefit.

d. Whether they go into space or not doesn't really affect my personal situation. I can't see how it bothers my family or my friends either. For example, my father works in accountancy, in an office. I don't think advantages and disadvantages of space travel come into his mind at all. I suppose if they were to find alien cultures, ==we'd all be massively affected==.

> Hints at how we could "all" be affected personally, but Cassie misinterprets what is meant by personal perspectives.

Khalid's response

This is fine as Simon uses his own words to convey an upwards trend from 2020.

a. Both countries are spending more based on the year before.

Makes a correct inference from Source 2 regarding potential dangers.

b. It leads to more space junk and we could find alien life that attacks us.

c. The graph shows that there are two global leaders of space exploration in China and the USA, from the perspective of global sharing. However, it would be good to see the wealthier countries collaborating with a wider range of countries to help them develop their space-age technologies. Yes, we should look at how humans can migrate to other planets, and open up our chances of finding alien life, but our main aim should be to do this as a united world experience, so all countries benefit from the advances we make.

This humanity-based benefit also considers the challenges in Source 2 with some data from Source 1. It is a sophisticated response.

Goes on to give relevant examples of how different people gain positive rewards.

d. The consequences of exploring space affect people differently depending on where they live. For example, in Europe, people are more used to space-age technology. There is the European Space Agency in France, and Switzerland has the atom collider called the LHC. So people have a personal benefit, which must be similar in China as they are developing fast in a space race with the USA. Scientists working in universities in physics departments feel the personal benefits in their research. Elon Musk and Richard Branson are motivated a lot by their space missions and provide lots of jobs for people.

However, for many people the consequences are damaging or, in some cases, irrelevant. During the economic crisis and cost of living crisis in 2022 and 2023, I would say the majority of people didn't care about what was going on in space and preferred the money and time to be spent on other things. People living in poorer countries are more concerned about their basic needs such as getting enough food and clean water. I can't see how they would have a positive viewpoint about sending a team of astronauts to the Moon again.

A clever way to end this paragraph on a range of personal consequences that show very different viewpoints.

Engaging with Question 1

1. The first two parts of Question 1 usually test locating specific details from the sources. Your answer will either be correct, partially correct but require more information, or incorrect. Write your own alternative questions for Question **1a** and **1b** which use the two sources.

2. Now provide answers to your own questions that fit all three categories – correct, incorrect, and partially correct but incomplete.

In this section you will:

- consider how much travel has changed over time
- explore what happens in community tourism.

A line of enquiry

People have always enjoyed travelling. Books have been written for hundreds of years by travellers, often taking months and years to enjoy "foreign lands". To what extent has the modernization of transport been influenced by the human desire to travel? Which people in history did not travel far? Why might that have been so?

The ultimate tourist trip might be travelling into space. Would you like to be among the first humans to visit Mars? As we move into space, do you think life on Earth might change? What about travelling to places on Earth we know little about – the bottom of the oceans or beneath the first few layers of Earth itself?

Empathy

Have you ever found that by travelling to a new place, you see things in a new way? One of the goals of tourism and travel is to see the world from a different perspective. It can be hard to understand why others act as they do if we do not share their experiences. Travel can help us to experience the lives of local people and develop our empathy.

▲ **Fig. 20.1** *Tourists looking for animals in Cuyabeno Wildlife Reserve, Ecuador*

Community tourism

Imagine waking up one day to find a group of people outside your house. They are speaking in a language you do not understand, stepping on your garden plants, and taking photographs. How would you feel? This is what tourism might feel like to people living in tourist hotspots. Community tourism presents a new model of tourism which arguably is better for tourists and the communities they visit.

Read the article, written by someone arguing for community tourism in Ecuador.

Community tourism

Traditional tourists stand outside a culture, take photographs of it, maybe sample some food and arts, and then leave. As far as I can see, most of the money remains with large international travel agencies, which subcontract local guides for a small fee. In traditional tourism, local communities gain few economic benefits and often have no say in where or how tourists come.

Community tourism aims to take charge of tourism and change how it takes place. Community members host tourists in their own homes and organize activities. Tourists experience life as part of the community and learn about community values as part of an authentic experience. The money from tourism stays within the community, helping to reach development goals and make the community feel valued.

In Ecuador, some communities in the Amazon rainforest and in the Andes encourage tourists to participate in the preparation of traditional foods, experience the jungle and indigenous healing rituals, and learn about indigenous ways to live, known as *sumak kawsay*. Tourists can develop friendships with community members that last a lifetime.

Sustainability

Community tourism refers to tourism that focuses on respecting and supporting local communities in the tourism destination. Ecotourism focuses on respecting the environment and might focus on tourists enjoying specific natural wonders in a sustainable way. The two types of tourism often overlap, as indigenous communities highlight the importance of respecting the environment where they live.

Task 1

In pairs, answer these questions.

1. Think of some ways community tourism is different from traditional tourism.

2. Decide whether each of these consequences of tourism are economic, environmental, cultural, or psychological.

   - Communities suffer stress from multiple visitors.
   - Communities earn money by selling goods.
   - Hotels in the country gain from visitors.
   - Community members learn new languages to help tourists.
   - Local languages are lost as younger generations focus on learning tourist languages.
   - Tourists influence the culture of the local community (for example, with new fashion trends).
   - Local communities are affected by rubbish.
   - Pollution due to traffic increases in the area.
   - Tourists learn about local practices and culture.
   - Communities do not feel respected.

3. Which of the consequences in the list are positive? What other positive or negative consequences would you add? What perspective do they fall into?

4. Which negative consequences are addressed by community tourism?

5. Imagine you are visiting Ecuador as a traditional tourist and your friend is visiting as part of a community tourism project. How might your journals be different?

Quote

"Broad, wholesome, charitable views of humanity and things cannot be acquired by vegetating in one little corner of the earth all of one's lifetime." *(Mark Twain)*

"When a man is tired of London, he is tired of life." *(Samuel Johnson)*

"Traveling – it leaves you speechless, then turns you into a storyteller." *(Ibn Battuta)*

"Not all those who wander are lost." *(J.R.R. Tolkien)*

"Travel makes you realize that no matter how much you know, there's always more to learn." *(Nyssa P. Chopra)*

To the future and beyond

In this section you will:

- analyse the advantages and disadvantages of virtual tourism, considering different perspectives
- think about the limits of time travel.

A line of enquiry

Some of the technology we have now allows us to travel in ways that were previously unthinkable. We can sit at our computers and visit distant lands through virtual travel.

Virtual travel

Imagine you have decided to visit the Pyramids of Giza. You wake up early, turn on your computer, and put on your VR headset. And there you are – exploring one of the seven wonders of the world! This is virtual tourism.

▲ Fig. 20.2

Virtual travel cuts down your carbon emissions as you are not getting on a plane for hundreds or thousands of miles. We must remember, however, that using computers is not entirely green, as they require energy to run and to maintain data.

Virtual travel makes travel more financially and physically accessible to many. For example, people with limited mobility are now able to virtual-visit the heights of Machu Picchu or climb Mount Kilimanjaro.

Virtual travel can also safeguard ancient treasures. Real travellers can damage historical sites simply by repeatedly exposing them to touch and light. Virtual travel avoids this. On the other hand, some argue that there is nothing like being in a place, smelling and tasting local cuisine, or exploring new neighbourhoods.

As technology improves, virtual travel is likely to become more realistic and certainly more appealing. The impact it will have on the travel remains to be seen.

Causes and consequences

You have discussed some of the consequences of virtual travel. However, you could also consider why humans want to travel, virtually or in reality. There are many reasons, including the desire to have new experiences, to understand history and the world, to expand scientific knowledge, and to satisfy natural curiosity to explore the unknown.

Task 2

In pairs, read the article and answer these questions.

1. List the benefits of virtual travel given in the article.

2. Whose perspective(s) does the article consider?

3. What other perspectives do you think could be considered to decide on the advantages and disadvantages of virtual travel?

4. Consider the consequences of virtual travel for the people in the table.

Code programmer	Tour guide	Environmental activist	Airline pilot	Elderly tourist
More work programming different tours and events in more parts of the world				

Time travel

As far back as 1888, H.G. Wells wrote about the possibility of time travel in his short story *The Chronic Argonauts*. In 1895, he wrote *The Time Machine*, in which a scientist was able to create a time machine in which he visited the future, finding that humanity had become a very different species.

Task 3

In small groups, answer these questions.

1. Discuss the advantages and disadvantages of time travel. Use a table like the one below to help you consider the advantages and disadvantages from different perspectives.

Perspective	Advantages	Disadvantages
Personal		You might end up living in a place you don't like.
National		
Global	We might find a solution for climate change.	

2. You are hired to create a sales brochure for a company that offers time travel. Design and write the brochure, including text and photographs to convince others to become time tourists.

   Look over your finished brochure.

   a. List the arguments you used to convince people to participate in time travel.

   b. What is the tone of your brochure? Do you use expert evidence, emotion, or personal points of view to sell time tourism?

3. Discuss how you personally feel about time tourism. If it was possible in the future, do you think the benefits would outweigh the costs?

Transportation

A line of enquiry

▲ Fig. 20.3

Imagine a world where all motor vehicles – cars, motorcycles, trains, planes, and boats – suddenly stopped working. Most people depend heavily on transportation, not just to move within their country and to visit places around the world, but also to obtain food and other goods they use every day. As populations grow and the world is increasingly interconnected, countries struggle to find ways to keep up with the need for transportation.

Japan's new answer to transportation challenges

Japan's trains are famously efficient, but they're also famously crowded during rush hour. A future solution might be on the cards as Japanese transport company Zip Infrastructure Inc. is looking to introduce a public ropeway system with capsule cars running on zip-lines by 2025. Known as Zippar, these electric-powered zip-lines would be set up throughout a city and could transport up to 12 people per capsule.

Unlike trains with human drivers, the service would be fully automated. It's also apparently more cost-effective than building a monorail. A network of zip-lines would mean the cable cars could navigate difficult routes such as tight turns and have paths which branch out in multiple directions.

Unlike a typical mountain ropeway, these capsules are designed to operate at high speed and could potentially run every 12 seconds, allowing them to transport 3,000 people per hour.

Task 4

In pairs, answer these questions.

1. Set a timer for 30 seconds and list all the types of transport you have ever used.
2. Set another 30-second timer. Now list the types of transport you know about that you have not used. You can look back in history.
3. What do you already know about Japanese trains? What can you infer about them from the article?
4. What problems do Japan's Zippar aim to solve?
5. Do you think Japan's Zippar could help to improve transportation in your country? Explain your reasoning.

Connecting the world

Transportation allows us to travel around the world. As technology advances, travel takes less time and is generally more comfortable. New roads, for example, can connect cities and countries, and support tourism, economic development, social interactions, and political exchanges. However, transportation has costs other than just raising the money for it. To build roads, forests might have to be cut down and villages might have to be moved, changing the landscape forever.

The geography of an area often determines the complexity of the transport system. For example, a road built across a flat area, such as the plains of central USA, is likely to be straight. In contrast, a road through a mountainous or hilly area, such as the foothills of the Himalayas, will tend to follow the easiest route. Bridges are needed to cross rivers or even stretches of open water. Historically, transport networks often developed around ports and crossing points on rivers, linking road and rail to boats and barges.

Task 5

In pairs, answer these questions.

1. Copy and complete the table contrasting the advantages and disadvantages of each type of transport. Add more types of transport if you can.

Type of transport	Efficiency	Economic costs	Environmental costs
Petrol / diesel cars			
Electric cars			
Driverless cars			
Taxis			
Trains			
Trams			
River boats			

2. What challenges in developing transport are faced in your local area?

3. There is more demand than ever to supply countries with a greater number of products. What impact does this have on transport and what are some of the different perspectives it raises?

4. Join another pair to discuss the statement: "International travel using motorized vehicles should be limited to those transporting foods or necessities such as medical supplies."

Research

Rivers have been fundamental to the development of civilizations. They are central to transportation and agriculture. For example, the flow of information, goods, and people along the Nile allowed ancient Egypt to flourish. The Nile was even used to transport materials for the Great Pyramids of Giza. Other key rivers for transportation include the Tiber in Rome, the Amazon through South America, the Mississippi in the USA, and the Rhine in Germany.

Evidence

Evidence suggests that making public transport free would increase the number of people using it. Free public transport allows those with lower incomes to use their money for essentials such as food and housing. Free and efficient public transport might also reduce the amount of traffic and therefore pollution. However, if there are long waits and overcrowded journeys, some travellers will still opt to drive themselves, even if it is more expensive.

Ever-changing world

Transportation has changed from when humans used animals to ride on, move goods about, and power vehicles. Wind and steam were used to power boats, and wheels and steam helped to move vehicles on road and rail. Then motor engines made transportation more efficient. Now we can fly at supersonic speed and send humans into space. Further developments are very likely, but there is also a growing awareness that transportation needs to be sustainable.

Moving towards assessment – Individual Report

Consistency in citation and referencing

In your **Individual Report** of 1,500 to 2,000 words, you are expected to reference and record the source materials you used in a clear, logical, and consistent manner. When done well, anyone reading your report can go and look up your sources for themselves.

Skills focus – using clear and consistent referencing

Look at these examples from articles on the rise in popularity of electric vehicles (EVs). Then answer the questions that follow.

Proposed research questions

Look at the four research questions that have been suggested for Individual Reports on the topic of *Transport, travel, and tourism.*

Evaluate each one. How suitable are they as research questions? How could they be modified to ensure that they meet the expectations of a full report?

1. All public forms of transport are unnecessary.
2. Tourists should have to pay admission charges to visit other countries in order to pay for the damage they do.
3. Old vehicles should be scrapped and recycled every five years.
4. Short internal flights should be banned in favour of more sustainable methods of travel.

Recent vehicle sales data suggests that the market in EVs is steadily on the rise. In 2020, sales of EVs increased by 172.5 per cent from the previous period. Again, in 2021, EVs showed another significant sales increase with more than 10 per cent of all new vehicles being electric or hybrid. This data shows that the proportion of electric / hybrid vehicles within the general new car market is rapidly increasing.

Across all car types, electric / hybrid and conventional, 1.93 million new cars were registered in 2021. This figure is just 2 per cent up on 2020, as a consequence of the Covid-19 pandemic and the shortages in components that were a consequence of it. However, more EVs were sold in 2021 than the total for all of the previous five years. This resulted in new electric / hybrid registrations accounting for 17.6 per cent of all new car sales in the year.

The green motoring consultancy AutoGreenTC released an independent report today. According to their data, in 2021 EVs made up 16.4 per cent of sales, with more than one million now on UK roads. However, while EV sales continued to increase their market share, the rapidly rising rate in sales seen in the previous year has slowed. The report suggests that the total combined sales of all-electric and hybrid vehicles were down by 12 per cent compared with the same sales last year.

1. To make an effective reference, what information do you need to include?
2. Given the referencing in each extract, do you think you would be able to find the original information independently?
3. How effective do you think the referencing in each extract is? How might it be improved?

Sample student referencing

Three students have chosen to write their Individual Reports on the subject of EVs. The research question is: "Are electric vehicles a good alternative to conventional fuel-driven vehicles?" Read the extracts below, taken from sections where the students referenced their work. Then answer these questions.

1. What information is missing from Ian's example?
2. What could Alex do to make his source selection clearer?
3. How could Mena improve her reference to the US EPA report?

Ian

EVs are increasingly popular across the globe, especially as gas prices rise and the environmental damage caused by carbon emissions is better reported. In an article published in *EV Special*, Paul Moss explains that the increased use of EVs may be having a positive impact on climate change because of the fall in direct emissions, but the manufacture of the components for these new cars comes with its own environmental costs. For example, nickel mining around the world, needed for the manufacture of batteries, has resulted in fresh water contamination.

Mena

While EVs are becoming a very popular alternative to conventional petrol- and diesel-powered cars (Sinclair 2021), electricity is not the only alternative fuel on the market. Tomas Mickelson, a motoring journalist with *Popular Transport* magazine, explains the benefits of using hydrogen as another fuel that may have less environmental impact (Mickelson, T., 2022). A report published by the US EPA in 2022 also supports this view.

Alex

YouTube is full of people testing EVs and showing how much faster and more efficient they are. They can accelerate faster and stop quicker than conventional cars. In addition, because they are not restricted by cooling considerations, they can be styled better and have more interesting features that customers are willing to pay more for. Reports show that buying an electric car is as much about the look and style as it is about the environmental impact.

Assessment tip

It is important that you give credit where credit is due in your report. If you use information from a book, journal, interview, or any other published / broadcast work, you must show in a clear and concise manner where you found that information. For example, "Why EVs are becoming a very popular alternative to conventional gas-powered cars" (Sinclair 2021).

Common misunderstanding

When adding references to your bibliography, do it in a logical and consistent order. If you are going to use an alphabetical list, make sure you put the surname of the author first. For example, list 'Peter Smith' as 'Smith, P.'. Also make sure that if you have more than one author with the same family name, they are listed alphabetically by their initial. For example, 'Smith, P.' comes before 'Smith, W.'.

Moving towards assessment – Team Project

The effects of ecotourism

People love to travel. As well as exciting cities, they love to explore wild and naturally beautiful landscapes. The benefits and pleasures that visitors experience in new and interesting locations are often matched by the economic and social gains of the local inhabitants.

Have you ever been on an ecotourist holiday? What is tempting about such holidays? Do you think some people might have reservations, or even objections, about going on one?

Skills focus – preparing for learning from research

Look at the photographs, then answer the questions that follow.

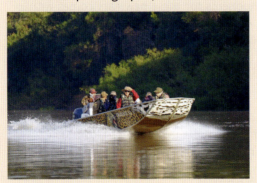

▲ Fig. 20.4

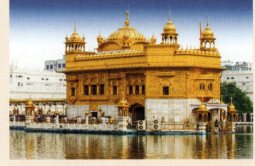

▲ Fig. 20.5

1. If you were researching for a Team Project on ecotourism, what could you interpret from the photographs? What perspectives do they show or imply?
2. If your Team Project was on ecotourism, what role would you like to have? What perspectives would you like to research and explore?
3. How would you monitor your own research during and after you have completed the project?
4. How motivated would you be to contribute to such a project?

Sample student reflections

A team of three students decided to raise awareness of the effects of ecotourism in their local countryside and community by developing and giving a slideshow presentation. The aim was to understand and share both the positive impacts and the negative consequences of tourism for the area and its inhabitants.

Read the extracts from their reflective essays, then answer these questions.

1. Which student do you think was the most motivated during the project? Why do you think that?
2. Which student do you think reflected most on their own learning?

Proposed projects

Look at the following four ideas that have been suggested for a Team Project on the topic of *Transport, travel, and tourism.*

Evaluate each one. How suitable are they as projects? How could they be modified to become more appropriate and viable?

1. To work for our cultural centre to raise awareness of the ecological and social pressures on our local area.
2. Should all air transport be restricted in some way?
3. How can cultural insensitivity by tourists be addressed?
4. Should our local town centre be fully pedestrianized?

3. How does Jo's reflection on the project differ from the others' reflections?
4. What room for improvement in their own research skills has any of the students identified?

Jo

I researched the environmental effect of ecotourists on our area. I discovered that a lot of damage is being done because of the increase in pollution that tourists cause. At first I felt despondent, but my teammate's research showed that much of this type of damage is happening everywhere, even without tourism.

Although Lena's research was limited, it was obvious that the money visitors bring to our community helps to restore some of the damage and also funds publicity to raise awareness of wider issues, such as climate change.

I have realized that, although our wilderness is very special and I am very protective of it, it is also very fragile and needs our help to maintain it. This needs funding so we have to share and use what we have in order to keep it safe. Our research has opened my eyes — we cannot just hope that all will be well.

Lena

My responsibility in the presentation was to look at the economic impact of ecotourism on our community. I struggled to find information that told me how much money comes in and what effect that has. I counted the number of stores, hotels, and restaurants that rely on tourists each year and figured out how many people would lose their jobs if tourism stopped. The wilderness project ranger who is responsible for the visitor centre would also lose his job. I found it difficult to get answers from many of the store keepers about their businesses and soon got fed up asking. I could have asked visitors how much they spend, but unfortunately I started too late and there were not many about. I think I worked well but I did not get much help from my teammates as they were focused on their topics.

Pavel

My role in the presentation was to co-ordinate with my teammates and make sure everyone was on track. We set up an online document to share information but Lena rarely used it. I had to keep asking the others for their work to make sure we made the deadline. I found it quite stressful and difficult to motivate the others, and also myself sometimes.

I was looking at the cultural and social impacts of ecotourism on our wilderness area. Initially, there did not seem much to consider until I began to talk to older villagers. I realized how much the area has changed in a short space of time and that things I take for granted are here because of the visitors. The fibre internet and mobile phone coverage are here because, without them, visitors would not come. So we are more connected than before. Visitors also bring a glimpse of other cultures, which tempts many younger villagers to leave in search of different lives. This causes depopulation and an increasingly elderly community.

Assessment tip

Approach the topic as part of a collaborative team and learn from your own and your teammates' research. Reflect on the project by writing about how your teammates' research can help you to evaluate and enhance your own skills. Explore relevant topics beyond the scope of your own research (for example, the wider impacts on the tourists themselves involving their mental health) and look for connections with a teammate's research.

Common misunderstanding

It is important to make a distinction between the challenges you encountered when working in a team and how your own performance affected the learning of other team members. For example, Lena raises the issue that she felt she didn't get much help from her team and was quite despondent, but fails to reflect on how her own lack of enthusiasm might have affected the overall outcome of the project.

Moving towards assessment – Written Exam

Scan here to obtain the source material you need to carry out this examination practice work.

Question 1 in your **Written Exam** is a structured question based on several sources. There will be three or four parts to the question. Candidates are required to read the sources and analyse the information, arguments, and perspectives presented about the global issue.

Q1. Study Sources 1 and 2.

a. From Source 1, which country shows the largest overall change in bicycle ownership? Which has the smallest?

b. From Source 2, identify two different perspectives about cycle lanes.

c. Identify one example of a statement from Source 2 that you think is a generalization. Explain why you think this.

d. Which of the advantages or disadvantages in Source 2 is most significant? Explain your reasoning.

Read the two sample student answers, then answer the questions that follow.

Padma's response

a. The UK has the largest change in bike ownership and Greece has the least as they had no rise.

b. Some people suggest that cycle lanes ease congestion, while others think it does the opposite and increases it.

c. "Building cycle lanes is cheaper than building new roads" is a generalized statement which depends upon many factors. Not least is that a cycle lane is using an existing road. Creating a new cycle route away from a road is expensive as the land needs to be bought and the cycle route built. This is cheaper than building a new road but more expensive than adding to an existing road. ==Also, if an existing road is made exclusively a cycle lane, the displaced traffic will have to travel on a new route, putting pressure on a different part of the road network. The cost is not reduced, it is just moved elsewhere.==

d. ==The importance of the reasons behind whether more cycle lanes should be built depends on whether you are a cyclist or not. Different road users will have different perspectives.== For cyclists, the suggestion that cycle lanes ease congestion by taking cars off the roads and so reduce pollution could be seen as the most important because the consequences affect everyone – a reduction in traffic means reduced pollution and safer roads.

However, a car commuter may think that the loss of road space actually has the opposite effect, slowing everyone down, causing increased congestion and longer car journeys for those who do not cycle to work. Then cars will use more fuel and therefore produce more, not less, pollution.

==Overall, road users have a very selfish view on how roads ought to be used because they are trying to get to where they are going in the shortest time.==

Gives a clear and credible opinion but lacks support.

Lays out the different possible justifications for two differing perspectives.

Makes a clear judgement as to the difficulties of the issue.

Davina's response

a. The UK has the largest rise in bike ownership and South Africa has the least because bike ownership actually went down.

> Shows she didn't read the question properly.

b. When it comes to deliveries for businesses, one argument suggests that cycle lanes will make deliveries more difficult, but the other argument is that it will make deliveries easier. The two opinions do not state which way the deliveries are going, to or from the business.

> Analysis highlights an inconsistency in the source.

c. The statement "They are only ever used by white, middle-class men" is very general and appears to be based on watching cycle lane use at specific times of the day. For example, if a car driver only drives near cycle lanes to and from work, they only ever see them used by other commuters, mainly office workers who may be white, middle-class men. At other times of the day, users could be different. For example, users near a school at school time would mainly be schoolchildren.

> Analyses the limitations of the source.

> Clearly explains justification for her answer.

d. We are trying to globally reduce climate change. That change will come from education, so we need to start with children. If we build dedicated cycle lanes away from traffic that are safer for children travelling to school, then we build a new normal into our travelling habits from an early age. Older people constantly tell us they walked 10 miles to school in all weathers and that we are soft because we don't walk or cycle. However, roads are much more dangerous now with more traffic and faster speeds. Dedicated cycle lanes away from traffic would teach children that they can travel around safely without using a car.

> Expresses a developed opinion but does not relate it to the source (climate change not directly mentioned in the source).

Where cycle lanes are not practical, then the money would be best spent on the next best alternative. The travelling and commuting public needs to be flexible and, if we can provide a good, reliable, and, most importantly, affordable public transport network as an alternative to cars, that is a good next best solution to cycle lanes.

> Offers her own alternative perspective related to the issue based on source material.

Engaging with Question 1

1. Look at both responses to Question **1b** and identify which student gives the most effective explanation. Explain your answer.

2. In Padma's response to Question **1c**, explain what she means by "generalized"?

3. Davina's answer to Question **1d** has made a point about climate change but is not directly linked to the source material. Evaluate how valid her point is.

4. Analyse Padma's response to Question **1d**. Do you consider she is for or against cycle lanes? Does she successfully answer the question?

In this section you will:

- explore personal values and beliefs
- understand how values influence behaviour.

A line of enquiry

▲ Fig. 21.1

If you look closely at the back of a US dollar bill, you can read the words "In God we trust" above the value of the bill. In fact, some people think materialism and spiritual concerns are opposites. Some religious people denounce all worldly possessions and live as monks and nuns, free from earthly concerns such as money. They believe ideals such as trust, honesty, friendship, and kindness are higher values and one should seek them rather than money, a commodity that holds no intrinsic value.

Which of these do you value most? Which ones are less important to you?

- My smartphone
- Eating healthily
- Keeping promises
- Sports and exercise
- Freedom
- Friends
- Respecting authority
- Treating everyone as equal
- Telling the truth
- Fast cars
- Fairness
- Money
- My looks
- Caring for the elderly
- My education

Task 1

1. In pairs, discuss the beliefs and values. Which ones do you agree with and which ones do you disagree with?
2. Which ones are you not sure about? Explain to your partner why.

What beliefs do you hold to be true?

"There is more to life than just this existence."

"I believe there is something out there – call it 'aliens' or 'gods' – we just haven't been able to prove it yet."

"Animals are just as valuable as human beings."

"The existence of the human race is a random and meaningless accident as a result of the formation of the universe."

"Something of you lives on after death – your consciousness or your spirit."

"Life is a miracle. It's beautiful and precious to be alive and we must protect our life."

"Ghosts and spirits exist. They are here to guide us."

"Do not harm any living thing is the best rule to live by."

"Your upbringing decides what kind of person you will be."

"Religion causes wars."

"You should be free to do what you want and say what you want."

"I don't believe in anything."

"Every person has a destiny. You can't escape it."

"Life is a circle. When you die, your soul is reborn into something or someone else. It's called reincarnation."

Underlying and hidden cultural values

Why do we care about certain things and not about others? Can we truly understand and communicate with people whose beliefs, values, and perspectives differ from ours? Values and beliefs exist in society but are often hidden. What we often see are the outward behaviours and practices such as festivals, traditional costumes, food, and music. However, unseen principles influence how we behave and what we do.

Task 2

To identify underlying attitudes, beliefs, values, and perceptions, look at the following examples. Match each person with the most appropriate underlying belief or value.

1. Tabitha had to change her job and sell her city apartment to look after her elderly parents who live in the countryside.

2. Mrs Green wasn't sure her student understood the task, because Sakiko hardly ever made eye contact with her teacher.

3. Despite the fact that he didn't know where to start with his project work, Tim didn't ask his peers for help.

4. Christina did not call her teacher by her first name. She called her Professor Turner.

5. Bruno's aunt was offended when he bluntly responded with "No!" when she asked if he liked the jumper she bought him.

6. Hong insisted on paying for everyone at the expensive restaurant even though she did not have much money left this month.

7. Siobhan was stuck in her maths exam. When she quietly signalled to her friend that she needed help, her friend refused to help her.

8. The pro-democracy protester was interrogated by an official, who thought the protest was an attack on his country.

a. A strong sense of duty

b. Cheating is wrong

c. Being polite and respectful

d. Family is most important

e. Respect for authority

f. Lying is always wrong

g. Self-reliance is a virtue

h. Saving face

Perspectives

Values are principles or standards of behaviour by which we judge what is important in life. Values can be universal or personal. An example of a set of universal values is the Universal Declaration of Human Rights. A belief is being convinced of the reality or truth of something regardless of whether we have proof of it being objectively true, for example, the belief in life after death or the belief in democracy.

Mindfulness

It is possible to be unaware of our core beliefs. Reflect on what beliefs and values you have followed because of your upbringing. Think about the values that your parents or people in your culture hold but that you disagree with. Are there any beliefs that influence you in a negative way? Remember that beliefs and assumptions can be changed.

Universal values

In this section you will:

- evaluate the significance of a set of universal values

- explore whether some human rights are universal.

A line of enquiry

Conflict arises where cultures cannot accept each other's different beliefs and values. In order to live peacefully together, we must focus on the common values all humanity shares, no matter where people live or what culture they belong to. But what could these universally accepted values be and do they change over time?

Many people think of "the golden rule", the idea of treating others in the same way as one wishes to be treated, as a value that transcends time and place. Other universally accepted values are freedom, charity, not harming others, and showing an understanding of people with different views.

Task 3

Working in pairs, answer the following questions.

1. In which countries or cultures do you think people share similar values in the areas listed in the table?

2. What about your own country or culture? Copy and complete the table with examples of the values held by people in your country. Add more areas that relate to your country.

Area	Example of values
Family	Our culture shows great respect for older generations.
Work	
Freedom	
Charity	
Politics	

3. Do you think there should be a set of universal values for every country to follow? Why or why not?

The Universal Declaration of Human Rights

On 10 December 1948, the United Nations (UN) declared a set of rights that all humans are entitled to.

Task 4

In pairs, think about the importance of promoting human rights globally. Answer the following questions.

1. Why do you think it was necessary to agree to a set of values that was internationally followed and believed in?

2. In your own words, which human right do you think each of the five photographs below represents? Name the corresponding UN Article and number.

> Article 1: We are all born free and equal.
>
> Article 4: The right to be free from slavery.
>
> Article 14: A right to seek asylum in other countries.
>
> Article 18: Freedom of thought, conscience, and religion.
>
> Article 26: A right to education.

3. Explain whether each photograph represents a positive or negative example of the human right.

4. Do you think these rights are globally supported or increasingly suppressed?

▲ Fig. 21.2

▲ Fig. 21.3

▲ Fig. 21.4

▲ Fig. 21.5

▲ Fig. 21.6

Sustainability

Many schools have set up a model UN club or conference. You might consider starting one. The aims are to sustain the values set out by the UN and debate recent issues. It's your chance to be a world leader and find solutions to global problems.

Research

Shalom H. Schwartz is a social psychologist and professor at Hebrew University in Jerusalem. He developed a theory of basic human values which works cross-culturally. It's interesting to explore the *Values Project*, which looks at the cultural dimension of values across more than 70 countries.

Viewpoints

Most values and beliefs are subjective to the person who holds them, whereas objective values relate to factual matters that can be proven true or false. For example, holding the point of view that giving to charity is important is a personal belief. Yet the claim that charity organizations help many people is a fact – it can be proven to be true.

Fake news and the value of truth

In this section you will:

- discuss experiences of fake news
- evaluate the use of deepfakes.

A line of enquiry

In times of misinformation and media manipulation, it is easy to fall victim to some of the fake news circulating on the internet. Fact checks are now a regular feature on social media platforms, as deepfake videos of celebrities, internet hoaxes, and online rumours try to influence online users and manipulate their thinking. Deepfakes have increasingly been used to alter images. For example in 2022, the musician Kendrick Lamar transformed himself in a music video into figures resembling Nipsey Hussle, O.J. Simpson, and Kanye West, among others.

Ever-changing world

Deepfakes create fake media content. Many are used maliciously and are intended to spread misinformation. On the internet sophisticated technology is used to change facial features (face re-enactment), fake a person's speech (audio deepfakes), move a person's mouth to match someone else's speech (lip-syncing), swap elements of two images to make a fake image (face-swapping), and animate videos of a person using someone else's movements (puppet master).

▲ Fig. 21.7

Threat Research trainee

The government is expanding its Threat Research Team, which researches and exposes threats to the wellbeing of social media users. If successful, you would be working with a dedicated team of expert researchers, data scientists, and exploitation specialists to make social media platforms safer for all users.

We are looking for a research trainee with the following skills and qualities:

- excellent critical thinking and writing skills
- reliability, honesty, and trustworthiness

- knowledge of social media platforms and how they work
- ability to spot fake news
- knowledge of online deceptive and manipulative techniques.

If successful, you will receive full training on how to identify:

- misinformation or disinformation
- fake behaviours and other advanced manipulation
- other online threats, including bullying and harassment.

Task 5

What media do you use to access information? Work in small groups and answer the following questions.

1. How regularly do you read the news?
2. Where do you usually get your information from?
3. What sort of information do you trust?
4. How would you spot fake news? What claims might make you suspicious? How do you cross-check the information?

5. Tell your group about something you believed that turned out to be not true.
6. Read through the job advertisement and write a short application letter from a candidate who is very keen on becoming a Threat Researcher.

Sweep it under the carpet

In the English language, the idiom "to sweep something under the carpet" describes how something can be concealed, denied, or ignored if it is unappealing or harmful to one's image or reputation.

Look again at the photograph of the graffiti created by the artist Banksy. It appeared in 2006 on a wall in north London. Banksy is believed to be pointing to the refusal of the Western world to deal with global problems. He is criticizing governments that conveniently believe that if you don't see the truth, it's not there.

▲ **Fig. 21.8** *'Sweep it under the carpet' by Banksy*

Task 6

In pairs, discuss the following questions.

1. How well do you think Banksy has illustrated the meaning of the idiom?
2. Do you think Banksy is right if he is suggesting that the Western world ignores the truth? Explain your answer with some examples.
3. Suggest two other examples where artists, such as musicians, poets, or painters, have tried to hold society to account.

Moving towards assessment – Individual Report

Finding and using sources

In your **Individual Report** of 1,500 to 2,000 words, you should include a range of sources, such as articles, blogs, interviews, and films. You must avoid copying large chunks of text from your sources. Copying ideas or words from other sources without citing them is called plagiarism and is against the rules of academic writing.

Skills focus – referring to external sources

Read about the issue then answer the questions that follow.

Issue: Does conscious AI deserve rights?

Here is Jack Harrison's response to a question about robots taken from his 2022 blog from the website roboticworld.org.uk. His blog was entitled "A robotic mindset".

> The robots that we have at the moment quite clearly don't have any human thoughts. I'm referring to robotic machines that carry out tasks where we don't want to risk any human error, for example, in medical procedures and making electric vehicles. Even where robots are made to look like humans – and some of those being developed for use in the later 2020s look very human-like – they still don't have a brain or human consciousness. However, the way that bio technology is going, and quantum computing, we may well have robots with some brain-like thought processes. At that point, yes, I think we should look at the rights issue. We can't just say to the robot: "We are 100 per cent biology but you are only 35 per cent biology." In my view, that lacks respect.

Practise citing and referring to this source using each of the methods below:

- quoting from the source directly
- paraphrasing some of the information in your own words
- using footnotes
- using reported speech
- using attribution phrases.

Sample student use of sourcing

The following students have written reports on the issue of human rights abuses worldwide.

Proposed research questions

Look at the four research questions that have been suggested for Individual Reports on the topic of *Values and beliefs*.

Evaluate each one. How suitable are they as research questions? How could they be modified to ensure that they meet the expectations of a full report?

1. Should euthanasia be legalized in all countries?

2. It's best that we limit the right to freedom of speech and expression on social media.

3. Sanctity of life versus quality of life – which is more sustainable?

4. What are the advantages and disadvantages of using deepfake technology?

Read each extract. Then answer the following questions.

1. Evaluate Elise's use of sources.

2. Which student has the right balance and variety of sources?

3. Which student has to change the way they cite because it interrupts the flow of their report?

Wasim

According to Amnesty International, authoritarianism rose in Europe and Central Asia in 2021 (www.amnesty.org/en/location/europe-and-central-asia/ accessed 08/11/22). Furthermore, in a report by Human Rights Watch, freedom of speech and women's rights were globally repressed (www.hrw.org/ topic/free-speech and www.hrw.org/topic/womens-rights). To conclude, I agree with the statement "the internet and other technologies are critical tools to defend rights and hold powerful actors to account. But technology can also be used in ways that curtail rights and deepen inequality. We defend human rights in the digital age" (www.hrw.org/topic/technology-and-rights).

Elise

Amnesty International is a non-government organization that campaigns for abolishing the death penalty worldwide. On its website it states that "the death penalty is the ultimate cruel, inhuman and degrading punishment. Amnesty opposes the death penalty in all cases without exception – regardless of who is accused, the nature or circumstances of the crime, guilt or innocence or method of execution."

Maya

It is reported that there were 2,052 death sentences in 56 countries and 579 executions in 2021 (Amnesty, 2022). These figures have risen significantly compared to previous years. According to an article by Annie Kelly and Pete Pattisson, the UN Secretary described the increase of human rights abuses as a "pandemic" (*Guardian*, 2021). In the following essay, I will examine why human rights are globally under threat. There is no doubt that the pandemic has created more pressure on people and governments around the world. Many young activists, from Malala Yousafzai to Payal Jangid, influence people on social media and raise awareness of human rights abuses from education for girls to forced marriages (YouTube, 2020).

Bibliography

1. www.amnesty.org/en/what-we-do/death-penalty/ numbersofdeathsentencesandexecutionseachyear (last accessed 08/11/2022).

2. Kelly, A. and Pattisson, P., '"A pandemic of abuses"': human rights under attack during Covid, says UN head', *The Guardian*, 22 Feb 2021.

3. www.youtube.com/watch?v=X8w3j5j64zU (last accessed 08/11/2022).

Assessment tip

Listing too many sources in your bibliography may lead people to think that you have not read them all. On the other hand, citing only a few internet sites is not sufficient. Take the middle way and include a variety of sources such as articles, videos, and blogs in your bibliography. Look at the way Maya cited her sources and follow her example.

Common misunderstanding

A student listed the four main internet websites that he used at the end of his Individual Report. He thought that this was all that is necessary for a reference list. He did not use an access date, nor did he identify any sources in the main essay. He would therefore not gain the marks available because he did not understand how to cite his sources within the text.

Moving towards assessment – Team Project

Local community values and beliefs

Values and beliefs cannot easily be seen or examined as they lie beneath the surface of a local community. For example, a local faith group might offer an evening soup kitchen for the homeless, so volunteers would possibly hold values such as charity, empathy, and equality. Think about the values and beliefs that are relevant and perhaps dominant in your local community.

Skills focus – reflecting on working in a team

Some of the skills that you will practise during your teamwork are communicating with others, being reliable, being able to listen, and the ability to propose solutions to problems. In your Reflective Paper, you can then reflect on how well you think you have developed these skills. You should weigh up how effective your contribution was and show that you are aware of your own strengths and weaknesses in relation to working with others.

▲ **Fig. 21.9** *'Three wise monkeys' at Toshogu Shrine, Japan*

Look at Figure 21.9. The monkeys are associated with the phrase "see no evil, hear no evil, speak no evil", which has been interpreted in different ways.

Now think about your own values, and your strengths and weaknesses when it comes to working as part of a team.

1. What values do you think the wise monkeys highlight? How could these values be useful advice for teamwork?

2. What about other animals in nature? Do they possess values which relate to living together in groups? What can we learn from nature? Give some examples.

Sample student reflections

A team of three students has worked on the topic of equal rights for all people in their local area. Each team member has started to reflect on what went well and what they could have improved on during their work. Read through each student's reflection and answer the following questions.

Proposed projects

Look at the following four ideas that have been suggested for a Team Project on the topic of *Values and beliefs*.

Evaluate each one. How suitable are they as projects? How could they be modified to become more appropriate and viable?

1. Should local faith communities overcome their differences and worship together?

2. What actions are best to promote equality and diversity in our school?

3. Our team will look at the values that underpin our society and how they differ to other cultures.

4. We will look at where our education system fails to promote understanding, tolerance, and friendship of all nations, racial, and religious groups.

1. Evaluate whether each student fully reflects on their learning. Why or why not?
2. Identify each student's strengths and weaknesses.
3. Which of the students would you like to have on your team? Explain why.
4. Which student do you think you might have problems working with? Explain your reasons.

Dina

My learning journey throughout this project had some complications. I was ill when the teacher assigned the topic to our group. As a result, I had to work on the scientific perspective, although I would have preferred the ethical perspective. I was annoyed, but then I changed my attitude and worked as hard as I could. I like to work in a team and I have always tried to share my sources, so we all benefit from each other's research. One of the weaknesses of my team was that we all put off getting on with things and had to make changes at the last minute, which created a bit of an issue.

Asim

I have worked in teams before and because I am quite organized as a person and can manage my time effectively, I was chosen as team leader. I was a good team leader in my view, but there was a problem with two students who did not finish their tasks. It wasn't all their fault. One was not in school for a couple of weeks due to illness and the other had personal issues that took priority over schoolwork. It made my work difficult and I had to put in extra hours to help them complete the work in time. I'm glad I did because we succeeded as a group and that's what matters to me most. I am not so good with making slideshows, so Dina helped me with that. In the end, I felt we did our best and I am pleased with my own performance.

Muhammad

During our research, we all worked independently on our perspectives. When we needed help we turned to our team leader, and he did a pretty good job. I felt a bit overwhelmed with it all, and I got distracted by the internet. Also, I'm not really good at speaking with other people. I like to hide behind my research and get on with it. I guess not everyone in our team was outgoing. I also had an argument with one of the girls. She wanted me to do the presentation differently, but I didn't feel comfortable with that, so I talked to my teacher. In the end, we managed to resolve the issues between us. What have I learned through this team project? I think I learned to take responsibility for something and that working with others is not always easy.

Assessment tip

Keep regular, informal notes after each time that you and your team get together. Write about how you felt and the team dynamic. What went well? Is there anything you wish would change? For example, "Today two team members got into an argument as they both wanted to do the ethical perspective. In the end we sorted it, but it took nearly the whole lesson. I felt irritated; there are too many strong characters in our team."

Common misunderstanding

A student's reflection noted, "We worked very well together. I took the ethical perspective and my teammates took the environmental and socio-economic perspective." This is a description, not a reflection. To improve it, "We worked well together because we are friends and have worked together on other projects. We both have strong opinions, but we respect each other's ideas so we had no problems assigning different perspectives."

Moving towards assessment – Written Exam

Scan here to obtain the source material you need to carry out this examination practice work.

Question 2 in your **Written Exam** is a structured question based on a source that describes some research or evidence about the global issue. There will be two parts to the question. Candidates are required to evaluate the research or evidence, and suggest ways to research or test a claim related to the global issue.

Q2. Study Source 3.

a. As people get older, they value things less, and friends and family more.

Evaluate the strengths and weaknesses of the research outlined in Source 3.

b. "Most young people nowadays do not feel the need to be still or seek answers to existential questions."

Explain how this claim could be tested. You should consider the research methods and evidence that could be used.

Read the extracts from three sample student answers, then answer the questions that follow.

Highlights a clear strength in identifying the purpose of the research.

Highlights a potential weakness and goes on to explain why.

Silvi's response to Question 2a

a. The idea behind the ==research was clearly stated so we know what the researcher was looking for.== They involved a wide range of ages and ethnicities in the group discussion. This allowed access to several different viewpoints based upon their individual circumstances and backgrounds. ==This variety of individuals helped to add balance to the research.== However, ==the open forum format meant that not everyone had a fair say.== They talked over each other in some cases and it might have been a bit intimidating for the quieter members of the group.

Recognizes that balance comes from using different perspectives.

Jamal's response to Question 2a

a. The problem I have with this research is that the group discussion idea doesn't work if you are trying to find out what individual people think. ==It is too easy in a group discussion to nod along and agree when someone says something even if you don't really agree== with it, for fear of looking a bit out of place or not in tune with what everyone expects you to think. It might have been better to ask them to complete a questionnaire or hold personal interviews as well as the group discussion. The research says that the old people rolled their eyes when a young person mentioned career and money, as if to say that really isn't important. But at a young age it obviously is to them. The research has a biased tone to it because they make statements like =="it was clear"==, but that is just their interpretation.

> Gives a clear explanation of why this method has its limitations, highlighting group bias.

> Uses a quotation to illustrate a possible weakness.

Lee's response to Question 2b

b. To test this claim, ==I would need to consider "people" in a global context as not every society looks at things in the same way. I would also try to narrow down what is meant by "fulfilled" because again that means different things to different people.==

I would look to find ==academic studies that define these words and then look at national census data that covers this topic globally. There must be a lot of data from national surveys in lots of countries that ask about people's sense of happiness. It would be very difficult to approach a wide range of people in different countries on an individual basis, so looking at work that has already been done in collecting this data and taking an overview would be more effective.==

I think that the most realistic way to assess how much people value their relationships it to actually give them a money value. ==By figuring out how much people would be willing to pay for something, you get a sense of how much they value it or not.==

But again this has limitations as it depends upon who you ask and what their circumstances are. Therefore it might be more effective to do a small local survey asking a few simple questions about the importance of family connections and then try to get others to repeat that process in other countries around the world and compare the results.

> Shows understanding of the need to refine the research method and narrow it down to make it valid.

> Uses a good range of primary and secondary data source, and explains which is which.

> Justifies reason for looking at this method, by explaining the limitations of alternatives.

> Explains the chosen method.

Engaging with Question 2

1. Identify the strengths and weakness of Silvi's argument.
2. Do you think that Jamal's answer has the correct degree of balance? Explain your answer.
3. List the research methods Lee mentions in his work. What others could you add to further enhance the effectiveness of his research idea?
4. Which student do you think best explains their answer to **Question 2a**? Why?
5. Suggest changes to Lee's answer to make it easier to follow.

In this section you will:

- understand the importance of water as a source of life
- analyse the usefulness of amunas as a sustainable water collection system.

A line of enquiry

Where there is water, there is life. It was this knowledge that made our ancestors build their earliest settlements near ancient river systems such as the Ganges, the Yellow River or the Nile. As ancient civilizations started to flourish, their agricultural and industrial development became reliant on their understanding of how to collect and preserve rainwater.

Following on from our ancestors, we have built hydraulic structures, tunnels, dams, and water reservoirs to store and protect our drinking water. With glaciers melting and deserts expanding, climate change is exacerbating water scarcity on Earth. How will future generations cope with the potential drying up of the Earth? In 100 years' time will scientific development have found ways to ensure that water resources are no longer an issue?

Task 1

Think about your own access to fresh water. Work in pairs and answer the questions below.

1. Which of these water sources do you and your family use? Explain why or why not:
   - rainwater butt in the garden
   - well
   - hosepipe
   - water storage tank in the loft
   - bottled drinking water
   - outside water taps
   - pond
   - water pump
   - stream.

2. What are the advantages and disadvantages of each of these sources?

▲ **Fig. 22.1** *A dried-up lake during a drought in China*

▲ **Fig. 22.2** *Part of the amunas, the water collection system in Peru*

Solving water supply in Lima, Peru

In the 4th century BCE, the Wari people installed a water system called the amunas in the mountains around Lima. It collects and redirects any water from the glaciers to the city.

The impact of the amunas on Lima's water security

Water security in large cities such as Lima is a growing concern. Peru's capital city is home to 70 per cent of the country's population and is the source of most of its economic activity. There is growing awareness that water is not an infinite resource and that water quality is highly vulnerable. Lima's water comes from mountains, travelling as far as 160 km from source to city. Ecosystems such as snow-capped mountains, lagoons, wetlands, grasslands, and scrubland feed into it along the way. A series of dams, canals, and tunnels (known in Peru as the amunas system) then direct it to the treatment plant located inside the city. These ecosystems are being devastated by human activities and climate change.

There are 60 km of amunas to restore, which, if completed, could increase the volume of groundwater by 3 million square metres. This would help improve water distribution in the low-water season, reduce the likelihood of landslides in the upper basin, and increase resilience to climate change. Given the complex economic situation that Covid-19 has placed us in, implementing this type of solution not only helps improve water security, it also helps increase communities' economic income: around 70 per cent of each amuna's restoration costs are spent on local labour. There has been a high level of participation from women in the restoration of the amunas.

Task 2

In pairs, read the newspaper article and answer the following questions.

1. Why can the city of Lima be described as a water-stressed area? Give reasons from the text.

2. Give four examples of how repairing the amunas would contribute to sustainable living for the inhabitants of Lima. Refer to different viewpoints such as economic, social, and cultural.

3. What other water-saving solutions do you know? Think about two other areas in the world where different water-saving solutions are being used and compare them to the amunas.

   a. What are the advantages and disadvantages of each method?

   b. Which one do you think is best? Explain why.

4. United Nations Sustainable Development Goal 6 is "ensure availability and sustainable management of water and sanitation for all". Write a story or a poem in which you explain how the amunas have helped a family in Peru. Include different viewpoints, for example, from a woman, a teenager, a farmer.

Sustainability

Providing clean drinking water to everyone is just one side of the challenge. The other side is to manage water sustainably when it rains. Devastating floods in Pakistan and Bangladesh, and stormwater surges in the USA, have shown that many cities are not prepared for such intense rainfall. Often the urban drainage systems cannot cope and need to be modernized in order to manage a sudden excess of water.

Geoengineering

In this section you will:

- understand how cloud seeding works and evaluate its advantages and disadvantages
- create a strategy for a water-resilient city.

A line of enquiry

The weather is getting more extreme around the world. Torrential rain, hurricanes, and tsunamis not only destroy roads and houses and disrupt food supply chains, they also threaten people's lives. To try to reduce the effects of these extreme weather events, scientists have proposed ways of manipulating and controlling the environment. This is called "geoengineering".

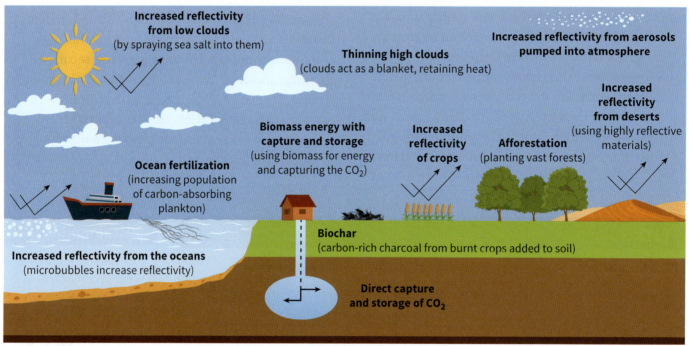

Increased reflectivity from low clouds (by spraying sea salt into them)

Thinning high clouds (clouds act as a blanket, retaining heat)

Increased reflectivity from aerosols pumped into atmosphere

Increased reflectivity from deserts (using highly reflective materials)

Biomass energy with capture and storage (using biomass for energy and capturing the CO_2)

Increased reflectivity of crops

Afforestation (planting vast forests)

Ocean fertilization (increasing population of carbon-absorbing plankton)

Biochar (carbon-rich charcoal from burnt crops added to soil)

Increased reflectivity from the oceans (microbubbles increase reflectivity)

Direct capture and storage of CO_2

▲ **Fig. 22.3** *A range of geoengineering ideas for controlling the environment*

Task 3

In small groups, read through the list of ten potential geoengineering projects and discuss the reasonableness and viability of each of them.

Surface radiation management: roofs, roads, and sidewalks are painted white, and desert regions are covered in bright polyethylene tarpaulins, to reflect sunlight back into space.

Marine cloud brightening: drone ships spray sea salt into the sky, causing the clouds above to thicken and become more reflective.

Stratospheric aerosol injection: planes, rockets, artillery shells, or balloons introduce millions of tons of sulfates into the atmosphere, creating a layer of particles that scatter sunlight.

Cirrus cloud thinning: drones inject heat-trapping cirrus clouds with dust or pollen, which creates gaps where heat can escape.

Glacier geoengineering: a 100-metre-high wall around the glaciers in Greenland and Antarctica to stop them from melting.

Space sunshade: a large shade to reflect sunlight back into space.

Tree bombs: drones drop seeds to encourage reforestation.

Ocean seeding: the oceans are fertilized with iron sulfate to stimulate the growth of algae which absorbs CO_2.

Injecting sulphur dioxide particles into the atmosphere: cools temperatures.

Coating fresh ice with white sand: reflects more light so the ice strengthens rather than melts.

Cloud seeding

Cloud seeding is a weather modification technique that is used to mitigate the effects of droughts by improving a cloud's ability to produce precipitation. The seeding can be done either from the ground or from the air when an aircraft shoots dry ice or silver iodide into cloud chambers. In Saudi Arabia, cloud seeding is predicted to increase the annual rainfall by 20 per cent.

Task 4

You are part of a city planning and development team. Your city has an arid climate and is surrounded by deserts. There is very little annual rainfall and the inhabitants experience regular water shortages. The city has been chosen to host a major international event in five years' time. The building of extra hotels and the increase in tourists will put an additional stress on the already depleted water supplies of the city. There are also obvious benefits.

1. In small groups, divide the following roles among you:
   - the director of the event
   - a construction manager hired for the project
   - an environmentalist worried about negative impacts on your city
   - a political activist lobbying for workers' rights
   - a minister for travel and tourism
   - a local resident who has no running water.

2. Decide whether you want to use cloud seeding to improve the water security of your city or whether there alternative methods that would be better.

3. What are the advantages and disadvantages of holding such a large event in a city with a water shortage and water management issues?

Vertical farms and agricultural robots

In this section you will:

- evaluate the advantages and disadvantages of vertical farms
- look at several perspectives on the use of robots in agriculture.

A line of enquiry

By 2050, the world population is expected to reach 9.7 billion people. The demand for water for agricultural use is expected to rise by 20 per cent and outdoor farming faces increasing challenges because of more extreme weather caused by climate change. However, smart indoor farming promises to offer a sustainable solution by growing food vertically rather than horizontally, using less water in the process.

Vertical farming

▲ **Fig. 22.4** *Example of vertical farming*

Vertical farming is where plants are grown in vertically stacked layers. It saves space and water, and promises to be more sustainable than traditional farming methods. There are already some large vertical farms in Singapore, Japan, South Korea, and the USA.

The graph shows that vertical farming in the USA has grown year on year and how it is projected to continue up to 2027. Tomatoes, lettuce, and leafy greens have seen the biggest increase, while the markets for herbs, peppers, strawberries, cucumbers, and other crops also expanded. Vertical farming is expected to continue its upward trend into the future.

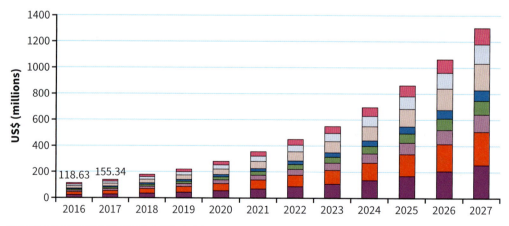

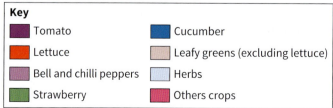

Key

- ■ Tomato
- ■ Lettuce
- ■ Bell and chilli peppers
- ■ Strawberry
- ■ Cucumber
- ■ Leafy greens (excluding lettuce)
- ■ Herbs
- ■ Others crops

▲ **Fig. 22.5** *Bar graph showing vertical farming in the USA, by crop, 2016–2027*

Task 5

In pairs, study the graph and discuss the advantages and disadvantages of vertical farming. Decide whether the following statements are for or against vertical farming.

a. Vertical farming currently produces only leafy vegetables.

b. It costs millions of dollars to set up a vertical farm.

c. It needs less space, soil, and water.

d. It is not dependent on sunlight, as systems use energy-efficient LED lighting.

e. It depends on advanced technology.

f. It is labour intensive, and chemistry knowledge and technical skills are required.

g. There are no insects in vertical farming.

h. It produces purer food, free from pesticides or herbicides.

i. Nutrients have to be added artificially.

j. It can produce crops all year round.

Robotic farming

Indoor vertical farming won't be able to feed the growing global population. The future of sustainable farming will include new and upcoming technologies, such as robotics, computer vision, and machine learning that can contribute to solving agricultural problems.

▲ **Fig. 22.6** *Is this the future for robotic farming?*

Task 6

In pairs, answer the following questions.

1. How many different ways of using robots in farming can you think of?

2. Many modern farmers have a positive attitude to using robots in farming. Why might they hold this view? What do you think?

3. What about the argument to protect traditional ways of farming? Do you have empathy with this argument?

Sustainability

Did you know that 70 per cent of Earth is covered by water, but only 2.5 per cent is fresh water? Only 1 per cent of fresh water is easily accessible and traditional agriculture consumes 70 per cent of it globally. That's unsustainable!

Vertical farms need significantly less water and no soil to grow plants. Hydroponics are crops that are grown in nutrient-rich water. Aeroponics works by suspending plant roots in air and misting them with nutrient water. Aquaponics is a form of agriculture that combines farming fish with the growing of plants.

Developing a global and a national perspective

In your **Individual Report** of 1,500 to 2,000 words, you should show that you understand a variety of different perspectives on the topic. You must include a global perspective and one other – a national or local perspective. Engagement with the perspectives needs to be sustained and detailed.

Skills focus – covering different perspectives

International organizations such as the UN, WHO, WTO, IMF, and NGOs and charities are concerned about the global supply of clean drinking water and sanitation. Not having regular access to both will inevitably lead to medical, socio-economic, cultural, political, ethical, and environmental problems.

Read the text about "World Toilet Day" and answer the following questions.

1. Which activity would you enjoy most?
2. Select four of the ideas and show how each enables a range of perspectives and viewpoints relating to sanitation and safe water supply to be covered.
3. Which idea raises a global issue and which idea focuses on a local / or national context?

> ### Proposed research questions
>
> Look at the four research questions that have been suggested for Individual Reports on the topic of *Water, food, and agriculture*.
>
> Evaluate each one. How suitable are they as research questions? How could they be modified to ensure that they meet the expectations of a full report?
>
> 1. It's obvious that by the end of the century poor countries will be fighting water wars.
> 2. To what extent should geoengineering be used globally?
> 3. Is vertical farming really sustainable?
> 4. What are the advantages and disadvantages of using artificial intelligence in farming?

Different ways to celebrate World Toilet Day on 19 November

- Set up a photo exhibition of toilets from around the world.
- Organize a fundraising event to sponsor a total makeover of your school's toilets and to install a disabled toilet.
- Join #WorldToiletDay and share your experience on how important sanitation for all is.
- Plan a toilet design competition to raise money for charity.
- Watch an online video from a global NGO such as Water Aid.
- Play the game "This is a true story" on Netflix and follow Bontu on her journey to collect clean water.
- Create a slide presentation about how 770 million people lack access to clean and safe water.
- Find out about Scott Harrison, the founder of a water charity, and be inspired by his mission to eradicate the global water crisis through his company cleanwater.org.

Sample student extracts

Three students decided to write their Individual Reports on the issue of geoengineering. Read through the extracts, which start to explore some perspectives. Then answer these questions.

1. Evaluate the strengths and weaknesses of each student's work.
2. Identify which student provides a clear and supported global perspective.
3. Identify which student includes a clear and supported national perspective.
4. Identify where any perspectives are covered superficially.

Javier

Geoengineering is a technological manipulation of the climate to reverse the negative impacts of climate change. Cloud seeding, for example, brings economic benefits to farmers and enhances water security for people who live in countries with arid climates. However, from an ethical perspective, there are several concerns that interfering in nature might eventually come back to haunt us. Callies, D. (2018) raises the ethical objection to geoengineering that once starting this course of action, there is little that can stop it. However, this is a weak argument as Callies is too concerned about the negative impacts of geoengineering.

Raina

Many countries are using cloud seeding and ocean fertilization to reverse the impact of climate change, but the belief that geoengineering has mainly advantages is highly controversial. A project conducted by three universities in the United Kingdom concluded that technologies that tamper with ecosystems could be a danger rather than a help. Dr Matthew, a reader in natural hazards at the University of Bristol, concluded that pumping sulphate aerosols into the atmosphere to reflect more sunlight back into space and therefore reduce global temperatures could potentially be dangerous. Therefore, from a scientific perspective alone, geoengineering can hardly be justified.

Ellie

On the one hand, geoengineering has been hailed as the answer to our prayers as new technologies can stop and reverse the effects of climate change. At the COP27 climate conference in November 2022, the United Nations agreed that drastic action is needed. Greta Thunberg, a climate activist from Sweden, did not attend COP27 because she thought it provided a platform for "greenwashing, lying and cheating". She published *The Climate Book* in October 2022. In it, Jennie C. Stephens, a professor of sustainability science, opposes geoengineering and thinks it is just a "technical fix" which "has this technological optimism, even a colonial, problematic power structure about who would govern it, who benefits and who gets screwed with it" (*The Climate Book*, 2022).

Assessment tip

Different perspectives do not have to be opposing. In other words, you could have a range of sources that all say geoengineering methods, such as cloud seeding, are good but the sources approach it from different viewpoints, such as environmental, economic, and technological.

Common misunderstanding

A student included her own country's response to water scarcity and also researched a European country and an Asian country. She thought that this fulfilled the criteria of covering a global perspective, but all she did was present three national perspectives. To develop a global perspective, she could include the viewpoint of an international organization such as the United Nations or a global non-governmental organization.

Water worlds, tsunamis, and sunken cities

The Greek philosopher Plato once described an island with a densely populated city called Atlantis. Atlantis was thought of as the most powerful and technologically advanced city of its time, but a tsunami destroyed it and the island sank into the ocean. No one knows if it really existed. Rising sea levels, tsunamis, and floods threaten modern cities. Which cities or places in the world do you think are threatened and might become sunken cities in the future?

Skills focus – a game designed to solve a water issue

Design a game about water. It could be an online game or you could create a traditional board game.

▲ Fig. 22.7

1. Give your game a name. Include different characters and an aim. What do you want to achieve?

2. Write instructions for how to play the game. What are the rules? How do you win?

3. Is your game working out as you expected? What changes might you make to improve its design?

4. Do you think a game is a suitable action for a Team Project in highlighting a local issue?

Sample student planning

Two teams chose to address the issue of saving water in their school.

Look at the tables opposite, in which the teams explained their research and outlined their planning. Then answer the following questions.

1. Do you think each team has clearly identified the topic and issue? Why or why not?

2. How well designed are their plans? Have they included enough detail? Explain your answer.

3. Evaluate how well each team identified the roles and responsibilities of each team member.

4. Comment on the clarity and effectiveness of each team's proposed action.

Proposed projects

Look at the following four ideas that have been suggested for a Team Project on the topic of *Water, food, and agriculture*.

Evaluate each one. How suitable are they as projects? How could they be modified to become more appropriate and viable?

1. How can our schools offer more vegan and vegetarian dishes in their canteens?

2. Can the desalination of saltwater save the world from water insecurity?

3. Our team will obtain financial support for local communities who want to establish community farms to combat food insecurity.

4. We will conduct research about the issue of waterborne diseases globally.

Toby's team

Topic: How can we best save water in school?

Issue: School is old with leaking taps, no rainwater harvesting, and no water-saving flush system in toilets.

Aim: To raise awareness of water wastage and raise money to update toilets.

Plan	Roles	Action
Raise awareness with posters explaining how school wastes water and toilets have no dual flush system.	**Toby:** Inform head teacher of the plan and request school water bill. Include pictures of toilets and water puddles.	Evidence: letter to head teacher, water bill, posters, questionnaire, emails to other schools, approach specific teachers, create slideshow.
Write to the head teacher to explain our action plan and ask to see school water bill. Also offer to organize an assembly.	**Rosie:** Create a "toilet design" competition and poster at school and on school website to raise awareness.	We will know whether or not we have been successful by:
Speak to students at assembly and raise awareness with a questionnaire for students before and after the action.	**Sancho:** Research how other schools save water, asking geography teacher to help. Create a questionnaire for students.	• questionnaire results (before and after action) • toilets improvements
Raise money for updating school's toilets.	**Salima:** Create a slideshow and speak to students in assembly. Suggest art club paints murals.	• even if the toilets take time to be modernized, we can show evidence for raising money and awareness around school.
Additional fun: paint walls of toilets with murals.		

Team B

Topic: Is our town's water system sustainable?

Issues: When it rains, there is constant flooding in certain areas. Do people have rain water butts?

Aim: To raise money so every household can install a rain water butt in their garden.

Plan	Roles	Action
Raise awareness	**Harriet:** Write a letter to the council to do more about flooding.	Write letter to the council.
Raise money		Go to check if people have water butts installed.
Write to the council	**Jasmine & Carl:**	
Check people's gardens	Go round houses and ask people if they have a water butt.	Bake cakes.
		Find out on internet how much water butts cost.
	Song & Alberto:	
	Bake cakes and sell in school.	

Assessment tip

Everybody in your team will be awarded the same mark for your Explanation of Research and Planning. Toby's team has managed to divide the responsibilities equally between the team members. This is an opportunity for you to listen to each other and build on each other's strengths.

Common misunderstanding

Some students think that if they don't make any changes to their Explanation of Research and Planning, they are successful. For example, Team B wrote that they did not change anything as everything went to plan. It would have been better for Team B to acknowledge that there were limitations to their scope of research as that would show awareness.

285

Scan here to obtain the source material you need to carry out this examination practice work.

Question 1 in your **Written Exam** is a structured question based on several sources. There will be three or four parts to the question. Candidates are required to read the sources and analyse the information, arguments, and perspectives presented about the global issue.

Q1. Study Sources 1 and 2.

a. What trend can you observe in the bar graph illustrating the use of AI in agriculture from 2020 to 2040?

b. i. Identify one example of an assertion in Source 2.

   ii. Explain why the example you identified is an assertion.

c. From Source 2, describe the employment agency's perspective on robots in farming.

d. Sources 1 and 2 suggest that in the future there will be an increase in using robots in agriculture. Do you think this is a positive or negative development? Explain your answer.

Read the two sample student answers to Questions **1c** and **1d**, then answer the questions that follow.

Kamala's response

1c. The employment agency thinks negatively about the increase of robots in farming. They are worried that robots can take the place of workers, who would be made redundant, which is obviously a big problem. The employment agency is referring to two perspectives: one is the economic aspect and the other one the ethical aspect. They say that precision agriculture will be worth $20 billion and this has caused a decrease in farming jobs, although there are many workers who would like to apply for such jobs. These workers don't have any other skills, so they are not likely to find a job elsewhere. That's why the agency thinks it is unethical and unjust, and not in line with our human rights. If robots compete with humans, then that's an unfair working condition because machines have advantages over human beings. Machines can work quicker and with more precision. So the agency thinks that the effects on a human worker would be to lose their human rights.

1d. I think it's a negative trend. Technology has taken over all of our lives and now we have to worry that there won't be any jobs in future. In my country, there are people who work very hard on farms. They pick cotton and vegetables to feed their families. If robots take away their jobs, what other job can they do?

> Highlights the perspectives discussed in the source and begins to pick out and use relevant material.

> Describes the problem in detail, a Level 3 skill.

> Needs greater support to justify the opinion.

> Exaggeration. Stay focused on the sources and do not generalize ideas.

> Direct questions are not explanations. Needs to justify her suggestion to get to a higher level.